DEPRESSION, THE MOOD DISEASE

A JOHNS HOPKINS PRESS HEALTH BOOK

FRANCIS MARK MONDIMORE, M.D.

# Depression, the Mood Disease

## Third Edition

THE JOHNS HOPKINS UNIVERSITY PRESS    BALTIMORE

© 1990, 1993, 2006 The Johns Hopkins University Press
All rights reserved. Published 2006
Printed in the United States of America on acid-free paper
9 8 7 6 5 4 3 2 1

The Johns Hopkins University Press
2715 North Charles Street
Baltimore, Maryland 21218-4363
www.press.jhu.edu

Library of Congress Cataloging-in-Publication Data

Mondimore, Francis Mark, 1953–
    Depression, the mood disease / Francis Mark Mondimore. — 3rd ed.
        p.   cm.
    Includes bibliographical references and index.
    ISBN 0-8018-8450-0 (hardcover : alk. paper) — ISBN 0-8018-8451-9 (pbk. : alk. paper)
    1. Depression, Mental—Popular works. I. Title.
    RC537.M65 2006
    616.85′27—dc22        2006005264

A catalog record for this book is available from the British Library.

Illustrations by Jacqueline Schaffer

For JAY, of course

# Contents

## PART II   VARIATIONS, CAUSES, AND CONNECTIONS

## PART III   GETTING BETTER

# Preface

When the first edition of *Depression, the Mood Disease* appeared in 1990, there were very few medications available to treat depression. The medications that *were* available were toxic, had a lot of side effects, and were hardly ever prescribed by medical professionals other than psychiatrists. There was a lot of disagreement about how long people with depression should continue to receive treatment with medication. Some professionals still argued that depression and anxiety should never be treated with medications—that medication only "covered up" the symptoms of deep-rooted psychological maladjustments that needed to be treated with talk therapy. The idea that medication could help with depression was unfamiliar to most people.

Fortunately, those days are over for good. Now dozens of different medications are used to treat depression, medications with far fewer side effects and far less toxicity. The medical field now has more than fifty years of experience in treating these illnesses, and we are much better informed about their course and prognosis. Family practice physicians have become much more aware of the illness of depression, and most persons with depression are now treated by a doctor who is not a psychiatrist. The idea that depression is a medical illness that needs medical treatment is accepted by the vast majority of mental health professionals as a proven fact, and even the general public has become at least somewhat familiar with the medical (as opposed to psychological) treatments for depression—you can see commercials for antidepressants on television any day of the week.

We have also learned that depression is a complex illness, one that varies tremendously from one individual to another. Also, with so many choices available now, the treatment of serious depression and other mood disorders is more complex and varied. Many sufferers still lack knowledge of the diagnostic methods and the options and principles of treatment. Many questions and controversies about the causes of these illnesses remain. Persons being treated for depression naturally want to understand all of these issues.

I was very gratified, then, when the Johns Hopkins University Press agreed that an update to the book was a good idea. But as I started to revise the previous edition, it became apparent that a simple "revision" wouldn't do. There is so much new information that nearly every section of the text needed to be rewritten, making this essentially an entirely new book.

I'd like to thank the many people who have assisted and supported me in this work. First, thanks to the Johns Hopkins University Press and its editors, who have believed in me from the first: thanks to Anders Richter, who shepherded me through the publication of the first edition, and to Jacqueline Wehmueller, who inherited me from Andy after his retirement and encouraged me to write a second and now a third edition of the book. She has been a constant and steadfast source of inspiration and support for this and many other projects.

Immeasurable thanks is owed to my teachers and mentors at Johns Hopkins, Paul R. McHugh and J. Raymond DePaulo, and to my psychiatric colleagues (from whom I never stop learning), especially Jimmy Potash, Melvin McInnis, Dean MacKinnon, Jennifer Payne, John Lipsey, and Karen Swartz. Thanks to Trish Caruana, LCSW, and Sharon Estabrook, OTR, for teaching me the extraordinary importance of their respective disciplines, clinical social work and occupational therapy, to the comprehensive treatment of persons with mood disorders.

And thanks, of course, to my partner, Jay Allen Rubin, for much more than I could ever put into words.

# Introduction

Depression, "mood swings," and other mood disorders are estimated to afflict up to 15 percent of the adult population at any given time. Even though safe and effective treatments for this group of illnesses are readily available, study after study has concluded that many, perhaps most, of the people who suffer from them do not receive adequate treatment. This book is for these people and their families.

Every year hundreds of thousands of people are given prescriptions for antidepressant medications but stop taking them because they never receive a thorough explanation of their purpose or side effects and are not carefully instructed in how to take them properly or in what kinds of improvement to expect and how soon. This book is for them.

Uncountable thousands seek relief for their mood problems from family members, counselors, and clergy when they actually suffer from a medical illness and need to see a physician. Perhaps many more simply suffer in silence, not knowing what to do or whom to ask for help. Most of all, this book is for them.

This is not a "self-help" book. Perhaps it is closer in style and content to a "consumer's guide." My purpose is to explain that in many cases a mood disorder such as depression is a serious medical problem. It is not something one can talk oneself out of, not a "phase of life problem," not "getting old," "growing pains," or some other minor and temporary difficulty that will pass with time or that people can "snap out of." It is a medical illness that causes lost productivity and time off from work at a tremendous dollar cost. It brings great misery: wasted days, months, and even years of impaired functioning at a human cost that cannot be measured. It is a disease with a frightening mortality rate. Its most serious complication, suicide, often takes its victims in the prime of life and is consistently one of the top ten causes of death at all ages. Suicide is the third leading cause of death in teenagers and young adults. Nevertheless, these illnesses are misdiagnosed by doctors, misunderstood by many well-educated laypeople, and, tragically, too often ignored or explained away as a passing inconvenience.

I have written this book to help people with depression and other mood disorders understand their illness and their treatment so they can get the fullest benefit from all available types of therapy.

In these first paragraphs, you may have noticed some words that are perhaps unexpected: *disease, illness, complications, mortality rate.* These are "medical" words, not "psychological" words, used in discussing diseases of the body like tuberculosis, myocardial infarction (heart attack), or diabetes. I hope that by the time you have finished this book you will agree that they are completely appropriate for discuussing mood disorders and that depression or abnormal mood swings can be as much a disorder of the body as any other "real" disease you can think of.

I recommend that you read the book from beginning to end in sequence. The beginning chapters lay some important groundwork for those that come later. Also, don't assume that some of the "special case" sections (such as "Depression and Stroke" in chapter 5) don't apply to you and therefore be tempted to skip them. Many facts learned by studying special cases have shed light on all the mood disorders. Scientists have learned much from them, and so will you.

If you bought this book to understand your own feelings of depression, your mood swings, or the "moody" behavior of someone close to you, that in itself probably points to a medically treatable mood disorder. I think you will find this volume informative and comforting, but don't think it can substitute for medical treatment! Remember, it is a consumer's guide, not a repair manual. Read the book *and* make an appointment to see your doctor. Today.

# PART I

# SYMPTOMS, DIAGNOSIS, AND TREATMENT

# CHAPTER 1

# Mood

## Mood: What Is It?

"I'm in a great mood today; I feel on top of the world." "Stay out of my way this morning, I'm in a terrible mood." We use the word *mood* all the time to describe a complicated set of feelings, both psychological and physical, that affect our behavior toward others, our productivity, our ability to relax and have fun, and our attitude about ourselves.

When our mood is good we feel energetic, optimistic about the future, and eager for the challenges of work or play. In a good mood, we are outgoing and enjoy being with people. We have a hearty appetite, sleep soundly through the night, and awake refreshed and ready for a new day. People in a good mood are affectionate and loving, and sex is relaxed and fun. Perhaps the most basic aspect of a good mood is that it makes us confident—sure of our positive attributes and not preoccupied by our faults. Minor setbacks are taken in stride, and even major problems can be tackled with determination and commitment. A person in a good mood is happy to be alive.

A bad mood causes an opposite set of feelings. The half-filled glass looks half empty. Energy is low, and it's hard to get things done—the most minor tasks seem interminable or even overwhelming. Time passes slowly. In a bad mood we find other people irritating and may lose our temper over the smallest things, then feel guilty for having done so. Not surprisingly, we simply avoid others and prefer to be alone. It's difficult to be affectionate and almost impossible to be sexy. More basic is a feeling of emptiness, of not being our usual self; self-confidence is absent, self-esteem low. This is the set of changes and feelings psychiatrists call *depression*.

Unfortunately, discussions of mood states and changes in mood have suffered from a lack of precise medical terms to describe them. This has hampered medicine's ability to discuss mood problems in a way that is as precise and therefore, to some people's way of thinking, as "medical" as, say, a discussion of headaches or chest pains. But it's not easy to discuss such very basic and complex feelings the same way one talks about a physical pain. One can often point to a location on the body, rate the pain in intensity, and say when it began. "It hurts more when I cough"; "I've got a throbbing headache." These are symptoms that can be characterized very accurately.

Doctors have always had a hard time naming symptoms that are more generalized and difficult to pinpoint, so this trouble in describing mood is not surprising. To describe how one feels when the flu is coming on, the aching in muscles and joints, hot and cold feelings, headache, and so forth, English-speaking physicians merely borrow the French word for illness and call this collection of symptoms *malaise*. It's not surprising, then, that we have not come up with good terminology for the symptoms of the disease that affects mood. Mood is such a basic aspect of how one feels that it is difficult to describe it, talk about it precisely, or identify mood changes within oneself or others in specific terms. In questioning patients, psychiatrists often resort to slang. A good mood is referred to as "on a high," "in high spirits." A bad or low mood is referred to as "down in the dumps," "in low spirits," "the blues."

So what is meant by the commonly used word *depression*? Many people say "I'm depressed" when they really mean "I'm sad." *Depression* does not really mean *sadness*. Usually a person feels sad about something in particular, and the feeling is usually associated with some loss. For example, people become sad about the death of a loved one or the breakup of a relationship. Other words used to describe this sense of loss are *grief* and *bereavement*. Another kind of sadness is the sense of longing for the way things were, for the "good old days," that is commonly called *nostalgia*.

Unfortunately, the word *depression* is often inaccurately used to describe these other unpleasant feelings. The concept as psychiatrists use it is a bit different, a more fundamental and also more pervasive experience. Sometimes depression can go far beyond sadness and the other feelings described above to affect the way we feel about our entire future and alter some very basic attitudes about ourselves. Sometimes depression can deepen and widen to poison one's attitude about all aspects of life, to the point where words like *despair* and *hopelessness* accurately reflect one's feelings. Another word used to separate this collection of feelings from other sad feelings is *melancholia*. This very old word means "black bile" and refers to the ancient Greek theory of medicine that considered disease states to be caused by a deficiency or excess of one of four bodily fluids. (Depressed persons were thought to suffer from an excess of black bile.) Although *melancholia* was the word used to describe depression in several very early clinical works on psychiatric conditions, and thus might seem a natural choice as a modern clinical term, it has never gained common acceptance, perhaps because of its poetic, romanticized connotations.

I hope this discussion helps you begin to understand what psychiatrists mean by mood. Yes, it does include concepts like happy and sad, but mood goes further or perhaps deeper than this and includes our sense of physical well-being, our attitudes toward others, our feelings about the future, our self-esteem and confidence, and our attitude toward ourselves as well.

What is a *normal* mood? It would be easy to get into a complicated philosophical and scientific discussion on the question What is normal? To keep things simple, I will use the word *normal* to mean that which is usual, common, or expected—not some ideal state against which other states or conditions are compared.

Let's get back to the question, What is a normal mood? The first part of the answer is, it depends. A good mood is frequently normal, but a bad mood can be normal as well. For example, when good things happen to us, we generally find ourselves in a good mood. When we are beset by problems, disappointments, and setbacks, it is normal to be in a bad mood. The "it depends" part is perhaps one of the most important characteristics of normal mood, for normally mood is *reactive*. Our mood responds and reacts to events—to what happens to us and to those important to us. Furthermore, mood is reactive in a predictable way: when something good happens, our mood is good; when something bad happens, our mood turns sour. Thus a second aspect of normal mood is that the direction of changes in mood is *understandable* in light of what we know about human nature and the way people usually react to events.

Another characteristic of normal mood changes is that they are in some way *proportional* to the circumstances that provoke them. For example, the normal change in mood following the death of a spouse will be very severe, much more than following the death of a pet. Getting a big promotion would be expected to lead to a greater boost in mood than merely being let off early one afternoon. Everyone has an intuitive sense of the direction and degree of mood change to be expected in particular circumstances; our sense is based on our own experience and observations. Although psychiatrists have been trained to observe people closely and are experienced in judging the usual range or proportion of mood change, we too rely quite a bit on intuition in drawing conclusions about normal and abnormal moods.

So it's not so much the mood state itself that can be said to be abnormal. More important, really, is to see the mood in the context of life events. Again, normal mood is reactive to life events, the way it changes is understandable in light of those events, and the change is proportional to the events.

## The Chemistry of Mood

During the seventeenth and eighteenth centuries, physicians began to realize that the workings of the human body followed the rules of science. Indeed, the word *science* came to be used in its modern sense during this time, replacing the term *natural philosophy*. Today we take for granted that the heart is a pump and that we can understand a lot about the way it works if we know how pumps work. After the French scientist Pouseuille described the laws of physics that determine the flow rate, pressure, and other properties of fluids flowing in tubes, it quickly became apparent that the flow of blood through arteries and veins followed the same principles. "Philosophical" speculations about the heart as the source of love, loyalty, and other poetic qualities and feelings disappeared and were replaced by cold, hard, usually mathematical rules and principles. You may be wondering, What does this have to do with mood?

It took much longer to get started, but a similarly revolutionary change has been taking place over the past thirty years or so in the fields of *neuroscience* (the study of the brain and nervous system) and *psychiatry* (the branch of medicine that concerns itself with treating disorders of emotions and behavior). We are learning today that the activities of the human brain—activities like thinking, remembering, getting angry, and feeling calm—can also be understood in scientific terms and that the laws of biology and chemistry apply. This application of the laws of science, especially *biochemistry* (the chemistry of living things), to the understanding of behavior and mental states isn't really surprising or even new.

Humans have known for thousands of years that various substances can change thinking and behavior. Almost as soon as we figured out how to grow crops, we discovered how to ferment some of them and began using ethyl alcohol (the alcohol in alcoholic beverages) to change the way we feel. We found substances that dull the perception of pain (aspirin from the bark of willows, morphine from poppies), substances that boost mood and energy level (caffeine from coffee beans and cocaine from coca leaves), as well as substances that could induce very abnormal mental experiences such as hallucinations (mescaline from the peyote cactus, psilocybin from hallucinogenic mushrooms). The number of naturally occurring psychoactive substances has now been far surpassed by man-made ones. (*Psychoactive* means having an effect on the chemistry of the brain and on mental processes.)

As more chemicals were discovered and used as medicines to treat everything from tuberculosis to arthritis, many of them were found to be psychoactive as well. In the 1950s, reserpine, a pharmaceutical used to treat high blood pressure, was discovered to cause profound depression in some people. Some people who had been perfectly happy and content became depressed and suicidal while taking this medication. This was one of the first pieces of evidence that there is a chemical basis to mood, and it is still one of the most compelling.

## An Early Breakthrough in Brain Science

Parkinson's disease is a progressive deterioration of a person's ability to produce smooth muscle movement. The first sign of this devastating disease is usually a change in muscle tone that shows up as stiffness of posture and slowness of movement. The affected person walks with a shuffle and becomes stooped. The limbs tremble. Writing is scrawled. In severe cases the victim becomes almost paralyzed. These symptoms do not occur because the muscles or the nerves in the limbs are diseased, but rather because the organization and initiation of movement in the brain centers controlling these functions fails. Although the first description of the illness was published in 1817, it wasn't until 1919 that a Russian-born scientist named Tretiakoff discovered that Parkinson's disease is caused by the deterioration of a single brain center, the *substantia nigra* (Latin for "black substance," because the area appears to the naked eye to have dark pigment). Under the microscope, many cells of the substantia nigra in people with Parkinson's disease could be seen to be dead or dying. Other researchers discovered that this center is connected to many other areas of the brain that control movement and hypothesized that it somehow coordinates all these centers to produce smooth, fluid motion, the function that is lost in Parkinson's disease. Although this finding was very instructive for understanding how the brain controls movement, it didn't mean much to sufferers of the illness because it did not result in any useful treatments.

That changed however, when new biochemical techniques made it possible to move beyond simply visualizing brain cells under the microscope and allowed scientists to investigate the *chemistry* of brain function. In 1960, the Austrian neurologist Oleh Hornykiewicz discovered that the amount of a brain chemical called *dopamine* is lower than normal in people with Parkinson's disease. In fact, the brains of persons who had died with the disease were found on autopsy to have much less dopamine than people without Parkinson's disease in the cells of the substantia nigra. It seemed that the loss of dopamine-producing cells somehow upset the balance of activity of brain centers necessary for smooth movement, causing symptoms. These findings led Hornykiewicz and others to wonder if it might be possible to boost dopamine levels in the brains of person's with Parkinson's disease. They administered the drug *l-dopa,* which the body changes into dopamine, to patients and found that the symptoms of Parkinson's disease improved dramatically in many. This was one of the first examples of *neuro-pharmacology,* the treatment of a brain disease with a pharmaceutical. It developed from an understanding of the chemistry involved both in normal brain functioning and in the disease state. For the first time, neuroscientists figured out the chemistry of a system in the brain and set out to treat a disease by manipulating that system. They were successful.

## Mood Disorders

I have talked about chemicals that affect emotions and behavior and about how the brain uses various chemicals to carry out its functions. I discussed Parkinson's disease, which is caused by a lack of a particular chemical in a particular brain center and which is treated by boosting the level of the missing chemical in the brain. With these facts in mind, let me pose several questions:

1. Since the brain uses chemical messengers to carry out its work and to regulate things like muscle tone and level of alertness, shouldn't there also be chemical systems that regulate mood?
2. Can't we assume that the chemicals that affect mood (like the blood pressure medicine reserpine, which causes depression in some people) work by affecting these systems?
3. Might there not be a type of disease that affects these brain systems and has as its symptom an abnormal change in mood?
4. Couldn't we try to treat this disease with medication that attempts to restore the normal functioning of these systems?

As you might have guessed, the answer to all these questions is yes! In fact, several different illnesses affect mood and are treated with medications that have been shown to change the level and balance of various chemicals in the brain. Some psychiatrists think all of these illnesses and their variations are so closely connected that they should be considered subtypes or variations of a single disease, which has been called *affective disorder.* The word *affective* has been used for many years by psychologists and psychiatrists to talk about mood. It refers both to the subjective experience (how one feels on the inside) and also to the changes in behavior and functioning that can accompany a marked change in mood (the sad look of a depressed person, loss of appetite, restlessness, and so forth). More recently these illnesses have come to be called *mood disorders.*

Why aren't these illnesses called affective disease or mood diseases? After all, we don't call the movement problem I discussed earlier Parkinson's *disorder*. The answer is that medical scientists are reluctant to call a process a disease if its basic cause is unknown or if we cannot see its basic *pathology*—abnormalities that can be observed under a microscope or measured in a laboratory. Scientists investigating Parkinson's disease saw deterioration and death of cells in the brains of its victims and measured unequivocal pathological changes in the amount of dopamine. In mood disorders, the alterations in functioning in the brain are just beginning to be measured. It's quite clear that the changes in the actual structure of the brain are extremely subtle; almost no changes in the structure of the brain can be seen with a CAT scan or MRI scan or under a microscope.* Because the amounts of the brain chemicals involved are so small and difficult to measure, chemical analysis has not been much help either.

This leads me to share with you a somewhat embarrassing fact about the treatments for depression (in fact, about the treatments for almost all psychiatric problems): unlike the scientific discoveries and elegant reasoning that led to a treatment for Parkinson's disease, the medications and other treatments used for depression were all discovered essentially by accident. Only after they had been used safely and effectively for some time were some of their effects on brain chemistry discovered.

## What Is the Biology of Depression?

In 1985, psychiatrist and neuroscientist Nancy Andreasen wrote a book called *The Broken Brain* about the new discoveries in biological psychiatry. (*Biology* can be defined as the science that deals with living things, including their classification, anatomical structure, and chemistry.) The title makes the point that psychiatric illnesses like major depressive disorder, bipolar disorder, and schizophrenia are caused in large part by biological and chemical malfunctions of the brain. Although we still don't know exactly what these malfunctions are, we are getting very close to understanding some of the biological mechanisms that might be involved. In this overview of brain functioning, I want to tell you about what scientists think might be "broken" in mood disorders. (In this section, I will discuss some of the scientific theories about the causes of mood disorders. You can skip it without losing continuity.)

Many people imagine that the human brain is a kind of wonderful computer. Although this is a vast oversimplification of the true capabilities of

---

*Very subtle changes in the size of certain brain structures have been demonstrated in depression. However, the changes are not enough to be useful for diagnosing the illness in individuals.

the brain, it's a good place to start in trying to understand how this fantastic organ works.

Like the computer that I'm using to write these words, a human brain receives input, processes the information it receives, and then delivers output. Like a computer, it stores information and often uses this stored information to help process further input. The human brain receives its input from the sense organs: the eyes, ears, taste buds, touch receptors, and so forth, and delivers output in terms of behavior.

You may know that a computer has many thousands of microscopic switches embedded in its processing chip. Information is stored according to a pattern of "on" and "off" switches; the flow of signals through these switches is what we call processing. The human brain contains about eleven billion nerve cells, or *neurons,* but as powerful as a computer with eleven billion switches would be, our brain is much more powerful than that. This is because a neuron is not just a switch that is either on or off but an impressive microprocessor in its own right. Each neuron receives input from many other neurons, processes this information, and sends output to others. The brain, then, is not like a computer with billions of switches; it is more like a network of billions of computers, all capable of being individually programmed. Each neuron in the brain may receive input from and transmit signals to up to fifty thousand other neurons. The number of all of the possible connections in the human brain is incomprehensibly large, a hyper-astronomical number on the order of the number of molecules in the universe! (Even if we could figure out how to build such a computer, there'd be no place on the planet big enough to put it.)

I'm going to jump the gun a little and tell you that there is a lot of evidence that mood disorders, as well as anxiety disorders, are caused by some defect in the mechanisms by which the individual neurons are programmed. Neurons have the ability to be "reprogrammed" in response to various situations (such as stress), a capability called *neuroplasticity* (the original meaning of the word *plastic* is a material that can be shaped and reshaped, like modeling clay). But before we get to that, we need to talk about neurotransmitters.

Although the human nervous system uses electrical signals to do much of its work, it uses chemical signals as well; molecules called *neurotransmitters* are the means by which nerve cells communicate with each other. Neurotransmitters operate in an area where two neurons nearly touch (called the *synapse*). The first neuron releases packets of neurotransmitters, which flow across the narrow space to link up with targets called receptors on the second neuron. When enough of the receptors are occupied by the neurotransmitter molecules, which fit into them like keys fit into locks, the second nerve cell is activated and fires off its own signal. Neurons com-

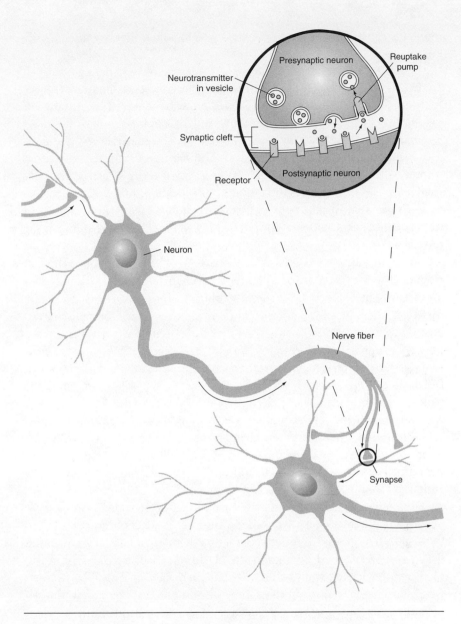

Figure 1.1 Synapse

municate constantly with the other neurons to which they are functionally linked.

There needs to be some mechanism for this chemical signaling system to be turned off and reset. After neurotransmitter molecules link up with receptors across the synapse, they must somehow be removed in preparation for the next batch. This happens in a variety of ways, but one of the most important mechanisms is by *reuptake* into the cell that released the neurotransmitters. This word may already be familiar to you; you may know that some antidepressants are called SSRIs, short for *selective serotonin reuptake inhibitors.* These antidepressants inhibit, or block, the molecular pump on neurons that removes the neurotransmitter *serotonin* from the synapse and transports it back into the interior of the cell where it can be repackaged for re-release.

Soon after antidepressants were discovered (I'll tell you about this accidental discovery in more detail in the next chapter), neuroscientists, most importantly the American biochemist Julius Axelrod, started to investigate the effects these pharmaceuticals had on brain chemistry. It was discovered that these first antidepressants were powerful inhibitors of the reuptake pump for a group of neurotransmitters called *neurogenic amines* (or *neuroamines*), of which *norepinephrine* was thought to be the most important. (Axelrod, together with Ulf von Euler and Sir Bernard Katz, received the Nobel Prize for Medicine and Physiology in 1970 for this work.) Again, neurons turn off their chemical signals by scooping up neurotransmitter molecules from the synapse and repackaging them. Just as partially closing the drain in a bathtub will cause the tub to begin to fill with water, if you block the reuptake of neurotransmitter molecules into cells, the net effect will be an increase of neurotransmitters in the synapse.

Subsequent work has shown that nearly all effective antidepressants cause neurotransmitter reuptake blockade in brain cells. This observation led to the "amine hypothesis" of mood disorders, a theory that basically stated that depression was caused by an abnormally low level of neurotransmitters. (This may be where the unfortunate term "chemical imbalance" had its origins.) Further work soon indicated, however, that this explanation was much too simplistic. Antidepressant-induced changes in neurotransmitter levels at the synapse occur almost immediately after the drug is taken—in a matter of hours. But it was a well-known fact that antidepressants take several weeks to start alleviating the symptoms of depression. If the problem were simply too little neurotransmitter in the synapses of certain brain circuits, why would it take several weeks after the drug raised transmitter levels for the symptoms of depression to subside?

It was then suggested that the neurons may respond to these higher levels of neurotransmitters by changing their receptor molecules, either making them more sensitive to the neurotransmitter or putting more of the receptors in the synapse, a process that could be expected to take several weeks. The idea that antidepressants work by triggering an "up-regulation" of receptor sensitivity in the neuron continues to be popular among neuroscientists interested in the chemistry of mood disorders—but there is increasing recognition that this, too, is only part of the story.

Because of the unique therapeutic effects of lithium in mood disorders (both major depressive disorder and bipolar disorder), there has been a lot of effort to figure out where it acts in the brain and what its effect on brain chemistry is. In fact, investigating lithium's effect on brain chemistry is leading scientists closer than ever before to understanding the "broken" mechanism in mood disorders.

Lithium doesn't seem to affect neurotransmitter levels in the synapse and doesn't interact with neurotransmitter receptors or affect the reuptake pumps. In fact, it doesn't have any of the direct effects on cells that the antidepressants do. It's only been in the last few years that the probable site of lithium action has been found, and it's not at the synapse at all. Lithium (and perhaps the newer mood stabilizers as well) seems to work at a different cellular level: *inside* the neuron.

Although the precise fit between a neurotransmitter and its receptor molecule has often been compared to the close fit of a key into a lock, it has become apparent that the receptor is much more than just a lock. Starting in the 1970s, scientists have been able for the first time to elucidate the structure of cellular receptors and discover the details of these complex and elegant mechanisms. Receptors on the surface of the cell are coupled with structures called *G proteins* that extend through the cell membrane and link up with a complex array of other proteins and enzymes that regulate various functions of the cell. The G proteins act as transducers, converting data from outside the cell into functional changes inside the cell. They do this through a host of chemical processes that includes turning genes located inside the cell on and off.

There is evidence that lithium has direct effects on G proteins and several other groups of molecules that work inside the cell as "second messenger" molecules. The neurotransmitters, molecules that bring messages from other cells to the neuron, are considered the first messengers. The second messengers are molecules inside the cells that get activated by G proteins and travel within the neuron to turn on or off various switches in the cell membrane (the covering of the neuron) and in the main control center of the neuron, the nucleus.

You can think of the G protein–second messenger system as a communications and activity monitoring system for the neuron, constantly assessing the level of neurotransmitter activity and, perhaps by turning genes on

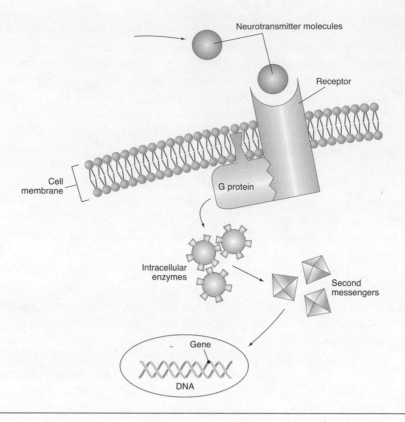

FIGURE 1.2 Receptors and G proteins

and off, continually altering and adjusting the functioning of the neuron in response to this activity. This is the neuroplasticity mentioned earlier in this chapter: the ability of the neuron to react and reshape itself, perhaps "tuning in" to certain levels of signaling. Several small molecules inside the neuron with names like *BDNF (brain-derived neurotrophic factor)* and *CREB (cAMP response element binding protein)* are thought to be important for this programming and reprogramming of neurons. There is more and more interest in another neurotransmitter, *glutamate,* which seems to factor significantly in neuroplasticity. Lamotrigine (Lamictal) and other mood stabilizers appear to work by changing glutamate levels.

You can think of neuroplasticity as the neurons' responsiveness and ability to react to change and stress. It is also thought to be involved in memory and learning. If you consider the symptoms of mood disorder, which include thinking and concentration problems in addition to mood changes, and also about how episodes of the illness can be triggered by stresses of various types, the idea that neuroplasticity is disrupted in mood disorder begins to make sense. It may be a necessary part of maintaining mood within a normal range, somehow adjusting the responsiveness of our mood state to experiences and environment. Perhaps mood disorder symptoms are the result of problems with neuroplasticity in neurons that make up the circuits that regulate mood.

Another area of research in mood disorders concerns the growth of cells in an area of the brain called the *hippocampus*. It was thought for many decades that the brain stopped producing new neurons shortly after birth—that the adult brain was not capable of growing new nerve cells. We now know that this is not the case; in fact, new cells are constantly being produced in certain areas of the brain. One of these areas is the hippocampus, a very specialized brain center involved in memory and emotion. Studies of humans with depression using imaging techniques that allow the size of brain structures to be measured in living people have shown the hippocampus is smaller in people with chronic depression. Animal studies indicate that lithium, antidepressants, and electroconvulsive therapy all increase the growth of neurons in the hippocampus. There is also evidence that chronic stress interferes with this cell growth in animals, a finding that may explain why stress triggers mood episodes in people with mood disorders.

This may also explain why medications that help with symptoms of mood disorders often take several weeks to do so. Antidepressants may artificially change neurotransmitter levels in the synapse, setting off a cascade of events, through the G protein and second-messenger system, that turns on genes that make molecules like CREB, BDNF, or other cell components needed to re-tune existing neurons and grow new ones. This could be why treatments for symptoms of mood disorders take several weeks to work.

It may be some time before we understand how all the molecular and cellular pieces of this complicated puzzle fit together, but the work to unravel the basic cause (or causes) of mood disorders is proceeding rapidly. And when we understand exactly what is "broken" in mood disorders, the job of fixing it will become much easier.

# CHAPTER 2

# Depression

THERE IS NO MORE VIVID WAY TO TALK ABOUT A DISEASE, ITS SYMPTOMS, and its treatment than the case study. Throughout this book, I will use case studies to explain a symptom or make a point. Some of the cases are composites of many patients; all them have been altered and disguised to protect the privacy of the people involved.

Margaret was a thirty-two-year-old woman who was referred to me by her family doctor because she was "very depressed." When I first saw her in my office she was attractive and fashionably dressed and looked healthy, but she had a sad, subdued manner.

"Your doctor told me you've been feeling depressed," I said. "How long has this been a problem for you?"

Margaret sighed deeply; she looked as if she didn't know where to begin. "About six months, I guess." Another deep sigh. "The crazy thing is, Doctor, I have absolutely no reason to feel like this. Feeling depressed is not like me."

"You'd better be careful using the word *crazy* in a psychiatrist's office!" I said, smiling, trying to be reassuring.

She looked blankly at the picture opposite her chair; if she had heard my attempt at humor, she certainly didn't think it was funny.

She continued: "I have a wonderful husband. We have two healthy children who do well in school and don't cause any problems at home other than the usual brother-sister bickering. No one could ask for a better family."

Margaret had returned to full-time work the year before, when her younger child was old enough to be in day care. She was executive director of the local arts council and had enjoyed her work immensely until her mood changes began. Margaret was well educated and had been very successful in her career in the arts. She had attended a prestigious local women's college and had a bachelor's degree in English and a master of fine arts degree. She had held administrative positions in several arts organizations before and just after she got married, but she quit working while her children were infants. While she was at home after the birth of her second child, she did watercolors in her spare time. She'd had a show of these works at one of the better galleries in town two years before and continued to sell her work regularly.

Her husband was an attorney with a medium-size firm and was well on the way to becoming a partner. I saw from her address that they lived in a distinguished older neighborhood; finances were probably not a problem. Why was this attractive, healthy, successful young woman depressed?

"Think for a minute about the beginning of this depression. What was the first thing you noticed that you thought wasn't right?"

"I think the very first thing I noticed was that I started having trouble sleeping. I've always slept very soundly."

"I want you to think carefully about your sleep problems for a moment. Have you been having trouble falling asleep at night? Do you wake up early in the morning and can't get back to sleep?"

"Let me think about that. I just seem to toss and turn all night, I think." She paused for a moment. "Well no, I know I lie awake waiting for the sunrise many mornings. I think it's more the second pattern."

"Do you think about anything in particular in those early morning hours?"

Another sigh. "Oh, I don't know . . . depressing things; it seems I obsess about every foolish thing I've ever done in my life."

"Like what?"

She was quiet for a moment and looked across the room again. "Well, my husband's sure this is the problem, so I might as well just tell you right away." (This might explain it, I thought, perhaps she's going to reveal some terrible secret, the reasons for her early morning ruminations and other symptoms of depression.) Margaret's "terrible secret" was that she had become pregnant as a teenager and had had an abortion.

"How long has your husband known about this?" I asked.

"Oh, I told him before we got married."

Well, this doesn't quite fit, I thought. I could have understood if Margaret's husband had just found out about a prior intimate relationship and had become jealous and accusing, perhaps taunting her about it or else becoming sullen and withdrawn. Opening old wounds like this has a way of making a person relive all sorts of regrets and losses and can definitely cause temporary depression. But that this successful, talented young woman would suddenly start worrying about such an old issue didn't quite make sense.

I tried to find other clues to her symptoms in the content of her early-morning thoughts. "Tell me what else you find yourself obsessing about."

"I worry about the children, especially Sarah, my youngest. I feel I should be at home for her until she's in the first grade like I was for David." She paused and sighed deeply. She looked down at the floor and said with a pained voice, "I have had such guilty feelings about her being in day care."

Margaret didn't realize that by using one particular word in her last sentence, only fifteen minutes into her first appointment with me, she had allowed me to diagnose her as suffering from a mood disorder and decide on a plan of treatment.

"Do you think there's a connection between your feeling about Sarah's day care and your memories of the abortion?"

As Margaret looked down at the floor, her mouth began trembling and tears welled up.

"Doctor, I sometimes have these awful guilty feelings that I'm a terrible person." She started crying quietly. "I've never felt so bad in my life."

---

Are you wondering what word made the diagnosis? "Made the diagnosis" is perhaps overstating the case. Let me say rather that it is a word that makes a psychiatrist highly suspicious of a mood disorder in a person complaining of depression. The word is *guilty*. A peculiar quality of the depressed mood seen in mood disorders is that it is very often accompanied by feelings of guilt. Sadness, disappointment, and the other unpleasant but normal feelings I discussed earlier do not usually have this quality, whereas patients suffering from a mood disorder frequently find their thoughts drifting back to things they have regretted or felt guilty about. Very often, as in Margaret's case, they feel guilty about things they thought they had come to terms with, and they can't explain the recurrence of bad feelings about these old issues.

Margaret had shared her experience with all the important people in her life she felt had a right to know, even her husband, whom she met years after the incident and who might never have found out otherwise. Margaret clearly felt guilty about the abortion now, but she hadn't for many years. No one in her life had brought it up. Why were these feelings coming up now?

Many mothers feel a bit guilty initially about sending their children to day care, even now when so many women work outside the home. But guilty feelings had not cropped up for Margaret until the past several weeks, and this was many months after her daughter had started day care. As it turned out, little Sarah had done some clinging when she first started at day care, but in a week she was completely adjusted to the new routine, had made lots of friends, and looked forward to going each morning. Again, Margaret's guilty feelings should have been strongest when Sarah was in the clinging stage, not now. Margaret's feelings were not entirely *understandable* in light of the facts of her life situation.

"You've already told me about your sleep problem. Have you lost your appetite?" I asked.

"Yes, most days I just force myself to eat, especially breakfast."

"Have you lost weight?"

"A few pounds, but I can stand to lose a few."

"Have you noticed that you've lost interest in sex?"

"Yes . . . that's really bothering me too. My husband and I have always had such a good sexual relationship. It's not like me not to be interested."

Evidence for the diagnosis of a mood disorder was accumulating fast; here were the typical *vegetative symptoms*. Vegetative symptoms refer to the symptoms that serious depression causes when it interferes with the basic needs or drives for sleep, food, and sexual pleasure. That this illness interferes with so many aspects of life illustrates how serious it is and how basic a change in brain chemistry must cause it. The pattern of Margaret's sleep loss is typical of the illness. Psychiatrists use the term *early morning awakening* to refer to this particular sleep disturbance. Patients report that they fall asleep more or less quickly and at the normal time but wake up very early in the morning, often at two or three o'clock. They often say that this is the worst time of the day, a time when they, as Margaret put it so succinctly, "obsess about every foolish thing I've ever done in my life." The mood often lifts as the day goes on. Sometimes people with depression have the opposite pattern—they find that their mornings are better and they lose energy and experience worsening in their mood as the day progresses. These patterns of mood change throughout the day, patterns that repeat day after day, are called *diurnal variation in mood* and are a classic symptom of the depression seen in mood disorders. *Diurnal* comes from a Latin word meaning "of the day."

---

"Has there ever been another time in your life when you had these kinds of problems?" I asked.

"Not that I can remember."

"How about after the birth of your children? Did you notice any depression then?"

"Well, now that you mention it, I did have crying spells for about two months after David was born. I'd just burst into tears for no reason. But isn't that normal? I think my mother called it 'the baby blues.' She said it would pass, and it did."

---

Here was another piece of strong evidence that Margaret was suffering from a mood disorder—a history of a prior episode. This is another of the hallmarks of mood disorders: an episodic pattern and tendency to recur. As is frequently the case, Margaret's first episode was milder and shorter than the one that brought her to medical attention. As is also often the case, it went unrecognized and, in fact, was explained away as "normal."

Other symptoms of what we now know to be diseases were once thought to be normal, too, especially very common ones. For example, many people, including many physicians, believed that "getting senile" was a normal part of growing old. We now realize that a specific disease process causes the insidious loss of memory and other types of intellectual deterioration sometimes seen in elderly persons. This condition, like Parkinson's disease, is now thought to be caused by the death of cells in a particular brain center, the *nucleus solitarius*. This illness is the now-familiar Alzheimer's disease, more properly called *Alzheimer's-type dementia*. It was named after the physician (who was a psychiatrist, by the way) who first described it. This "senility" is a disease process, and there is nothing normal about it.

Similarly, symptoms of mood disorders at particular times of life have been called normal or explained away as a psychological reaction to certain life events. The "baby blues" is one example. We now know that hormonal changes can be associated with changes in mood and that postpartum depression (*postpartum* being the medical term for the period immediately after giving birth) probably has a significant chemical component. It doesn't happen to everyone, and how well or poorly one adjusts to motherhood does not predict who will get it.

The most striking example of how serious depressive disorders have been misunderstood in this way is the story of "involutional melancholia." For many years, it had been noticed that severe depression sometimes occurred in women going through menopause. Like postpartum depression, it was often explained in psychological terms. In this case it was seen as a psychological reaction to the termination of reproductive life—a kind of mourning for the end of the childbearing years and the beginning of old age. This explanation ignored that the symptoms did not look at all like mourning but had all the characteristics of the depression of affective disorder. When effective medication for depression became available, it was found to work for involutional melancholia. It seemed illogical to call an episode of serious depression by another name just because it happened to occur at menopause, so the name was dropped as a diagnostic category. (I'll return to these issues in a section of chapter 5 called "Mood Disorders in Women.")

"How has this change in mood affected your working, your free time?" I asked Margaret. "What do you do for enjoyment?"

"Usually I can really relax and enjoy myself after dinner with my painting. It's always been such a source of pleasure for me. But I don't enjoy it like I used to. I just can't get interested in it."

"Would you say you don't get as much enjoyment out of a lot of things anymore?"

"Well, yes, I suppose that's true. I just sort of feel stuck. I can't do anything to pull myself out of it. David's team won their first soccer game of the season this past Saturday. Last year I got so tickled watching them, even if they lost. Now every game is a chore. I get so restless and irritated at the thought of spending an afternoon at the school. I lost my temper on the way home last week just because the poor little kid had gotten grass stains on his uniform. I've been a real bitch to live with."

Another classic symptom: *anhedonia.* The word is derived from a Greek root meaning "pleasure" (a hedonist is someone who lives only for pleasure). Anhedonia is the inability to experience pleasure. Again, a psychiatrist makes the diagnosis of a mood disorder by discovering the qualities of a patient's mood change that are abnormal. Sad persons who are not suffering from a depressive disorder usually do not have marked anhedonia. Rather, they are able to shake off their sadness for a time during the day and enjoy some pleasurable activity. They can go to a movie and forget their troubles for a few hours or take a drive in the country and come back refreshed. A person in the midst of the depression of affective disorder, however, cannot escape from a continuous, pervasive change in mood that is simply unrelenting. The mood is consistently the same—miserable. Some little pleasure or happy accident during the day that ordinarily would cheer the sufferer just falls flat. Remember, normal mood is reactive. In affective disorder the mood loses this quality—there is no reaction to events in the environment. This phenomenon has been called a *constriction* of mood.

---

"I want to shift gears a bit and ask you some questions about your family background," I said. "Do you know if anyone else in your family—parents, brothers and sisters, anyone at all—has ever needed to see a psychiatrist or take medication for depression or emotional problems?"

"No, nothing like that."

I persisted. "Now I want you to think carefully about your mother and father. Aunts and uncles on your mother's side?" Margaret's face became a little more strained in concentration. "Aunts and uncles on your father's side?"

"My uncle Edgar, on my father's side, was in a mental hospital once . . . no, I think it was two or three times."

"What can you remember about your uncle?"

"Well, it's funny, because he's always seemed perfectly normal to me. Uncle Edgar is usually the life of the party at our family reunions. Come to think of it, I never could make sense out of what my mother said about him."

"How so?"

"Well, she told me he had had shock treatments in the hospital. I thought you really had to be crazy to need that. But as I said, he always seemed just fine to me. He owns a big dry-cleaning chain in the West. He works hard, makes tons of money. He sure seems happy and healthy now."

---

Well, I thought, this pretty much ties it up: a family history of a psychiatric problem severe enough to require hospitalization that was treated with electroconvulsive therapy. There were a number of questions to be asked for the sake of completeness. But Margaret's family history, her own history, and her symptoms made quite a case for a diagnosis of a mood disorder.

## The Symptoms of Major Depression

Let me review the process that led from Margaret's family doctor's description of her as "depressed" to a diagnosis of a mood disorder. First, and most important, Margaret reported feeling depressed. She did indeed feel a change in her mood as I described mood in the first chapter. Also, she could date the onset of the change and clearly stated that she felt very different now than she did when she was her usual self. Some patients with the depression of affective disorder say they do not feel particularly depressed. By this they usually they mean they are not sad and do not feel like crying, but they certainly are unhappy. They seem to be simply miserable, very irritable and short-tempered, impatient and restless, unable to relax, and unable to say anything nice about anything or anybody.

Secondly, Margaret reported that her mood change was with her every day. It was pervasive, there all the time, interfering with everything she did or wanted to do. Many patients find that the mood change even intrudes on their sleep in the form of unpleasant dreams. Themes of death, loss, and pain are frequent. Abraham Lincoln, who undoubtedly suffered from a mood disorder, had dreams of death and dying during the depressions that haunted him episodically for years. Shortly before his assassination, he told an aide that he had dreamed of finding a corpse lying in state on a catafalque in the East Room of the White House. Whether this was some kind of mystical revelation of his impending death I will leave to the parapsychologists, but it was certainly a typical symptom of the depression seen in mood disorders.

Margaret's depressed mood had some qualities that are seen in mood disorders and are not usually seen, or at least are not very prominent, in depressed states that are normal reactions to losses and disappointment. These qualities were her feelings of guilt and failure and her anhedonia. This loss of interest in usually pleasurable activities is very important. It seemed to grow out of the pervasiveness of Margaret's mood change. As I said earlier, psychiatrists sometimes call this a constriction of mood or, as I have described it, a loss of the normal reactivity of mood.

Margaret was preoccupied with some thoughts and issues that did not bother her before she got depressed, specifically her adequacy as a mother. Many patients with depression find that their minds continually return to the same unpleasant thoughts. Even though they try to put such thoughts out of their minds, their mental activity is drawn to the same depressing themes as if by some force like magnetism or gravity. In psychiatry such ideas are called obsessional thoughts or simply obsessions. Many people who are not depressed have similar experiences—we have all heard some melody, maybe something silly like an advertising jingle, and found ourselves humming or just thinking it throughout the day; even though we try to push it out of our minds, it keeps coming back. An obsessional thought is similar, but it is usually unpleasant and resisted by the patient, who tries without success to think about other things. Several years ago I treated a depressed man, a devout Catholic, who was tormented by recurring blasphemous sexual images. Not only were the thoughts extremely distressing in themselves to this religious man, but these blasphemous and therefore "sinful" ideas compounded the feelings of guilt caused by his depression. Another patient had the recurrent fearful thought that she was going to accidentally start a fire, so she began to avoid matches and soon even the stove in her own kitchen. Patients with obsessional thoughts cannot push them away for long and sometimes will complain of the fear of "losing my mind" to express their alarm at these out-of-control experiences. When obsessional thoughts are symptoms of affective disorder (and many are), they disappear when the disorder is properly treated.

Another common experience is the feeling that one's thought processes are slowed and inefficient. One may believe one's memory is bad, since when we aren't concentrating well it is hard to remember things. This slowing and inefficiency are also responsible for the indecisiveness depressed people often feel. This symptom seems especially prominent in older persons who become depressed (see "Major Depression in the Elderly" in chapter 5). In less severe cases, this can take the form of difficulties concentrating at work or school, problems reading a book or even the newspaper. Sometimes people who are severely depressed take longer to think and speak, and even their movements can be slowed down, an effect called *psychomotor retardation.* (*Retardation* here has its literal meaning of "slowed" and has nothing to do with the term *mental retardation,* which refers to low IQ.) Those around the sufferer sometimes interpret this lethargy as laziness, and this criticism can compound the guilt associated with the illness.

Margaret was having vegetative symptoms of depression; that is, she noticed changes in her usual bodily activities and rhythms. She observed a change in her appetite and a change in her sleeping habits. There was a particular pattern in her sleep disturbance, too: early-morning awakening. Some people have sleep and appetite changes in the opposite direction when they are depressed; they find that they sleep and eat more than is usual for them.

The uncomfortable physical sensations accompanying the depression of affective disorder can at times be so distressing that they dominate the clinical picture. Many people simply feel "sick" or "tired" in a vague and general way, but others notice a variety of true pains. Headaches are very common, as is a sense of heaviness in the chest. Any little ache that might otherwise be ignored seems to be exaggerated and becomes more difficult to endure, so that back pains or arthritis pains seem much worse (see "Depression and Pain" in chapter 5). Constipation is another common complaint.

TABLE 2.1  Common Symptoms of Major Depression

Depressed Mood
  Pervasive, constricted quality of depression
  Feelings of guilt and inadequacy
  Fearful, overwhelmed feelings
  Onset of a fear of being alone
  Diurnal variation in mood
  Preoccupation with failure, illness, or other unpleasant themes (may become
    obsessional thoughts)
  Nightmares, especially with themes of loss, pain, or death
  Anhedonia (loss of ability to experience pleasure)
  Indecision
  Onset of unexplained anxiety, panic attacks
Vegetative Signs
  Sleep disturbance (too much or too little, especially with early morning
    awakening)
  Appetite disturbance (increased or decreased, usually enough to cause
    weight change)
  Fatigue, low energy
  Vague aches and pains, heaviness in the chest
  Constipation
  Loss of interest in sex
  Poor concentration, slowed thinking (psychomotor retardation)

Margaret reported a loss of interest in sex. This symptom may be thought of as an aspect of anhedonia as well and is very typical of the depression of affective disorder.

These symptoms point to a mood disorder, but other information Margaret supplied was also helpful in making the diagnosis. She gave a history of a prior unexplained mood change (her "baby blues") that lasted several months and went away spontaneously. Affective disorder follows what physicians refer to as a relapsing and remitting course. It is episodic: relapses are separated by long periods of remission during which there are no symptoms. More about this aspect of the illness later.

Last, Margaret told me that a blood relative had had a psychiatric illness severe enough to require hospitalization but had recovered completely. Another important piece of information is that he received electroconvulsive therapy. We'll discuss this much maligned but safe and effective treatment later. For now I'll just say that it is now used almost exclusively for severe episodes of the depression of affective disorder. The genetic (hereditary) link in mood disorders is very strong. As we will see, having a relative with one greatly increases the chances of having a mood disorder (see "The Heredity of Mood Disorders" in chapter 6).

Psychiatrists now have agreed on a term for this type of serious depression. Margaret would be diagnosed as suffering a *major depressive episode,* and her illness—her type of mood disorder—is called *major depression.*

## "Normal" Depression?

In discussing Margaret's symptoms, I used the phrase "other types of depression." In the very first section I posed the question, What is normal mood? and answered that a good or happy mood is not the only normal mood. (As you will see later, a good mood can be abnormal too.) Now that we have talked about abnormal depression—the mood disorder called major depression—a reasonable question to consider is: Can there really be such a thing as "normal depression"? Let's examine this question by considering another case:

---

Patty is a fourteen-year-old high school student who came to my office with her mother. Mom did most of the talking:

"Doctor, we're so concerned about our Patty; her father and I are very worried that she's depressed." Patty's mother was an animated woman and impressed me as a "take charge" type of person who wanted the best for her family and would leave no stone unturned to get it.

"What kinds of things have you noticed that make you worry she's depressed?"

"Well, she just looks so gloomy and sad all the time. She mopes around the house. She doesn't go out with her friends like she used to. She's not as interested in school as she was. She's just not the old Patty."

Patty had always been a good student; in fact, she still was. She seemed to do less homework and to be less concerned with school, but her marks were still at about the same level as they had always been. Patty agreed that she didn't feel like going out with her friends the way she had during the previous school year and over the summer.

Her mother mentioned that Patty had broken up with a boyfriend recently, but Patty, rolling her eyes with an "Oh, Mom" look, corrected her and said that the breakup had occurred months ago and she was over it. Patty had done a little experimenting with alcohol and marijuana, but I believed her when she said she had tried them only a few times.

Her mother told me that Patty's older brother had had a severe bout of depression but was doing much better now that he was taking medication. This piece of information was a red flag, and as I continued to question Patty and her mother, I felt there was a fair bit of evidence that her depression was a mood disorder but that there wasn't quite enough evidence to start Patty on medicine—at least not yet. On one hand, she had a family history of major depression and had experienced a change in mood that seemed not to be in response to anything. But on the other hand, there wasn't a significant change in her concentration or her ability to enjoy other things (her schoolwork had not been affected, and she told me she had gotten through the six-hundred-plus pages of the latest Harry Potter book in only three days). When I asked Patty if she were having any suicidal thoughts, her eyes had widened in alarm and she'd said "Oh no, I have so much to live for, I want to be a doctor, a pediatrician."

"I'd like to see Patty back again next week," I said. "I want to get to know her better before deciding how best to help."

Her mother's brow knitted slightly. She obviously thought this was an inadequate way to finish the first appointment. "I thought you'd start her on medication right away. It helped her brother so much."

"I understand your worries, and while antidepressant medications are certainly low risk, they're not 'no risk.' I want to see Patty again next week and we'll talk some more."

At the next appointment, I saw Patty alone for most of the appointment and tried to get to know her better.

As sometimes happens, when I found out more about her, my initial formulation of Patty's problem changed. Patty's best friend was Audrey, and they did everything together. They had both started high school several months before, and for reasons they couldn't quite understand, there was a change in the pattern of friends they shared. Patty and Audrey suddenly found themselves part of the "popular crowd" at school. Patty had always been popular, but she considered herself a bit shy. Now she got invited to the best parties, ate lunch with the popular crowd in the cafeteria, and so forth. A teenage girl's dream come true, isn't it? Well, Patty certainly felt that way at first, but she started to change her mind as the school year went on. She found her new friends flashy but shallow. The "best" parties turned out not to be as much fun as last year's parties with her old friends, and Patty thought there was way too much drinking. Her family was Baptist and strongly discouraged any use of alcohol; although Patty was not as rigid as her parents, teenagers getting drunk definitely bothered her. She found a lot of the girls catty and cruel and the boys "stuck-up" and sexually aggressive.

Audrey, on the other hand, thought their newfound clique was *the* group to be with and couldn't understand why Patty had become so "uncool." Patty found herself in a real dilemma; she felt uncomfortable with her new friends and their values but felt she couldn't go back to her old friends or get different new ones without losing Audrey's friendship. (Remember that Patty thought of herself as shy.) Mom and Dad were rather strict parents, so Patty felt she couldn't really discuss these things with them (especially the "sex and booze" part).

Patty missed the "good old days" of last year. On the one hand she enjoyed the academic challenges of her new school, but on the other hand she worried about what the next four years would be like for her. What if Audrey didn't want to be her friend anymore? What if she *never* fit in? Patty felt trapped in the current situation and had some worries about the future. As adolescents often do, Patty had a very hard time seeing her current loneliness and feelings of alienation as temporary and situation-limited.

Also, Patty told me she had spent the previous weekend at her grandmother's farm in the country and it turned out that, as usual, she'd had a wonderful time. It was like a return to the carefree days of childhood, and she felt refreshed by the change in atmosphere and time away from her social pressures. This bit of information was very important and went a long way toward swaying me away from starting medication (remember what I said earlier about anhedonia and the pervasive, nonstop quality of depressed mood in mood disorders?); I decided to keep seeing her every week to talk about the problems at school and not to start medication. We talked about how to handle peer pressure, how friends sometimes grow apart as they grow up, about "shyness" and self-confidence. Her mood got better and better with psychotherapy and without medicine.

---

This case leads me back to the question, Can depression be normal? Let's examine what I said about a normal mood change. I described it as understandable and proportional. In Patty's case it took a while for me to figure it out, but when I did I realized that her mood change indeed had these qualities. Patty's nostalgia for past relationships, feelings of not fitting in, fears of losing her best friend, and not going out with friends as much, were really quite understandable. Also, although she worried that she was shy (and this was not new, according to her mother), Patty did not have the preoccupation with inadequacies or guilty feelings that is typical of major depression.

As we shall see, mild cases of affective disorder sometimes lack many of the typical symptoms, but given Patty's continued improvement without medication, one is hard pressed to say she suffers from an illness.

Nevertheless, one is also reluctant to say this behavior is normal, if by "normal" one means "the way it should be." Clearly, teenagers shouldn't be depressed. On the other hand, when we consider Patty's story and think about the emotional reactions people usually have to conflicts, our intuition and our own experiences lead us to an understanding of why Patty's mood and behavior had changed. We do not have to invoke a disease process that disrupts normal functioning to explain these changes. On the contrary, knowing Patty well and considering the situation that developed in her environment, we might almost predict some of her uncomfortable feelings.

Yet, Patty definitely had a problem in the emotional realm that impaired her to some extent and required and responded to treatment, albeit psychological treatment, not medication. What was my diagnosis of Patty's problem? In the latest version of the classification of psychiatric problems of the American Psychiatric Association, the *Diagnostic and Statistical Manual of Mental Disorders (DSM)*, Patty would be said to be suffering from an adjustment disorder with depressed mood. The key features of this diagnosis are that there is an identifiable stressor (the stress in this case is social change and disruption of relationships) and that there is some impairment of functioning. In Patty's case the impairment was quite mild, little more than her decreased socialization with her peer group and her moping around the house. Although not listed in the formal classification of psychiatric disorders, the term *reactive depression* is still often used to discuss this type of mood change. It is a useful concept and brings me to another important topic.

## The Classification of Depression

As you have seen from reading about Margaret and Patty, the phrase "I'm depressed" can describe what almost seem to be two different conditions. Margaret clearly has an illness, Patty seems to be reacting in an understandable way to life circumstances—yet they are both depressed. Their problems appear similar and yet, intuitively, they seem different. Even before neurochemical evidence accumulated for a biological basis for some changes in mood, psychiatrists recognized these types of differences and wondered if there were different kinds of depression. When medical treatments for depression were developed it was discovered that not all who complained of depression could benefit from the new treatments. This led to attempts to differentiate the types of depression that did benefit from those that didn't, and some new clinical terminology was developed.

In older textbooks of psychiatry, one reads various clinical terms that attempt to classify depression, usually into two basic types. *Primary* depression, as opposed to *secondary* depression, refers to depression that seems to arise "out of the blue" rather than being caused by a life event and thus secondary to or following something else. The terms e*ndogenous depression* and *reactive depression* express similar concepts. The word *endogenous* is from Greek roots meaning "produced or growing from within"; *reactive* is used with its customary meaning indicating that something is a result of an external event. These terms still are used quite frequently, but as we shall see, there are some problems with them.

Perhaps a better way to talk about these differences is to speak of "depression the *symptom*" and "depression the *syndrome*." A symptom is basically an uncomfortable or unusual feeling noticed by a patient. Chest pain, a cough, and ringing in the ears are all symptoms. Depressed mood is a symptom, too, and like the physical symptoms I mentioned, depressed mood may indicate several different underlying problems. Just as a cough can be a symptom of a minor illness such as a cold or of the life-threatening illness lung cancer, depressed mood can be a symptom of a minor problem or of a very serious one. A syndrome, by contrast, is a whole collection of symptoms and other findings that, when they occur together, point strongly to a particular diagnosis or small set of diagnoses. Pain in the wrist, for example, accompanied by swelling, redness, and heat, constitutes the inflammatory syndrome, or more simply, inflammation. To specify that the inflammation is in a joint, we use the term *arthritis* (from the Greek *arthron,* "joint"). The pain is the symptom: the swelling and so forth that the doctor notices on examination are called "signs." The syndrome is arthritis, and there are several causes for this syndrome.

The depressive syndrome includes the symptom of depression (or more precisely, depressed mood), but it also includes many other symptoms: anhedonia, guilt, and self-reproach, as well as other signs that go beyond the mood alone: vegetative signs, diurnal variation of mood, and so forth. Taken altogether, these symptoms and signs define the *depressive syndrome.* Everyone has experienced depression the symptom, but only people with mood disorders have the syndrome of depression. (Actually, some other causes of the syndrome are possible, as you'll see in chapter 6 under "Medical Causes of Mood Disorders" and elsewhere.)

Why all this interest in classification? Perhaps instead of *classification* I'll substitute a more familiar word that doctors use to talk about the classification of illnesses: *diagnosis.* Diagnostic categories are really systems of classifying diseases. The basic purpose of diagnostic categories is prediction of treatment and outcome. Making a particular diagnosis allows the doctor to predict which treatment will be most effective in helping the patient get better. The obvious advantage of accurate diagnostic classifications is that the most effective treatment can be chosen quickly, eliminating unnecessary treatment by ineffectual methods.

In the treatment of depression, several facts have been discovered that make diagnosis important: the medications and other treatments I will discuss in the next chapter provide the most benefit in the syndrome of depression. Persons with reactive or secondary depression often do not derive any benefit from these sort of treatments but instead get better with a very different kind of treatment: psychotherapy. Although it is tempting to try dividing cases of depression in this way to decide on treatment course, it would be much too simplistic. A major depressive episode can follow a traumatic event and seem reactive, yet respond to medication. Also, psychotherapy can be very useful in the treatment of major depression. Most importantly, it's clear that biological factors (like one's genetic endowment) often interact with life stresses, losses, and traumas to trigger major depression. In fact, this is probably most often the case.

Let's examine another case history in order to understand these issues more clearly:

Robert was a thirty-six-year-old engineer who had just been through a nasty divorce from his wife of ten years. They had three daughters, aged nine, eight, and two. Robert and Nancy had not been a very compatible couple from the start and began to have difficulties early in their marriage. Robert was a serious, methodical, rather meticulous person who wanted a quiet home life, while Nancy was a vivacious, independent, at times tempestuous woman who was impulsive and could be almost reckless in her pursuit of new experiences. In the early years of their relationship, the temperamental differences between them were complementary and mutually enriching. Robert and Nancy were the opposites that attract. As the years passed, however, these differences caused more and more problems. The large age gap between their older daughters and their youngest occurred because Nancy decided (several years after she and Robert agreed they would have no more children) that she also wanted a son. Without informing her husband, Nancy stopped taking birth-control pills. When she became pregnant, she couldn't imagine why her husband wasn't as happy as she. Robert, however, interpreted Nancy's actions as complete disregard for his feelings about their family's future. Sexual intimacy between them practically stopped because Robert felt he could not trust Nancy not to get pregnant again. They began to bicker and grow distant. Robert spent more and more time at the office. One day he came home to find Nancy and the children gone. He discovered that Nancy had left him and taken the children to her hometown three hundred miles away.

A long and acrimonious divorce process began. Nancy's volatile nature and need for confrontation made every disagreement on terms a battle of wills. Every issue was a source of bitter contention, and custody of the children was the most emotional and nastiest battle of all. The arrangement that eventually was painfully worked out was joint custody, with Robert having the children with him each summer and during the week between Christmas and New Year's.

Despite a legal document clearly outlining each one's rights and responsibilities, and even with several hundred miles separating them, Nancy and Robert continued to have disagreements that precipitated violent verbal confrontations. In many ways Nancy missed Robert very much, but her pathological independence made it impossible for her to compromise to solve their problems. The thought of Robert leading a life of his own seemed to enrage Nancy, and she used every interaction with him to act out her fury in the pettiest ways. Robert would travel three hundred miles to pick up the children at an agreed upon time, only to find Nancy's house empty. She would return hours later with the children and simply say she had been grocery shopping. Robert would get abusive phone calls from Nancy in the middle of the night accusing him of not sending his support payment; he would investigate the matter at the bank and stop payment on the check, then Nancy would tell him the check had mysteriously appeared in the mailbox.

Throughout his trial by fire, Robert maintained his usual steady and methodical manner in his work, went through the wrenching process of selling the house their family had been growing in, and simultaneously met Nancy's assaults on his peace of mind with what could only be described as equanimity. His unflinching even-temperedness prevailed as Nancy's histrionic energy waned, and their relationship settled into an uneasy truce, or at least a cease-fire.

Six months after the divorce, Robert still found himself preoccupied by the devastation wreaked on his life. Instead of beginning to put the event in perspective and rebuilding his life, however, Robert ruminated on the past and tortured himself with questions. Had he been too hard on his wife? Had he been too rigid and unyielding? What had he done to change her high spirits and zest for living into bitter, recriminating sarcasm and conflict?

Robert found it difficult to concentrate on his work. He lost weight. His colleagues commented that he looked tired all the time. He wondered if he had some kind of infection and went to see his family doctor.

"I heard about Nancy the other day, Bob," the doctor said as he walked into the examination room. "I'm sorry things got so bad between the two of you. Listen, I'm sure she'll be much better in a few weeks."

"I don't know what you're talking about."

The doctor looked pained. "Gosh, Bob, the hospital staff said they were going to call you yesterday."

"I was in New York yesterday. What hospital staff? What's the matter with Nancy?"

"Bob, she took an overdose Tuesday night. The hospital they took her to called me for her medical records. Fortunately, her medical condition wasn't serious. They were going to admit her to the psychiatric unit."

---

Robert and Nancy both had serious emotional problems. They were both very unhappy people and both suffered from depression. Whose depression was more severe? The answer is obvious, or so it would seem. Nancy became so distraught that she decided life wasn't worth living and tried to kill herself, didn't she? Robert had a bad mood that went on for a while, but he was a "neurotic," introverted guy anyway, wasn't he? Isn't his depression understandable?

Robert's mood problem did not really begin until after most of the conflict with Nancy had ended. I described Robert as a logical, methodical person who did not like surprises or discord. If anything would "drive him crazy," that is, cause him to have severe reactive symptoms, it would have been all the conflict during the time immediately following their separation and divorce. One would expect him to begin to feel better once the dust had settled. When we look at the quality of his depression, we can identify symptoms of guilt and self-recrimination. Robert also had persistent and marked appetite and sleep disturbances. His history is strikingly like Margaret's. Robert's depression was major depression: he was having a major depressive episode.

How does the fact that he had a severe emotional trauma fit into the clinical picture? It was once emphasized in psychiatry that when a precipitating event could be identified, the diagnosis of major depression was unlikely. This has not turned out to be so. Instead, we now recognize that emotional trauma—the death of a loved one, the loss of a job, or as in this case, a divorce—can precipitate an episode of affective disorder.

A metaphor I often use to explain this concept to my patients is the common experience of getting caught in a soaking rain, becoming chilled, and then coming down with a cold. We know that getting chilled doesn't *cause* colds; viruses cause colds. But the chill can cause a set of biological circumstances that allows a virus in the air to get a "foothold" in the upper respiratory tract and bring on a cold. Emotional trauma may cause a set of circumstances that allows an episode of major depression to occur at a particular time in a vulnerable person. Physical stress can also precipitate an episode of affective disorder, especially certain kinds of physical stresses.

Because the depression of affective disorder can follow on an emotional or physical stress, the term *reactive depression* should be used cautiously. The term *adjustment disorder* (Patty's diagnosis) is now used in the diagnostic manual of the American Psychiatric Association to denote the relation between precipitating event and subsequent depression.

Now what about Nancy? Her problems seem much more complicated and much less clear-cut. In the hospital, an important part of the process of diagnosis will be to assess Nancy for the symptoms of the syndrome of depression. But an equally important part will be to attempt to understand the extent to which her symptoms and behavior might be the understandable result of who Nancy is (her personal strengths and vulnerabilities, her ways of coping with adversity), and of what has happened to her.

In Nancy's case, this second type of assessment will turn out to be more helpful. As the professionals caring for her will find out, Nancy is in some respects Robert's opposite; he likes predictability and routine, and Nancy thrives on the new and unexpected. One of Nancy's problems, which can be understood as an aspect of these qualities, is that she is impulsive. Robert tends to approach a problem logically and carefully—he will consider options, weigh pros and cons, and then make a well-reasoned decision. Nancy, on the other hand, will listen to her feelings and intuition and decide issues almost spontaneously, often based on emotion rather than logic. She will pick a particular option because it "feels right."

Another problem is that Nancy reacts very badly to loss and rejection. She had a difficult childhood, to a large extent because her parents died in a car accident when she was two years old. Nancy was shuttled between several different sets of relatives and raised by various aunts and uncles who often considered her a burden and an intruder into their own families. As a child Nancy never knew when she would be uprooted and sent on to yet another family. After a few years, she started to act up whenever she sensed that her guardians were getting tired of her. Rather than face yet another rejection, she would reject first. She was not conscious of this pattern, but it was almost as if she reasoned on some unconscious level, "You don't think I'm good enough for your family; well, I'll show you what bad really is!" In an unfortunate and self-destructive way, Nancy protected her fragile self-esteem by giving her aunts and uncles good reason to get rid of her. This led to an even more difficult tendency; it became extremely hard for her to admit when she was wrong. She blamed others for her own lapses of judgment and her impulsive and foolish decisions: "If you hadn't treated me that way, I wouldn't have done it." The idea of admitting she had been wrong and asking forgiveness as a prelude to working out differences was very difficult for Nancy.

How does this added knowledge about Nancy help us understand the problems between her and Robert and, even more important, her suicide attempt? Her impulsiveness may explain the pregnancy that seemed to set off the unfortunate chain of events culminating in divorce. When Robert rejected her sexually, Nancy, sensing that he might want to end the marriage, reacted (impulsively) by leaving him. As she had often done before, she blamed Robert completely for their problems; she remained furious at him, and her anger poisoned his attempts to placate her or reason with her. The custody and child-support battle became an emotional battering ram that Nancy could not resist using against him. Yet, in her moments alone, Nancy missed Robert and yearned for the happy early years of their marriage.

Now that we have some more background, let's look more closely at Nancy's depression and her suicide attempt. In addition to her reaction to the interpersonal loss, Nancy did not like being a single parent. Finances were tighter, so she had to work part time. This left little time or energy, let alone money, for a social life. This "all work and no play" was very difficult for Nancy. Robert, who had always found work stimulating and even soothing, could throw himself into it and gain a therapeutic effect. For Nancy, work was something one did to get money for fun, and given her financial situation, she wasn't getting much fun for her efforts.

As she might have expected, her relatives were less than supportive of her, either emotionally or financially. "So you've screwed up again," was the reproach she could detect behind their cool politeness when she visited her aunts and uncles. Their thinly veiled sarcasm was more than she could stand, and she stopped her contacts with them. As the months passed, Nancy became more and more unhappy. She felt trapped in a situation not of her own making, abandoned once again by those she had been foolish enough to trust. She became increasingly angry, lonely, and desperate. One day she dropped the children off at school, went home, and took an overdose of sleeping pills. She then tried calling Robert to let him know what he had done to her, but couldn't reach him. She began to panic and dialed 911 before she lost consciousness.

Now that we have gotten to know more about Nancy, it becomes apparent that her problems were in some ways very different from Robert's. Nancy had a set of attitudes about herself and others that made life difficult for her. Because of some destructive childhood experiences, she reacted in maladaptive ways to certain kinds of problems, especially problems in her relationships. Often her reactions, even the well-intentioned ones, made things worse rather than better. If we understand Nancy's particular personality vulnerabilities and consider the events leading up to her overdose, we don't necessarily need to invoke a disease process that disrupts normal functioning to explain her mood change and actions. Nancy's feelings and actions almost seem normal—for Nancy. Well, *normal* is of course not the right word—better to say they were somewhat understandable in the light of her personality traits and the unfortunate set of circumstances to which she was reacting. And there's that word—*reactive*.

Should Nancy be prescribed medication? That decision would depend on whether she had the other symptoms of the syndrome of depression. Although her problems were much more complicated, deeper really, and seemed to grow out of her personality and approach to life, she could still have had an underlying mood disorder. Her psychotherapy would consist of helping her put aside her anger at Robert, giving her support and encouragement in addressing the immediate problems in her life, and over the longer term helping her understand how some of her feelings and reactions to problems were rooted in the past rather than appropriate to the present. Clearly this is in the realm of the psychological rather than biological. Nevertheless, the therapist would need to carefully assess her response to treatment. If, like Patty, she started feeling better and better and returned to her normal level of functioning, this would argue for continuing to wait before trying medication. If, on the other hand, the therapy didn't seem to be helping, or if during the course of treatment it became clear that other symptoms of major depression were present, that would argue for starting medication as she continued to work in therapy.

At this point, you may be wondering: If classifying and diagnosing depression is so tricky, why not treat everyone who complains of depression with both medication and psychotherapy? Many studies indicate that a combination of both is most effective. Nevertheless, medications and other medical treatments have side effects and risks. Psychotherapy can be a long, often very expensive process and also has associated risks. When bank robber Willie Sutton was asked why he robbed banks, he replied, "Because that's where the money is!" Both physicians and patients want to put their efforts "where the money is" when making treatment decisions. Although there are certainly many cases of depression that fall into the gray zone, there are many that are more black and white, in which emphasis on medical or psychological treatment needs to predominate.

Another sort of depressive disorder causes individuals to have less severe but much more persistent symptoms. Often the symptoms are not severe enough to bring sufferers to seek medical attention of any kind, much less psychiatric treatment. They can simply go on in misery, perhaps thinking that everyone feels as bad as they do but that they can't cover it up as well as others. Many people with this disorder have a smoldering, debilitating problem that goes on for years and years, like an ulcerated sore that does not heal. They become so accustomed to their chronic misery that they just learn to live with it.

There is a set of terms that describe this smoldering, chronic type of depression: *dysthymia* and *dysthymic disorder*. The prefix *dys-* in medicine denotes "abnormal or impaired," and the root *thymia* refers to the mood. Dysthymic disorder is a diagnosis in the *Diagnostic and Statistical Manual of Mental Disorders*. It refers to a mood disorder that is not as severe as a major depressive episode but goes on for a long time. To meet the diagnostic criteria for dysthymic disorder, the patient must be symptomatic, with a depressed mood most of the time for at least two years. Other diagnostic criteria are similar to those used to describe major depression—appetite and sleep disturbance, low energy, low self-esteem, and so on. Simply put, *dysthymic disorder* refers to depression that is chronic but not florid or terribly debilitating. There is growing evidence that the distinction between major depression and dysthymic disorder is arbitrary, especially since most people with dysthymic disorder eventually develop symptoms severe enough to meet diagnostic criteria for major depression (this has been called *double depression*).

Earlier in this section, I mentioned other terms that psychiatrists have used to try to classify depression: endogenous depression and reactive depression; primary and secondary depression. I've also discussed major depression and now dysthymia, and I've hardly even mentioned bipolar disorder yet. Why all these terms? The existence of so many classification systems for depression illustrates a simple fact: psychiatry has not yet come up with diagnostic categories that accurately separate the different forms that depression can take. (I'll discuss some of the facts that might explain this in chapter 6, under "The Heredity of Mood Disorders.")

If this discussion of the classification of depression seems confusing to you, don't be discouraged. There are some simple facts upon which experts agree: although not all people who are depressed will derive benefit from, or need, medical treatments for depression, some people who have depression suffer from an illness rooted in the biological or chemical functioning of the brain. Medical interventions are necessary in the treatment of these patients, and psychological treatment alone will usually not be very effective.

# CHAPTER 3

# Treatment

Now that I have discussed the symptoms of depression, it is time to turn to its treatment. As I said in the first chapter, a large body of evidence has accumulated to indicate that mood disorders have as their basis a change in the functioning of the brain. It makes sense then to approach this problem with medical treatments that also affect the chemistry of the brain.

## Medications

As has often happened in medicine, drugs used to treat mood disorders were discovered practically by accident. Effective medications were found and successfully used for years before scientists had many clues as to how they worked. In the last chapter, I discussed how there has been a sort of reverse investigation in understanding the chemistry of depression and the chemical effect of these medications. The discovery of how treatments for depression change brain chemistry has pointed the way toward a biochemical theory of mood disorders.

### ANTIDEPRESSANTS

The development of the drug chlorpromazine (Thorazine) in the 1940s was a revolutionary breakthrough in the treatment of emotional problems. This drug was found to alleviate many of the symptoms of the often devastating and chronic psychiatric illness schizophrenia. Although schizophrenia is a very different illness from the ones that concern us here, the development of the first pharmaceutical to treat specific symptoms of a psychiatric disorder was nevertheless also a milestone in the treatment of mood disorders.

The calming effects of medications such as the barbiturates and morphine had been used in treating schizophrenia for many years, but these drugs were little more than "knockout drops" that simply put patients to sleep. The development of chlorpromazine made available for the first time a medication that did not just quiet an agitated person but actually relieved the symptoms of the illness without affecting other brain functions such as level of consciousness. Chlorpromazine was found to treat the hallucinations and disrupted thought processes of schizophrenia in a very specific way—a vast improvement over the older medications, which provided only general sedation.

Professor Roland Kuhn of Zurich reasoned that if a pharmaceutical could control the symptoms of schizophrenia in this specific way, there must also be a chemical way to treat abnormal mood states. He embarked on a search for the right chemical family and turned to a group of medications that had been synthesized as possible antihistamines but had been shelved when their antihistamine activity proved weak. He administered a number of these drugs to his patients and became convinced that one of them, at first known only as G22355, had the ability to relieve the symptoms of depression. In 1958, he published a paper in the *American Journal of Psychiatry* called "The Treatment of Depressive States with G22355 (Imipramine Hydrochloride)." The first antidepressant had been discovered: *imipramine.*

What do these drugs do? How do they work? For many years, the chemical activity of the brain was so mysterious that the mechanism by which antidepressants brought about their therapeutic effects was completely unknown. Today, although study of the effects of these drugs on the brain chemistry of animals has been more revealing, the chemistry of depression, and thus the chemistry of its treatment, is still profoundly mysterious. One problem is that different antidepressants that seem equally effective in treating affective disorder may vary considerably in their effects on brain chemistry. For example, *desipramine,* an antidepressant closely related to imipramine, considerably boosts brain levels of the neurotransmitter *norepinephrine.* It has comparatively less effect on serotonin. Another usually equally effective medication, *amitriptyline,* shows the opposite pattern. It boosts serotonin levels and has much less effect on norepinephrine. At one time this paradox led researchers to wonder if there might actually be two types of depression in affective disorder, one characterized by a relative deficiency of norepinephrine in the brain and another caused by a relative deficiency of serotonin. This line of reasoning led to many studies of the by-products of these chemicals in the spinal fluid of persons with mood disorders. It was hoped that by measuring the levels of these by-products in a particular patient, one might differentiate between these two types of depression and select the medication most likely to treat that patient's symptoms successfully. This line of reasoning turned out to be a dead-end and, to make matters more confusing, some of the newer antidepressants, such as *fluoxetine* (Prozac), have extremely potent effects on serotonin and almost no effects at all on norepinephrine. Another new class of antidepressants, which includes venlafaxine (Effexor), affects both serotonin *and* norepinephrine.

Unfortunately, then, I can't say much about how antidepressants work except that they change the chemical activity in the brain. I do, however, want to tell you about the experience of taking antidepressants and what a course of antidepressant therapy is like.

Perhaps the biggest problem with antidepressants is that they take a comparatively long time to begin to work. Unlike aspirin, decongestants, antihistamines, antacids, or other medications you are probably familiar with, the therapeutic effects of antidepressants are not apparent in a few minutes or hours. In fact, their effects usually become apparent only after weeks— roughly two to four weeks but occasionally up to eight weeks. In chapter 1, I explained why this is thought to be the case: recovery from serious depressive illness seems to involve structural changes in nerve cells in certain areas of the brain, and probably the growth of new cells as well.

Not only does improvement take several weeks but recovery also has a peculiar pattern, one described by Dr. Kuhn in the first patients to take antidepressants. He noticed that his patients' families often saw improvement before the patients themselves did. This has been consistently observed with all types of antidepressants.

Here is a typical story: A man notices that after a week of antidepressant treatment, his depressed wife is taking more interest in her appearance. He points out to her that the medication must be starting to work. "Are you kidding? This stuff isn't doing *anything* for me," she says. "I still feel terrible." Only after another week of treatment is she able to tell that her mood is better.

Often an improvement in sleep is the first sign of recovery. The patient falls asleep more easily and sleeps through the night. No more early morning awakening, the appetite is better, and weight loss stops. I can usually tell when antidepressant medication is working in my patients at least a week before they notice any improvement. Sometimes the change is almost too subtle to put into words—a slightly more erect posture, a smile now and again during the next visit. When I first went into practice I had a rather small office, and the lack of space meant that I always sat at my desk when I saw patients. Patients could sit facing me in a regular office chair beside my desk, or on a small, rather low sofa against one of the walls, also facing me but a little farther away. (I never tell patients where to sit; if they ask, I tell them to sit wherever they like.) Again and again I noticed that patients who were very depressed would choose the sad little sofa and sit slumped over and sinking into the cushions. After taking antidepressants for several weeks, they sat closer, taller, and more energetically in the office chair close to my desk. Before they said a word, I knew their treatment was working.

Notice that I have been using the term *treatment* rather than *cure*. There are some diseases that medicine can cure. Penicillin can kill all bacteria causing pneumonia, and that's the end of the disease. It's cured. It won't come back again unless a new infection occurs.

What about high blood pressure? There are medications that will lower high blood pressure to normal levels, but as soon as the patient stops taking them, the blood pressure rises again. The problem is treated with the medication, but the underlying disease process is not reversed. In most cases, the symptoms will return if the treatment is not continued. The treatment of mood disorders is much like the treatment of high blood pressure. Antidepressants seem to treat the symptoms, but if the medication is stopped too soon the symptoms can come right back.

Note that I said they *can* come right back. In chapter 2, I said that mood disorders follow a relapsing and remitting course, meaning the symptoms will often go away by themselves, sometimes for long periods of time. Thus, psychiatrists often talk about an *episode* of affective disorder. In this disease, the episodes of relapse may be separated by long periods, many years in some cases. Whatever change in brain biology brought on symptoms of affective disorder eventually seems to reverse itself, and the symptoms go away spontaneously. This means that patients must continue the medication during the entire episode, although some can possibly stop taking it at some point. It's important to remember that some forms of affective disorder have a very different course, and the length of time a person stays on medication is very variable.

What about side effects? The good news is that there are practically no *dangerous* side effects. Some of the older antidepressants can cause problems with the rhythm and organization of heartbeat in persons with certain kinds of heart conditions. Although there are very few people who cannot take antidepressants for this reason, some physicians prefer to have an electrocardiogram done on patients before they start one, just to be on the safe side.

The bad news is that there are a number of *annoying* side effects of some of the antidepressants. Fortunately, they usually diminish with time. The side effects of antidepressants tend to be worst during the first few days of treatment, and can often be minimized by starting the medication at low doses. This dose may be only a fraction of the amount needed to get the full benefit of the medication. For example, most patients need 100 to 150 milligrams of imipramine to get a full antidepressant effect, but most experience intolerable side effects if they start out at more than 25 or 50 milligrams a day. I usually will raise the dose of antidepressant every third or fourth day (more slowly in patients over the age of fifty-five or so) and increase it more gradually as the dose gets higher. It will sometimes take *three to five weeks* before there is significant improvement. Some experts recommend that a patient take a particular antidepressant for a full *eight* weeks before declaring it a failure. (Some of the newer antidepressants work at low doses, so there is no need to raise the dose gradually, saving some of this time.)

It's easier to discuss side effects if we divide the antidepressants into four groups: the tricyclics, selective serotonin reuptake inhibitors, other new antidepressants, and monoamine oxidase inhibitors.

## Tricyclic Antidepressants

I'll start with this group of antidepressants because they are the oldest. They are prescribed much less frequently now, largely because of their long list of possible side effects. However, there are some patients who do not respond to the newer drugs, and the tricyclics remain a very useful group of medications.

If you look at the chemical structure of these drugs, it's easy to see where the term *tricyclic* came from: three rings of atoms make up the molecules of medications in this class, and only differences in the side branches on the rings differentiate most of these drugs from one another.

Many of my patients report feeling "spacy" during the first few days of taking a tricyclic, the reaction some people experience when they take an antihistamine. (Remember that Dr. Kuhn found imipramine among a group of antihistamine-like drugs.) This symptom usually passes, but it may crop up again temporarily each time the dose is increased. Many tricyclics are sedating—that is, they promote sleep. These are very useful medications for depressed people who are having sleep problems. Tricyclics that are stimulating may be useful for patients who find themselves lethargic and sleeping too much, but some patients find this stimulation unpleasant and complain that the medication makes them jumpy and nervous and interferes with their sleep. The tricyclics can cause episodes of dizziness, an exaggeration of the common experience of feeling lightheaded when getting up suddenly from sitting or lying down. Most patients report that this side effect too gets better after a few days, and they cope with it simply by taking their time standing up, being especially careful to get out of bed slowly in the morning, when blood pressure is low anyway, and sitting on the edge of the bed for a few moments before standing up.

The most annoying side effects of the tricyclics are referred to as *anticho-*

TABLE 3.1  Antidepressants and Their Brand Names

| Pharmaceutical name | Brand Name(s) |
| --- | --- |
| Tricyclic antidepressants | |
|    amitriptyline | Elavil |
|    amoxapine | Ascendin |
|    clomipramine | Anafranil |
|    desipramine | Norpramin |
|    doxepin | Sinequan |
|    imipramine | Tofranil |
|    maprotiline | Ludiomil |
|    nortriptyline | Pamelor |
|    protriptyline | Vivactil |
| Selective serotonin reuptake inhibitors | |
|    citalopram | Celexa (Cipramil) |
|    escitalopram | Lexapro (Cipralex) |
|    fluoxetine | Prozac, Sarafem (Erocap, Fluohexal, Lovan, Zactin, and others) |
|    fluvoxamine | Luvox |
|    paroxetine | Paxil, Paxil CR[1] (Aropax, Seroxat, and others) |
|    sertraline | Zoloft (Altruline, Aremis, Gladem, Besitran, Lustral, Sealdin, and others) |
| More antidepressants | |
|    buproprion | Wellbutrin, Wellbutrin XL[1], Wellbutrin SR[1] |
|    duloxetine | Cymbalta (Davedax, Xeristar, Yentreve, and others) |
|    mirtazpine | Remeron (Remergil, Zispin, and others) |
|    nefazodone | (Serzone[2], Dutonin[2]) |
|    trazodone | Desyrel (Azona, Molipaxin, Sideril, Thombran, and others) |
|    venlafaxine | Effexor, Effexor XR[1] (Efexor, Efexor XR[1], and others) |
| Monoamine oxidase inhibitors (MAOIs) | |
|    phenelzine | Nardil |
|    tranylcypromine | Parnate |
|    selegiline | Eldepryl, Emsam transdermal system |

Note: Names in parentheses are brands marketed outside the United States.
[1]Slow-release preparation
[2]Brands withdrawn by manufacturer because of reports of liver failure

*linergic* side effects because they result from a drug-induced partial blockade of the neurotransmitter acetylcholine. Acetylcholine is instrumental in some of the automatic functions of the body such as the activity of the digestive tract, sweating, the emptying of the bladder, and the focusing of the eyes. One of the results of this blockade is dryness of the mouth caused by suppression of salivary gland activity. Some people experience constipation as well. These side effects usually get better in time, but I tell my patients they may need to chew sugarless gum to stimulate the flow of saliva and use a bulk laxative for several weeks. (Conversely, if a patient who has been taking an antidepressant with anticholinergic side effects stops the medication too quickly, the gastrointestinal tract seems to "speed up" again, and some people have mild, temporary nausea or diarrhea.)

The urinary effect of these drugs is usually a problem only in men. The prostate gland, which surrounds the duct emptying the bladder, can enlarge and narrow this opening in men over fifty or so, and a man who has trouble emptying his bladder after starting antidepressant therapy needs to stop the medication and call his doctor immediately.

A few patients report that they perspire more easily and more profusely on tricyclics, and this may also be related to acetylcholine blockade.

Many of the tricyclics stimulate appetite and cause weight gain. While this is a totally unacceptable side effect for many people, these medications can be just right for patients who have lost weight because of depression.

Another important characteristic of tricyclic medications is that they are toxic in overdose. Several weeks' supply can be fatal for an adult if taken all at once. Several days' supply can be fatal in a small child.

*Selective Serotonin Reuptake Inhibitors (SSRIs)*

Reading that long list of annoying and uncomfortable side effects makes it easy to understand why the name of a new antidepressant that had no anticholinergic effects, was not sedating, and didn't cause weight gain became a household word soon after it was introduced. Prozac (fluoxetine) became the most frequently prescribed antidepressant and one of the most frequently prescribed pharmaceuticals of *any* kind within a year of its appearance on the market. It was perhaps the first pharmaceutical to appear on the cover of *Newsweek*. What's really important about fluoxetine is that it was the first of a whole new family of antidepressants, a family that represented the first major breakthrough in the treatment of depression in nearly twenty years. Remember I said that some of the tricyclic antidepressants block the reuptake of neurotransmitters into nerve cells and thus increase the amount of those neurotransmitters in the synapse, which in turn probably affects the neurons that may be involved in mood. This new family of medications are named *selective* serotonin reuptake inhibitors because they

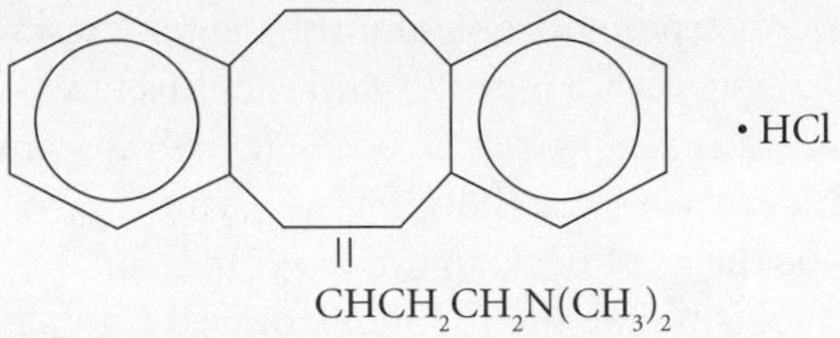

· HCl

AMITRIPTYLINE

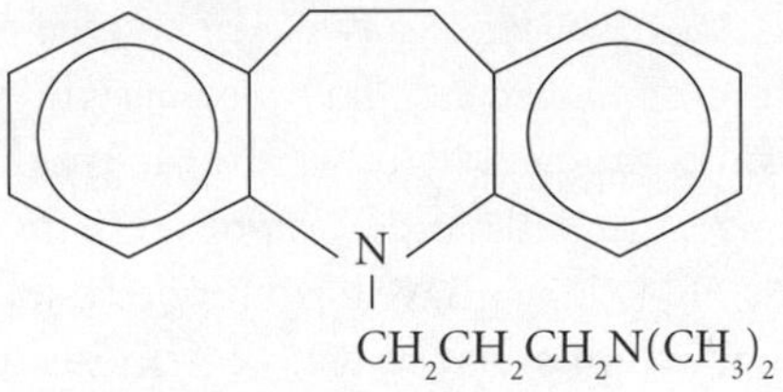

IMIPRAMINE

$CHCH_2CH_2N(CH_3)_2$

$CH_2CH_2CH_2N(CH_3)_2$

FIGURE 3.1 Chemical structure of two tricyclic antidepressants, showing their characteristic three-ringed structure

block neurotransmitter reuptake, like the tricyclics do, but are remarkably specific to the serotonin system. Remember that the tricyclics affect norepinephrine levels to some degree; this effect may cause the blood pressure drop that leads to the dizzy spells the tricyclics can cause. Tricyclics have antihistamine-like effects that cause the sedation and possibly the weight gain they can bring about in some people. And, of course, there are all those nasty anticholinergic effects caused by partial blockage of the acetylcholine systems: dry mouth, constipation, and so forth. But the SSRIs have practically no effect on any neurotransmitter system in the brain other than the serotonin system—this means fewer side effects. This is not to say that there are no side effects, but as with the other antidepressants, they tend to be temporary. The most common side effects again relate to the digestive tract, nausea or diarrhea being reported by about one-quarter to one-third of patients who took these medications in clinical trials. Very few patients need to stop the medication because of this. Headache is reported occasionally as well. Some SSRIs have a stimulant effect in some patients, who report noticing a boost in energy level fairly soon after starting therapy. There is, of course, a downside to this effect, and some patients experience insomnia or even an unpleasant jitteriness. Other SSRIs tend to be mildly sedating.

The most highly touted advantage of the SSRIs has been their ability to promote weight loss. In most people this amounts to a few pounds, but some patients experience a significant weight loss, especially if they are over-weight. People who are prone to gain weight as a symptom of depression can have a dramatic weight loss when their depression is treated with an SSRI. However, even with the SSRIs, weight gain can occur; paroxetine (Paxil) seems to be the most likely to cause weight gain.

One problem that might not be noticeable to patients until they've been on an SSRI for weeks or months is a change in sexual functioning, specifi-cally a noticeable decrease in sexual interest (loss of libido) or difficulty or inability to reach orgasm. As more patients have been treated with SSRIs during the last decade, it has become apparent that this is a significant prob-lem affecting about one-third of patients. There are a variety of strategies for dealing with these problems, so they should be reported to the physician. Weekend "vacations" from the medication have been reported to be helpful, as has the addition of other medications that seem to block these effects, but sometimes a switch to another antidepressant in a different class is the only solution.

When I asked one of my male patients if he was having any sexual dys-function from his new antidepressant, he replied that he thought fluoxetine had *improved* his sex life, increasing his sexual stamina and causing him to have *more* intense orgasms—a reminder that a list of potential medica-tion side effects should never be a reason not to try a particular medication. Pleasant surprises sometimes do occur. Also, a medication effect that causes problems for some patients can actually be helpful for others; for example, SSRIs have been reported to be helpful in treating premature ejaculation.

*Other New Antidepressants*

Since the early 1990s, many other new antidepressants have come on the market that aren't tricyclics and aren't SSRIs. Since most of these pharma-ceuticals don't really share many common features, there isn't a very good class name for them, although you'll sometimes see many of these new agents listed as "atypical" or "second generation" antidepressants. They have a va-riety of effects on norepinephrine, serotonin, and other neurotransmitters. Some have more than one effect on these systems and are therefore thought to provide different ways of manipulating the chemical systems in the brain concerned with mood. Venlafaxine (Effexor) and duloxetine (Cymbalta), for example, inhibit the reuptake of both norepinephrine and serotonin and are referred to as *dual reuptake inhibitors* or *SNRIs*, for *serotonin and norepi-nephrine reuptake inhibitors*. Buproprion (Wellbutrin) is most active on a different neurotransmitter altogether—dopamine.

The side effect profiles of these medications vary widely: some have a profile more like tricyclics, other more like SSRIs. Patients with a history of seizures should not take buproprion, because it has been reported to increase the likelihood of having another seizure. Trazodone (Desyrel) and nefazodone also have a rare but potentially serious side effect, *priapism*, which is the development of prolonged and painful penile erections in males.

*Monoamine Oxidase Inhibitors*

In the early 1950s, a new drug that had been developed for the treatment of tuberculosis was observed to cause mood elevation in some patients who took it for their lung disease. After several more years of investigations, mostly in England, several papers appeared that confirmed the therapeutic effects of iproniazid in patients suffering from depression. Shortly afterwards, it was discovered that iproniazid caused inactivation of an enzyme in the body. This enzyme, called *monoamine oxidase,* is responsible for gobbling up molecules of norepinephrine, serotonin, and several other neurotransmitters. Inactivating it increases the amounts of these compounds in the nervous system, and this effect, in some as yet poorly understood way, may be the mechanism by which they alleviate the symptoms of depression. This effect on the enzyme gives this class of pharmaceuticals their name: *monoamine oxidase inhibitors* or *MAOIs.*

There are two forms of monoamine oxidase in the body, *MAO-A* and *MAO-B.* Until recently, all of the pharmaceuticals used to treat depression were active in blocking MAO-A. In addition to its activity in the nervous system, MAO-A is also present in the lining of the intestine. This is because a number of naturally occurring substances in various foods are close enough chemically to norepinephrine to need deactivation before they are absorbed into the bloodstream. The importance of this becomes clear when I tell you that another name for norepinephrine is *adrenalin.* Adrenalin, the hormone responsible for the "fight or flight" reaction, also causes a rapid increase in heart rate and blood pressure. *Tyramine,* an amino acid that has adrenaline-like effects on blood pressure and heart rate, is present in high enough concentrations in some foods to cause dangerous cardiovascular problems in people taking MAOIs. A number of pharmaceuticals, including the ingredients of many over-the-counter remedies, also have adrenalin-like effects. People taking MAOIs therefore need to observe certain dietary restrictions and, even more importantly, *scrupulously* read the labels of any over-the-counter medication they are considering—or better yet, consult their pharmacist before taking any pharmaceutical they buy over the counter. MAOIs also interact with other medications that are prescribed or commonly used in emergency rooms for various problems. People taking MAOIs must be sure to inform all their treating physicians and should consider wearing an alert bracelet to let ER personnel know that they are taking an MAOI should they be brought into an emergency room after an accident or illness that may impair their ability to communicate with physicians.

Recently, a pharmaceutical that primarily blocks MAO-B, the other form of MAO in the body, has been developed. MAO-B is present almost solely in the brain and is not involved in blocking tyramine absorption in the intestine. The big advantage of an MAO-B inhibitor over an MAO-A inhibitor, then, would be that people taking it wouldn't have to be on a special diet. This drug, called *selegiline,* has actually been used for the treatment of Parkinson's disease for several years. There were early attempts to use it as an antidepressant, but it was discovered that the required doses were so high when taken in pill form that selegiline affected *both* forms of MAO (A and B); that is, the specificity for MOA-B was lost. This meant that patients taking selegiline would still need to watch their diet for sources of tyramine—no advantage there! Then someone came up with the idea of making a selegiline *patch.* The patch, whereby the drug is absorbed through the skin rather than taken orally, turns out to have two important advantages. First, because it is more directly absorbed into the bloodstream, the drug can be given at a low dose and maintain its specificity for MAO-B. Second, since it doesn't travel through the intestine, it doesn't affect the MAO-A located there. Both of these facts mean the selegiline patch is an easier MAOI to take, with fewer side effects and less worry about tyramine-rich foods.

MAOIs can have other side effects too. They can be stimulating and cause insomnia. For this reason, taking the oral preparations at bedtime should be avoided. Dizzy spells, especially when suddenly getting up from lying down, can occur. MAOIs block a blood pressure reflex that usually maintains blood pressure when we stand up, and the sudden drop in blood pressure on standing (called *orthostatic hypotension*) causes lightheadedness. Weight gain and sexual dysfunction may occur as well.

Because of these issues, MAOIs are most often prescribed to patients who have failed to benefit from other antidepressants. That said, they are sometimes uniquely effective, indeed they can be "miracle drugs" for some patients who have been helped by no other antidepressants. I think every psychiatrist I've ever spoken with has had the experience of effectively treating a particular patient with an MAOI after no other antidepressant had helped.

Occasionally, an MAO inhibitor is added to another antidepressant, and the two are taken together. This must be done with extreme care and close monitoring, as interactions between MAOIs and other antidepressants can be very dangerous.

*"Which Antidepressant Is Best?"*

This is a question I'm asked from time to time. "Which is the *strongest* antidepressant?" is another. Unfortunately, there is no best or strongest antidepressant. If there were, there would be no need for so many different medications on the market. The medication that is best for a particular patient depends on two things: *side effect profile* and *specific efficacy.*

Remember that there is a big difference between a side effect and an allergy to a medication. An allergy is an abnormal immune reaction to something new to the body. It is caused by the response of the body's immune cells to the new chemical and usually takes the form of a rash or fever. Sometimes other body systems are involved in the immune reaction: the bone marrow may be affected and blood cell counts can drop. Also, the liver can become inflamed (this is called *drug hepatitis*) in some drug allergies. A person can be allergic to just about anything, and it's impossible to predict who will be allergic to what. People who are truly allergic to a medication *cannot* continue to take it. Since antidepressants are synthetic compounds, and most allergies are a response to naturally occurring substances (usually proteins), true allergies to these medications are, fortunately, rare.

Side effects are common, however. Every drug has some. Unwanted effects of medication inevitably go along with the wanted effects and cannot be separated out (hence the origin of the term *side* effect). When you take a shower, you can't get clean without getting wet; it's impossible to separate one effect from the other! Fortunately, the desired effect (cleanliness) lasts longer than the side effect (wetness), and the side effect is well tolerated (by most adults at least). Unlike allergic reactions, side effects do not mean that you *must* stop taking the drug. Rather, they mean that you have a decision to make: Am I willing to put up with the side effects of this medication to get the antidepressant effect?

Side effects seem to affect different people very differently; a medication that makes one person miserable with side effects may cause absolutely none in another. Thus, the best antidepressant for an individual is the one that causes the fewest side effects while alleviating mood disorder symptoms in that individual. Be careful of the well-meaning friend or neighbor who tells you, "Your psychiatrist prescribed *what?* My cousin's brother-in-law's best friend took that medication and he had terrible side effects!" The old adage "One man's meat is another man's poison" is nowhere as relevant as in describing antidepressant side effects.

Antidepressants don't have any side effects that "sneak up" on you. For the most part, whatever side effects an individual is prone to develop will be apparent soon after starting a particular medication or after the dosage is raised. Patients who have been on a stable dose of medication don't often suddenly develop a side effect they've never had before. (One possible exception to this is the sexual dysfunction that can be caused by SSRIs; it may take several weeks to notice this problem.)

The other factor that determines which of the antidepressants is best for an individual is its specific efficacy for that person. Some people have better results (better *antidepressant* results, not just fewer side effects) from one drug than from another. I can recall several patients who asked me to prescribe fluoxetine for them when it first became available. They had been doing quite well, with good control of their mood symptoms, on tricyclics. They had read about this new antidepressant that had fewer side effects and wanted to try it. Several made the change and had good results, but a few wanted to go back to the older medicine. I remember one woman telling me, "I don't miss the dry mouth and I've lost five pounds, but Prozac just doesn't work for me as well as the imipramine did."

Specific efficacy seems to run in families, too. If a medication works well for one person in a family, there seems to be a greater likelihood that the same medication will also work for another. This is very helpful information for your doctor; don't be shy about asking family members about their medications if they've ever been treated for depression. (For that matter, certainly don't be shy about asking family members if they've ever been treated for depression—this too is valuable information for your doctor. See "The Heredity of Mood Disorders," in chapter 6.)

One of the most frustrating problems for both patient and doctor is that it is *impossible* to tell which antidepressant is best. It's difficult to predict which side effects a person will have or, at least, which will be so bad that another antidepressant will have to be tried. There's also the possibility that the first that is tried just won't work very well for that person. Often some trial and error is involved in antidepressant therapy. The important thing to remember is that these drugs, *all* of them, are *proven* to be safe and effective—*equally* effective in large groups of patients. The point here is that antidepressant therapy is not something to be entered into or abandoned impulsively. Unlike, say, a cold preparation, these medications may not provide any benefit for weeks, and in the meantime the side effects may be somewhat uncomfortable. Since there are so many antidepressants with so many side effect profiles, it is important to tell your doctor if side effects develop so that a switch can be made as soon as possible.

I find that the end of the first week or so of antidepressant therapy is the most difficult for my patients. This is the time when they are having the most side effects and seem to be getting little if any benefit. This is when the patients are prone to what I call the "flush urge." This is the urge to give up on a medicine and, well, you can guess the rest!

Some of the most frequent reasons for the "failure" of antidepressants are (1) inadequate prescribed dosage, (2) not taking the medication as prescribed, and (3) not persevering long enough with the medication for it to work. It has been discovered that people vary tremendously in the way their bodies handle antidepressants. Some patients need much higher doses than others to get the same amount of medication into the bloodstream. This may account for the need to vary the dosage of these medications from one person to another.

Reliable blood tests are available to measure levels of the tricyclic antidepressants in the bloodstream (this is another reason why this remains an important group of pharmaceuticals). For these antidepressants, a *therapeutic range* has been determined, meaning that the medication has been shown to work best when the amount measured in the bloodstream is within a certain range. These tests are useful for the patient who is taking what would usually be a reasonable dose of an antidepressant but who doesn't seem to be getting any better. A blood test may show that the antidepressant level is unexpectedly low if the patient is someone who metabolizes the drug quickly. This information allows the doctor to confidently raise the dosage. If, on the other hand, the level is within the therapeutic range, it may signal the need to try a different medication or another type of treatment altogether.

## OTHER MEDICATIONS USEFUL IN DEPRESSION
### Thyroid Medication

The thyroid hormones set the rate at which the body uses energy and "burns" calories and plays a major role in the body's energy regulation. Too little thyroid gland activity leads to sluggishness and weight gain, too much to metabolic overdrive—rapid pulse, nervous energy, and anxiety. While the precise role of thyroid hormones in the regulation of mood remains unclear, it's very clear that normal thyroid functioning is essential for effective treatment of mood disorders. Put another way, if a patient's mood symptoms don't respond to the usual treatments, or if a treatment that has been effective seems to lose its effectiveness, a thyroid problem, especially abnormally low thyroid functioning (*hypothyroidism*), should be suspected. A depressed patient whose thyroid gland is the slightest bit underactive will respond poorly to antidepressants.

But it is also clear that some patients with mood disorders whose thyroid hormone levels are in the usual normal range nevertheless can benefit from treatment with thyroid medications. It has been demonstrated that many patients with depression symptoms that are not responding to treatment have thyroid function that is "normal" by the usual criteria, but their blood tests show them to be in what might be called the "low normal" or even "barely normal" range. It may be that depressed individuals need a higher level of thyroid hormones than individuals who are not depressed. Perhaps thyroid medication somehow makes these patients more responsive to other treatments. Patients who have a partial response to antidepressant medication may have better control of their mood symptoms when thyroid medication is added, even if their thyroid hormones levels are normal. I tell medical students and psychiatrists-in-training to think of thyroid hormones as another class of psychotropic medications and to become as skilled in prescribing them as they are with antidepressants and mood stabilizers.

At one time, it was thought that very high doses of thyroid medication—enough to make the patient's thyroid overactive (*hyperthyroidism*)—were useful in treating depression. This approach has been shown to be unnecessarily risky.

### Lithium

Another drug that is often very helpful in treating depression is lithium. I will postpone a full discussion of this medication until the chapter on bipolar disorder (manic-depressive disorder), since lithium is much more frequently used for this type of mood disorder; nevertheless, lithium has very important antidepressant effects. Adding lithium can turn an incomplete response to an antidepressant medication into a complete one. Many experts recommend adding lithium as a first step in treating "nonresponders."

### Stimulants

For many years, the treatment of depression often included the use of powerful medications known as *psychostimulants*. *Amphetamine* is perhaps the best known in this group. These medications boost energy levels, concentration, and mood and were frequently prescribed for patients with depression years ago. As psychiatrists became more sophisticated in using antidepressants and more antidepressants became available in the 1970s, and perhaps more significantly, when the many problems with amphetamine-like drugs become more apparent, their use in the treatment of mood disorders fell out of favor.

The problems with these medications are their tendency to raise blood pressure and their abuse potential. Because they increase wakefulness and improve concentration and physical endurance, they were widely abused by college students cramming for exams, long-distance drivers, athletes, and other persons trying to improve their performance at any cost. Amphetamines tend to lose their stimulating effects with prolonged use, can cause symptoms of paranoia indistinguishable from paranoid schizophrenia, and when stopped after prolonged use or use of high doses, frequently cause the abuser to crash into a severe, even suicidal depression.

As with a number of powerful and highly effective treatments for psychiatric symptoms, enthusiastic overuse led to abuse and discredit for these medications, which in turn led to underutilization of an effective treatment and even denial of it to patients who could benefit from it. Physicians were reluctant to prescribe what had come to be seen as a "bad" pharmaceutical. But as usually happens with enough time and enough good research, the pendulum swung back toward the center and the legitimate and safe use of psychostimulants has become established. (We'll see in the section "Electroconvulsive Therapy" that a similar chain of events unfolded for that treatment.)

Psychostimulants as adjuncts to other treatments are used for the treatment of "treatment-resistant" depression, depression in the elderly, and also in the treatment of depression associated with medical illnesses such as cancer and AIDS. Psychostimulants are safe when used as prescribed, although side effects can include headache, flushing, loss of appetite, and insomnia. The severe problems noted in the preceding paragraphs are usually associated with prolonged use of high doses.

Another interesting use of psychostimulants has recently been reported: as treatment for the sexual dysfunction cause by SSRI antidepressant medications. In a small study of patients with this problem, dextroamphetamine or methylphenidate was 80 percent effective in reversing the sexual dysfunction caused by a serotonin reuptake inhibitor in twenty-four patients. (Psychostimulants are not the only remedy for sexual dysfunction symptoms caused by SSRIs; see the "Selective Serotonin Reuptake Inhibitors" section in this chapter.)

### Antipsychotic Medications

As you will see further on, the symptoms of depression can become extremely severe; the sleeplessness can be completely exhausting, and sometimes the patient can be overwhelmed with distress and even agitation. I've mentioned that one of the problems with antidepressant medications is that they take quite a while to work. Fortunately, there are other medications that can make the depressed person a bit more comfortable until they do.

Although in mild cases the usual medications for anxiety and sleeplessness (the *sedative/hypnotics, hypnotic* referring to sleep, not hypnosis!) are effective in relieving these symptoms, patients with major depression often get better relief with the stronger tranquilizing medications that were first used (and are still used) to treat schizophrenia. These medications have been called by several names, including *major tranquilizers* (as opposed to *minor* tranquilizers, which are used for mild anxiety and insomnia), and most commonly now, *antipsychotic medications.* These drugs have been used primarily to treat symptoms of hallucinations and delusions, often called psychotic symptoms, in schizophrenia but have long been used for treating some persons with mood disorders as well.

In major depression, the antipsychotics were at one time used as tranquilizers: that is, to reduce anxiety and tension and promote sleep. Also, some patients become so profoundly depressed as to lose touch with reality (as we will see in the case of Sylvia in the next section), and antipsychotics may have a specific effect on some of these very distressing symptoms. More recently, however, it has been demonstrated that some of the newest medications in this class have a specific antidepressant effect as well.

In the 1930s, a group of pharmaceutical compounds called *phenothiazines* were synthesized in Europe and were found to have antihistamine and sedative properties. One in particular, chlorpromazine, was found to be very useful in surgical anesthesia because it deepened anesthetic sedation more safely than other available agents. In the early 1950s, two French psychiatrists carried out several clinical trials using chlorpromazine to treat highly agitated patients suffering from schizophrenia. They had hoped the drug would provide sedation for these very sick patients—which it did—but these astute clinicians noticed that the medication did much more.

In addition to its quieting and sleep-promoting effects, chlorpromazine made the hallucinations and bizarre delusional beliefs of many patients with schizophrenia practically disappear. Chlorpromazine, in other words, had a *specific* effect on the cluster of symptoms usually referred to as "psychotic" symptoms, and thus the name for this group came about: antipsychotic medications. Occasionally, they are still referred to as *neuroleptic* medications (or *neuroleptics*), from *neuroleptique,* the French word coined from Greek roots that means, roughly, "affecting the nervous system."

In the 1980s, a new antipsychotic medication was developed that had much more effect on the neurotransmitter serotonin than did the other antipsychotics. In the years since, many more of these drugs, now usually called *atypical* antipsychotic medications, have been developed. This group of medications has been a very important development in psychiatry for reasons I'll discuss. Antipsychotic medications are now usually divided into two groups, the original group of medications being called *typical antipsychotics.* We'll take a look at each group in turn.

### The "Typical" Antipsychotic Medications

As we saw in previous chapters, antidepressants sometimes take weeks to begin working. This is where the typical antipsychotic medications have been useful. In cases of depression in which the patient is highly restless and agitated, they can have very beneficial effect.

The typical antipsychotic medications were called major tranquilizers at one time because they are, well, tranquilizers—in a major way. Some are more sedating than others, but all can be pretty powerful sedatives, especially at higher doses. They can cause some of the same anticholinergic side effects as tricyclic antidepressants: dry mouth, constipation, blurred vision. People seem to accommodate to these side effects after a period that ranges from days to weeks.

The main problem with most of these medications is their effect on muscle tone and movement: side effects of the dopamine blockade these agents

TABLE 3.2  Typical Antipsychotic Medications

| Pharmaceutical Name | Brand Name |
| --- | --- |
| chlorpromazine | Thorazine |
| fluphenazine | Prolixin |
| haloperidol | Haldol |
| loxapine | Loxitane |
| molindone | Moban |
| perphenazine | Trilafon |
| thioridazine | Mellaril |
| thiothixene | Navane |
| trifluoperazine | Stelazine |

cause. In textbook discussions of these medications, you will see these problems referred to as *extrapyramidal symptoms* or simply *EPS*. Dopamine is the main neurotransmitter used in a complex circuit of brain areas called the *extrapyramidal system*, which coordinates movement. The term *extrapyramidal* contrasts this system with another, called the *pyramidal* system because its main fibers are carried in triangle-shaped bundles into the spinal cord. The pyramidal system controls the quick, accurate action of individual muscles, and the extrapyramidal makes sure that other muscle groups relax or contract as needed for the smooth and graceful execution of these movements. Antipsychotic medications, by blocking the dopamine receptors in the extrapyramidal system, cause several movement problems. One is *pseudo-parkinsonism*. You may remember from the discussion of Parkinson's disease that in this illness, there is a degeneration of dopamine neurons in one of the brain's crucial components, the substantia nigra. Persons suffering from Parkinson's disease have a slowed and shuffling walk, seem to lose facial expression because of stiffness of their face muscles, and also have trembling of their hands. Pseudo-parkinsonism consists of these same symptoms; the neurons don't die as they do in the disease, but their chemical messenger, dopamine, is blocked from doing its work by a pharmaceutical agent.

Another set of extrapyramidal side effects are *acute dystonic reactions*. These are muscular spasms that usually involve the tongue, facial, and neck muscles, and are more common in young male patients. People taking antipsychotic medications can also develop a very uncomfortable restlessness called *akathisia*. This is felt mostly in the legs, and the individual feels the need to walk or pace.

Fortunately, these side effects are all treatable, either by lowering the dose of medication or by adding one of several medications that are also used to treat Parkinson's disease. Although they are uncomfortable, they are not dangerous and usually respond quickly to treatment once they are identified.

Most of the antipsychotic medications can, over years, cause a side effect called *tardive dyskinesia,* or *TD* for short. This consists of repetitive involuntary movements usually of the facial muscles, most often chewing, blinking, or lip-pursing movements. There is no good treatment for TD other than discontinuing the medication. We used to worry a lot about TD, because some patients who developed it seemed to continue to have these movements even after the medication was stopped. But two factors are calming these worries: the discovery that most TD symptoms *do* eventually go away with time and, more importantly, the development of the atypical antipsychotic medications that do not seem to cause TD. We'll talk about them in the next section of this chapter.

I want to emphasize that extrapyramidal symptoms sound a lot worse than they are, that they are usually easily treated, and that they are not dangerous. On the other hand, the symptoms of mood disorders that the typical antipsychotic medications are usually used to treat *are* extremely dangerous and much more uncomfortable. These medications are powerful agents, and they need to be used carefully and for the shortest period of time possible, but for the present at least they are nearly irreplaceable in treating the most dangerous and most terrible symptoms of severe depression.

### Atypical Antipsychotic Medications

It's probably apparent after reading the preceding paragraphs that there has been room for improvement in the antipsychotic medications. Not only are the extrapyramidal symptoms uncomfortable until treated, but it is usually necessary to add another medication to control them—and the more different medications a person takes, the more likely she is to have problems with side effects and drug interactions. So it created quite a stir when a new group of antipsychotic medications were introduced that don't seem to cause EPS. Even more good news: they seem to work better than their predecessors. These agents are called *atypical antipsychotic medications* because, although they block dopamine receptors just as their predecessors do (though not as potently), they are also active at *serotonin* receptors. This seems to have two effects: extrapyramidal symptoms do not appear nearly as often, and these medications seem to have significant effects on mood.

The first atypical antipsychotic, clozapine, was synthesized in the laboratory in the 1960s but was not marketed in the United States until 1990. One of the reasons it took so long for clozapine to get on the market is that it causes a very dangerous drop in the number of white blood cells (called *agranulocytosis*) in about 1 percent of patients who take it. This problem might have meant the end for clozapine as a new medication were it not

TABLE 3.3 Atypical Antipsychotic Medications

| Pharmaceutical Name | Brand Name(s) |
| --- | --- |
| aripiprazole | Abilify |
| clozapine | Clozaril |
| olanzapine | Zyprexa, Zydis |
| quetiapine | Seroquel |
| risperidone | Risperdal |
| ziprasidone | Geodon |

for the fact that it was found to be highly effective in treating patients with schizophrenia who had derived little benefit from traditional antipsychotic medications. Dramatic case studies of patients with chronic treatment-resistant schizophrenia basically "awakening" from years of unrelenting psychotic symptoms after they started clozapine sustained the interest of clinicians and pharmaceutical researchers. When it was discovered that the risk of agranulocytosis could be substantially reduced if the patient had his or her white blood cell count monitored on a weekly basis, clozapine treatment became available to larger groups of patients, and it was not long before patients with treatment-resistant mood disorders were treated with it as well.

In the years following the introduction of clozapine, several other atypical antipsychotic medications have come along, and their introduction has substantially expanded the number of treatment options for bipolar disorder. More and more evidence is emerging that the atypical antipsychotic medications are helpful in depression as well as in all phases of bipolar disorder.

Of the atypical antipsychotics, only clozapine causes the blood cell problem that requires frequent blood counts. None of the atypicals cause EPS except at high doses. High doses can also trigger the other side effects that traditional antipsychotic medications do: anticholinergic side effects and sedation.

The most significant side effect problem with the atypicals has been their tendency to make some individuals gain weight and develop obesity-related problems like high cholesterol and even diabetes. Not all individuals develop these problems, but attention to diet and weight issues is very important for persons taking these medications, especially patients who take them over the longer term. The primary cause of the weight gain associated with the atypical antipsychotics appears to be stimulation of the appetite center of the brain, although it has also been suggested that these medications affect several hormones that control how the body handles calories and stores fat. Some of the atypicals are more likely to cause weight gain than others. Several appear relatively weight neutral; that is, they seem to have little or no effect on weight. The latter agents would seem to be preferable in already

TABLE 3.4 Weight Gain Risks of Atypical Antipsychotics

| Higher risk | clozapine |
|---|---|
| ↑ | olanzapine |
| | quetiapine |
| | risperidone |
| | ziprasidone[1] |
| Lower risk | aripiprazole[1] |

[1]Negligible effect on weight

obese patients and in patients with diabetes or a family history of diabetes. Regular blood tests for diabetes and high cholesterol should be done at the beginning of treatment and regularly thereafter in patients taking antipsychotics for maintenance treatment. All patients taking atypicals should take steps to control possible weight gain by paying attention to their diet and being sure they are get regular exercise.

## Electroconvulsive Therapy

Perhaps no treatment in medicine has been so unfairly maligned as electroconvulsive therapy (ECT). Several years ago a jurisdiction in California went so far as to outlaw its administration. Fortunately, soon after this foolish law was passed, the facts about ECT were presented to the electorate and the law was repealed. More than fifty years after its introduction, after remarkable refinements in technique and, most important, after incontrovertible proof of its safety and extreme efficacy, there are still well-educated and sophisticated people who say they would never allow it to be given to them or their families.

As has so often happened in medicine, a series of coincidences led to the discovery that an electrical treatment could alleviate severe depression. The key word here is "severe": I will give some examples of the kinds of depression that may require ECT in the next section. Suffice it to say that only about two-thirds of severe depressions respond to medication, yet over 90 percent respond to ECT. I've always thought the best way to learn about a treatment is to understand its history, so let me review the history of ECT.

At the turn of the century, someone observed that people with epilepsy—those who had episodic uncontrolled spasms of electrical brain activity in the form of convulsions or epileptic seizures—seemed to have a lower incidence of mental illness. This observation turned out to be an error; as a matter of fact, a number of distressing emotional symptoms are often seen in those with some forms of epilepsy. Nevertheless, this led to the study of seizure activity in humans in search of a treatment for emotional symptoms. Experiments were performed in dogs to determine if a method could be developed to cause seizures without serious side effects. After work with various drugs and inhaled substances, it was found that a seizure could be induced relatively safely by passing a small electrical current through the skull from electrodes applied to the scalp. In 1938, two Italian psychiatrists reported their success in treating depressed patients with this technique.

After a number of years and initial resistance, the treatment became widespread, for a very good reason: it was a seemingly miraculous "cure" for an illness that until then had no treatment. (Remember, the first antidepressants were developed in the 1950s.) Patients who had been so depressed that they were literally starving from loss of appetite or had been suicidal for months were completely rid of their symptoms of depression in a matter of days. The reasons for the recovery were completely unknown, but it was clear that this treatment could produce astonishing improvement in some patients.

But ECT's success was also its downfall. It was so effective for some patients that it was overprescribed and used for many others with very different illnesses, such as schizophrenia, for whom it offered little hope. For a time, this overprescription made it seem that few patients who received ECT derived any benefit from it. The treatment became associated in peoples' minds with hopeless cases.

Another problem was the frequency of severe complications from the treatment as it was originally administered. An epileptic seizure can be a violent event. Patients suffered broken bones from the forceful muscle contractions during the seizure, severe headaches, and muscular soreness and wild fluctuations in blood pressure.

As years have gone by and more research has been done, both these issues have been addressed. It has become much clearer which patients will be helped by ECT and which will not. Modern anesthetic techniques have dramatically eased the problem of the physical complications of the treatments, which are immensely safer than in previous years.

Today ECT is administered in an operating room or a special treatment suite in hospitals. Using safe anesthetic techniques, patients are put into a deep sleep just as if they were to undergo surgery. One of the anesthetics used completely relaxes all the muscles, so that the actual "seizure" is an electrical event only. No jumping or severe jerking occurs in a properly anesthetized patient. On the contrary, the patient remains practically motionless, and only some minor changes in pulse rate and blood pressure and some twitching in the fingers or toes indicate that anything at all has happened during the few seconds that the tiny electrical current passes through the skull. The entire treatment lasts ten to fifteen minutes. Immediately before the treatment, patients may receive an injection of a medication that prevents abnormal heart rhythms (glycopyrrolate). An IV is started, and the patient is put to sleep with an anesthetic and then given a muscle relaxant. The patient is asleep and completely relaxed in less than five minutes. Electrode disks similar to those used to take cardiograms are applied to the scalp. Modern ECT equipment delivers a precisely timed and measured electrical stimulus: usually a half-second to several seconds in duration. In *bilateral* treatments, an electrode is applied over each temple, in *unilateral* treatments, in which the object is to stimulate only half the brain, one electrode is placed in the middle of the forehead and the other at the temple. (Unilateral treatment causes less post-ECT confusion and memory problems and is now used almost exclusively. Rarely, it doesn't work as well in some patients, who must therefore receive bilateral treatments.)

Most ECT machines used today record an *electroencephalogram* (a measurement of the electrical activity of the brain) through the same electrodes used to deliver the stimulus, so that the physician can see how long the induced "seizure" lasts—usually twenty-five to forty-five seconds. There might be a few brief muscle contractions observed during this time, but the muscle relaxant keeps the patient nearly motionless. Usually a brief quickening of the heart rate and increase of blood pressure also signal that the "seizure" has occurred. A face-mask breathing device delivers oxygen to the patient until he wakes up five or ten minutes later and the treatment is over.

Are there patients who cannot be given ECT? About the only people who absolutely cannot receive ECT are those very few people with medical conditions so severe that even ten to fifteen minutes of general anesthesia is too dangerous for them—people with very severe cardiac or lung diseases, for example. Patients with brain tumors are usually excluded as well. ECT can be given to persons who have recovered from heart attacks, to persons with epilepsy, and with careful monitoring and skilled anesthesia, to pregnant women. (In fact, ten to fifteen minutes of anesthetic several times a week exposes the developing fetus to less medication than if the mother were to take antidepressants and other medications for severe depression on a daily basis.) Old age is not a barrier; there is considerable evidence that ECT is especially effective in the elderly and perhaps safer for them than some of the antidepressants.

How does this treatment work? This remains one of the most deeply shrouded mysteries in psychiatry. The levels of various neurotransmitters are elevated after ECT, but as with the antidepressants, so many neurotransmitters are affected that no particular pattern has been implicated as either cause or cure. Perhaps the most interesting speculation now concerns the observation that when laboratory rats are given ECT, examination shows that neuron growth in certain areas of the brain is stimulated. ECT seems to enhance neuronal plasticity, which, you may remember, appears to be very important in mood disorders.

ECT does not produce its effect after a single treatment. Usually eight to twelve treatments are necessary, so psychiatrists often speak of a *course* of ECT. One treatment is given about every other day in most hospitals. Usually this is done on a Monday, Wednesday, Friday schedule. Therefore, a course of eight to ten treatments means a hospital stay of three or four weeks. Usually by the fourth or fifth treatment improvement in mood is noticed by others and perhaps even reported by the patient. Often there is a peculiar temporary recovery in mood immediately, even after the first treatment. For several hours the patient will have a striking improvement in mood state but as the hours pass, depression sets in again. With each treatment this improvement lasts longer and longer, and eventually it is sustained from one treatment to the next. Soon the patient feels completely back to normal.

I said that, on average, patients usually require eight to ten treatments. What determines the exact number? Who will need eight, or ten, or more? Unfortunately, this is another question about mood disorders that has no clear answer. The treatments are simply continued until the patient's symptoms of depression are completely relieved. This is *not* to be interpreted to mean that the treatments should be continued indefinitely even in the absence of any response. If there is no indication of improvement after several weeks of electroconvulsive therapy, the diagnosis of depression needs to be questioned. Other diagnostic tests need to be considered and other treatment options investigated.

A few patients do need a prolonged course of ECT. People with severe major depression that does not respond to medications very well may be prescribed what has been called "maintenance ECT." These patients receive a regular course of ECT and then continue their treatments on a reduced schedule, and often on an outpatient basis, for several months. They may have one treatment a month or may be treated less often than that.

Any antidepressant or other medication the patient is taking is usually discontinued before a course of ECT treatments begins. There is evidence that some drugs can make a person more likely to have ECT side effects.

Other important side effects of ECT concern memory. Although memory problems associated with ECT had been reported for many years, the types and extent of memory problems were not evaluated in an organized way until the 1970s. Most experts agree that ECT seems to interfere with the consolidation of memory for the time when the patient is receiving the treatments as well as for a short period before and after. This means that memories for events that occur during the three weeks or so that a typical patient is in the hospital getting ECT may be foggy or even completely lost forever. In addition, some memory for events in the weeks leading up to the hospitalization may be lost. This is called retrograde amnesia, *retro-* meaning "back," and in this case referring to the period before the course of ECT. In addition to this pattern, patients sometimes report that they temporarily lose memory for isolated events that occurred years before the ECT or lose other bits of memory in an almost random fashion. I heard of a patient who needed to look up a favorite recipe that she had made without a cookbook for years. It's almost as if a tiny snippet of memory has been clipped out for some people. Usually, however, these memories return with time. As you might imagine, it has been very difficult to devise tests to confirm the memory losses that ECT causes in some people. After many years of trying but failing to demonstrate or measure them with various tests of memory and learning, psychologists resorted to simply asking patients who had received ECT about whether they thought their memory had been affected, and how severely. When this has been done, several instructive facts emerge. The first is that patients' complaints of memory problems relate more closely to the severity of depression before the treatment began than they do to the number of ECT treatments they received. Second, although most patients report that they notice some memory problems in the first month or so, almost all report a year after ECT that their memory is completely normal.

Although many patients report no memory problems whatever, and most have only minor and temporary difficulty, some people do report feeling that their memory has never been the same. I'll only comment that these complaints seem rare in my patients, most of whom are very thankful that a treatment is available that alleviates their symptoms so quickly.

## Other Brain Stimulation Techniques

For many years, electroconvulsive therapy was the only treatment for psychiatric problems that involved actual stimulation of the brain. Recently, several other treatments have become available. One of these, *transcranial magnetic stimulation,* is still experimental, but another, *vagal nerve stimulation,* has now been approved by the Food and Drug Administration for the treatment of severe depression that has not responded to multiple medications.

### TRANSCRANIAL MAGNETIC STIMULATION

Transcranial magnetic stimulation (TMS) is another brain stimulation technique that appears to be effective in treating mood disorders. TMS is currently a research technique only, but preliminary results with it are very encouraging. The great advantage of TMS over ECT is that TMS is much simpler to administer: no seizure activity is induced by the treatment, and therefore no anesthesia is necessary. During TMS treatments, a magnetic coil is held against the scalp and the magnetic field that develops in the coil causes a very small electrical current to flow through nearby neurons within the skull. In TMS, no electricity passes through the skull as it does in ECT, only magnetic waves. Since the electrical current generated in the brain tissue by TMS is so small, a seizure does not occur. Pulses of magnetic energy are delivered over a period of about twenty minutes while the patient simply sits in a chair. The patient is awake and alert through the whole procedure. Other than some soreness from muscle stimulation, there appear to be no significant side effects. Several studies in patients with drug-resistant depression showed improvement after TMS. TMS is in its infancy. The strength of the magnetic stimulation that is most beneficial, the exact placement of the coil, and the most effective number of treatments and duration of therapy are all under investigation at various centers around the world. It is clear, however, that TMS is a very promising development in the treatment of mood disorders and may open up a whole new array of treatment options.

### VAGAL NERVE STIMULATION

The *vagal nerve* (or *vagus*) is a long nerve that emerges from the base of the human brain, travels down the neck and into the chest and abdomen, and regulates a number of vital bodily functions such as digestion and heart rate. Its connections in the brain are through important centers thought to be involved with emotional regulation and, specifically, with mood regulation. Animal studies done as early as the 1930s demonstrated that electrical stimulation of the vagal nerve produced changes in the electrical activity of the brain, and in the 1980s it was demonstrated that vagal nerve stimulation (VNS) could control epileptic seizures in dogs.

In the 1990s, VNS became available for the treatment of intractable epilepsy in humans, first in Europe and then in the United States. By the end of 2000, about six thousand patients worldwide had received VNS, almost all of them for the treatment of epilepsy. As with anti-epileptic medications that later turned out to be effective mood stabilizers, VNS was noted to have beneficial effects on mood in several of the patients who had received it to treat their seizures. Several epilepsy patients had substantial antidepressant effects from VNS even though the treatment didn't improve their seizure control.

In one of the first studies of the VNS treatment of depression, thirty adults received the treatment for severe, treatment-resistant depression. Some of these patients had taken dozens of different medications and ECT with little benefit. About half of these patients benefited from VNS. In a follow-up study, most of the patients who had shown a response had continued to do well, and several had experienced continued improvement when they were evaluated after one year of VNS treatment.

VNS is done by means of a pacemaker-like device that must be surgically implanted to deliver the tiny electrical signals that stimulate the vagus nerve on an ongoing basis. The surgical procedure to implant the VNS stimulator is so straightforward that it is usually done on an outpatient basis. The small stimulator is implanted under the skin of the chest wall just below the collarbone, and a thin, flexible wire travels about halfway up the neck and is connected to the vagus nerve (the surgery does not involve the brain). The strength and frequency of the stimulus is adjusted during office visits by the doctor placing a wand-like instrument that communicates electronically with the stimulator against the skin.

The most common side effects of VNS include hoarseness and cough during the stimulation (which ranges from a few seconds to half a minute every five minutes to two hours). Studies in patients have shown that the benefit of VNS may take many months, sometimes up to a year, to become apparent.

## Complicated Depression

Here are two more case histories that illustrate issues in the diagnosis and treatment of major depression. Alice taught me just how persistent one has to be to make the diagnosis of a mood disorder and how easy it is to be thrown off by an unusual set of circumstances.

Alice was a woman in her mid-forties who was referred for admission to the university medical center where I was a first-year resident in psychiatry. She was depressed, but she had good reason to be—or so it seemed. Alice was married and had an eighteen-year-old daughter. Years before her depression began, her husband's elderly father had come to live in their home. He was physically ill and needed almost constant attention. He had to be helped to the bathroom, required a special diet, and could not bathe himself; in other words, Alice became a full-time nurse with one patient. What made her task even harder was that her father-in-law was, to put it mildly, a difficult person. He was demanding to the point of being exasperating, and nothing she did seemed to please him. Food was too hot or too cold; he hated his low-salt diet and blamed Alice for being a bad cook. Nothing was right. Her husband spent long hours at his job, and though he was sympathetic, he provided little help at home either with the care of his father or with the usual housework.

Alice was from the mountains of West Virginia. She came from a simple, hardworking family and had been raised with what we might today call old-fashioned ideas. One such idea was that old folks deserved to be taken care of at home in their declining years and that it was the job of the woman of the house to provide as much care as was needed. No complaints.

Alice's father-in-law was chronically ill, but nevertheless hung on for many years. Alice cheerfully carried out her duties for a long time. Grandpa was a tyrant whose demands ruled the household. Alice's daughter Terry grew from childhood into adolescence in a home dominated by a sick, bitter old man. Terry's one relief from the oppressive atmosphere at home was the time she spent with the next-door neighbors. Judy and Bob were a childless couple in their late thirties who treated Terry as an unofficial niece. They showered her with gifts at Christmas and on birthdays, took her to the movies, invited her to barbecues. Alice was glad for their interest in Terry. As Grandpa became more feeble, her time and energy were taken up more and more by his needs, and besides, Bob owned the biggest furniture store in town, so he and Judy could take Terry places and buy her things that she otherwise might miss out on. Terry spent more and more time next door, began to stay overnight, and even went on extended vacations with Judy and Bob.

Years passed and Alice's father-in-law died. At last Alice could start enjoying her own family again—or so she thought.

On her eighteenth birthday, the day she was no longer a minor, Terry announced to her parents that she wanted to be legally adopted by Bob and Judy. Alice was devastated. She appealed to Bob and Judy to talk Terry out of her plan, but they said that it was Terry's decision and that they could provide for her better than Alice and her husband. Alice's husband was of little help. He was so angry at Terry's announcement that he was ready to disown his daughter and never speak to her again.

Alice became more and more distraught. She couldn't sleep at night; she awoke in the early morning hours and reviewed the past years again and again. "I shouldn't have let her go next door so much. I shouldn't have let her go next door so much," she repeated over and over to herself. She felt she had failed as a mother, and since her upbringing had stressed that role as the most important thing in her life, this was the most shameful failure she could know. She lost weight and looked thin and haggard. Finally she went to her family doctor to get some sleeping tablets. Her doctor noticed how depressed she looked, heard the story of Terry's leaving, and referred her to a psychiatrist. "You need to talk to somebody about all this. No wonder you feel so bad," he said. The psychiatrist saw her several times and decided that perhaps an antidepressant would help. Weeks went by; the antidepressant seemed to help a little, but Alice was still very depressed. She could think about nothing but her daughter and how she had failed as a mother. She started to be bothered by thoughts that perhaps she didn't deserve to live. The psychiatrist referred her to the university medical center for possible ECT.

Alice was admitted to my service. She looked depressed even to the untrained eye, but I had seen many patients who were much more depressed. When she told me her story, I reacted as a lot of cocky trainees do, by denigrating the physician whose treatment had "failed" and who had referred her to the university. I said (to myself, thank goodness), "Don't these small-town shrinks take the time to *talk* to their patients? They see a few tears and start throwing pills at them without taking the time to see what's going on in their lives." Clearly, I thought, this was an adjustment disorder. The precipitant was clear, and the severity of the depression was proportional, considering the facts. Certainly Alice had vegetative signs and anhedonia—but didn't she have good reason to? Surely a sensitive and intuitive budding psychotherapist like me was all she needed. There was nothing chemical about this depression!

I didn't see any reason to stop the antidepressant she had been taking, since she said it had helped a little. I saw her an hour every day for therapy, and after only a few sessions, I began to doubt my hasty assessment. Alice sat hour after hour, day after day in my office, wringing her hands and repeating over and over, "I shouldn't have let her go next door. I shouldn't have let her go next door." She could talk briefly about her own past, her relationship with her husband, and other life events, but she kept returning to her own failings as a mother. Her feelings of guilt totally preoccupied her. She was stuck, chained really, to one idea. Her mood never changed; her pained expression was as consistent from hour to hour and day to day as if she were a marble statue. Alice's unwavering distress was a clinical picture I would see again and again in patients with major depression.

Her psychiatrist had wanted her to have a course of ECT, and she was already scheduled. I had hoped to bring about a big enough change in a few days of intensive psychotherapy to persuade him to give psychotherapy another chance and perhaps avoid a long and expensive course of ECT. But I hadn't gotten any further than he, so the course of ECT was started. As ECT began, I was astonished to see the typical signs of improvement of a major depression responsive to ECT. Even after the first treatments, there were hours when Alice looked more relaxed and cheerful. At first this faded after the immediate post-treatment hours, as it usually does. But after a week, there were the unmistakable signs of improvement: her hand wringing became less noticeable, and she smiled more frequently. After a usual number of treatments, eight or ten, Alice was a new woman—or rather, she was the *old* Alice.

She had not completely adjusted to her daughter's moving out, of course. But she was confident that she had done the best job of raising her daughter that anyone could have done under the circumstances. She was sure that Judy and Bob would soon discover the difference between a houseguest and a daughter and grow tired of the responsibility of a full-time teenager. Terry would eventually come to realize how devoted Alice really was to her. The guilt and preoccupation were gone, and though she was certainly not happy, Alice was freed from the total entrapment by her mood that had been so striking when she was first admitted to the hospital. She could see beyond this one event in her life and put the affair into perspective in a way she was unable to do while weighed down by her low mood and guilty feelings. She was eating normally and sleeping without sedatives. Alice was discharged from the hospital and went back to the West Virginia mountains. I received a Christmas card some months later. Alice said she was feeling like her old self again, and she didn't even mention her daughter. ■

---

This is a fascinating case history. I tell it to many of my patients; usually to those who say they don't want to take medication because "medication won't solve my problems." Not only can the onset of an episode of affective disorder coincide with a traumatic life event but, as we have seen, a traumatic life event can precipitate an episode. I also relate this story to therapists, especially nonphysicians, as an example of how we can be *too* understanding and in the psychotherapeutic search for "insight" deprive a patient of the medical intervention necessary for recovery.

In discussing the symptoms of major depression, I mentioned obsessional thoughts. Remember that an obsession is an unpleasant idea that keeps intruding into consciousness despite efforts to turn one's thoughts to something else. Alice's preoccupation with her daughter's wanting to be adopted and her self-blaming ruminations are an excellent example of this particular symptom. For many patients there is a particular theme or thought that is the hallmark of their episodes of depression and does not bother them at other times. While they are depressed they can think of little else. I can remember another patient who developed a major depression after he moved to a new house. He became completely preoccupied with the move, convinced that he had made a terrible mistake and would never be happy in his new home. It is amazing to see how these "mountains" shrink to their true "molehill" size as the depression lifts. When they are feeling better, patients are sometimes embarrassed to have been so troubled by a problem that seems insignificant in their normal state of mind. Often people with major depression can spot the beginning of a relapse when a particular thought or set of thoughts returns. Their change in mood is like a rainstorm in the desert; all kinds of dormant seeds suddenly come to life and start growing. In this case, however, the flowers are not pretty. They are usually guilty self-recriminations about unpleasant things.

---

Several years ago I was called to the emergency room of the hospital where I worked to see a patient who had been brought in by her family. The emergency-room physician told me the patient was a woman in her late fifties who had cancer and was very depressed.

On the way to the emergency room, walking through the musty basement halls of the hospital, I began to conjure up a picture of what she would be like. I imagined a very thin, tragically heroic woman surrounded by her grieving family, weeping softly but trying to bear up and be strong for her distraught husband and children. What I found in the examining room did not resemble my imaginings at all.

Severe depression can be a violent, wrenching condition. When Dante imagined hell, he depicted a terrifying greeting at its entrance: "All hope abandon, ye who enter here." The loss of hope is the most profound horror a person can know. This woman was suffering the torments of the damned.

Sylvia was a housewife who, a year before I saw her, had been found to have a malignant growth at the back of her throat. The growth was small, but it was invasive and inoperable. Although the oncologist had told her family she had six months to live, Sylvia had surprised everyone by continuing to do reasonably well long after her diagnosis. She had a little pain but practically no impairment in her daily functioning. This was not really surprising once you knew Sylvia. She was hardworking, ordinary, and solidly predictable, a woman of common sense and plain dealings. Cheerful, encouraging, optimistic, strong, she was the kind of person no one could imagine even getting sick, let alone dying. It was thus all the more shocking that she had become the person I met in the emergency room.

I saw a moaning, writhing woman on the stretcher, her husband and daughter trying ineffectively to restrain and comfort her. I learned that even though her cancer continued in remission, she had been getting increasingly depressed over the past several weeks. She had had a setback about a month earlier, when it was discovered that a small tumor had spread to her lung, but she had started on medication to stop the swelling this caused and had again been doing well. It was not in her nature to give up on things, but her family noted a new sadness about her. She stopped paying attention to her appearance, lost her appetite, and became lethargic. Most worrisome, she began to expect death at any moment; she would wring her hands, sure each day would be the last. She had nightmares about death, funerals, and graves. Then her lethargy suddenly changed to agitation and distraction; she began pleading, "I'm dying, take me to the hospital."

By the time I saw her in the emergency room, the depressive process had reached its awful climax and Sylvia had crossed the line into psychosis. "I'm dead," she moaned. "Take me to the cemetery; take me to hell."

---

Psychiatrists use the term *delusion* to describe a persistent false belief that is preoccupying and usually extremely distressing. In the most severe forms of the depression of affective disorder, delusions can occur. The delusions of major depression are always—well, depressing. Severely depressed patients can become convinced that God has singled them out for punishment for terrible sins. (Remember, guilt is a quality of the depression of affective disorder.) Some are sure they have a fatal disease, often a shameful one—syphilis in years gone by and, more recently, AIDS. The belief that one has lost all one's money has been called the delusion of poverty.

At the beginning of the twentieth century, Clifford Beers, a member of a wealthy Connecticut family, suffered a severe psychotic major depression that lasted three years. After he recovered, he wrote about his experiences in a memoir called *A Mind That Found Itself.* He vividly described how psychotic depression could make its victims lose touch with reality: "I seemed to be no longer in the hospital [but] aboard a huge ocean liner [that] was slowly sinking. And it was I, of course, who had created the situation which must turn out fatally for all. Every now and then, I could hear parts of the ship give way under the strain . . . That I was not thrown into the sea by vengeful passengers was, I thought, due to their desire to keep me alive until . . . a more painful death could be inflicted upon me."

The themes of the delusions seen in severe depression—loss, guilt, illness, and death—reflect the change in mood and can be understood intuitively as arising from the abnormal mood state. For this reason, they are called *mood congruent.* This is in contrast to the delusions of schizophrenia, which are more often bizarre and do not seem to have any relation to mood. The belief that one's phone is bugged or that neighbors are sending x-rays through the walls to harass one are examples of *mood incongruent* delusions; they are very frightening, but they don't have much relation to mood.

Sylvia was immediately admitted to the psychiatric unit of the hospital. She was given a course of ECT and made a dramatic recovery from her depression. She regained her cheerful, simple "life is what you make of it" attitude and endeared herself to other patients and staff. Before she went home, Sylvia had her husband bring a camera to the hospital and take pictures of her with all her new friends; she had heard that ECT sometimes makes you forgetful, and she wanted to remember everyone she had met and come to know. Some months later we heard that Sylvia had died at home with her family, content and cheerful to the end.

There is much we can learn from Sylvia and her psychiatric problems. Let's look at some details one by one. I left out an important point in presenting Sylvia's medical history. I didn't tell you that the medication she was given when it was discovered that her tumor had spread was prednisone. This is a preparation of a hormone produced by the human adrenal glands; when given in high doses, it can shrink certain tumors. It is one of the class of hormones and hormone derivatives called steroids. Steroids are used to treat many illnesses, for in addition to shrinking some tumor tissues, they suppress inflammation. Thus, they are used in chronic inflammatory diseases such as arthritis, certain bowel diseases such as colitis, and also for lung problems such as chronic bronchitis and some cases of asthma. The steroids are powerful and effective, but they have many side effects. One is that they can cause a change in mood indistinguishable from major depression; in other words, they cause the *depressive syndrome*. A depressive illness that arises in the setting of another medical illness is usually called a "mood disorder due to *x*," with the name of the condition or substance substituted for the variable. (Thus, Sylvia's DSM-IV diagnosis would properly be "mood disorder due to steroid therapy with major-depressive-like episode.")

These illnesses frequently occur in individuals who have a predisposition to major depression. Often they have had a previous episode or they have a family history of a mood disorder, indicating that the predisposition is probably genetic. In fact, it may be incorrect to give these illnesses that look just like major depression a different name. There are indications that they are better understood as episodes of typical depressive illness that are *triggered,* rather than *caused,* by the medical illness or pharmaceutical. One of these indications is that once a steroid-induced depression starts, it usually continues even after the steroid is stopped. In Sylvia's case, it was probably adding prednisone to her medications that caused her to develop psychiatric symptoms. The mood syndrome must be approached with the usual treatments or it will run its usual course—and remember that Clifford Beers' psychotic depression lasted three years. (More on other medications that can mimic or trigger mood disorders is given in chapter 6 under "Medical Causes of Mood Disorders.")

Second, and Sylvia's case makes the point even more strongly than Alice's, if the patient has the qualities of mood change and other accompanying symptoms of major depression, even if the depression seems "understandable," one should not be tricked into interpreting severe depression as merely reactive. Sylvia's family made this mistake in the early weeks of her depression; after all, she had terminal cancer and had just had a setback. Who wouldn't be depressed? If her depression had been caught earlier and properly diagnosed, it might have been treated more easily.

Third, treatment of psychiatric problems, especially affective disorder, for which such effective and safe treatments are available, should always be aggressive and persistent. It would have been rather easy to rationalize not proceeding to ECT in managing Sylvia's case. Yet when her psychiatric problem was treated, Sylvia's optimism and courage were an inspiration to all of us on the staff and certainly a comfort to her family. In her final months, of which many weeks might have been lost had medication been tried and failed, she was full of life, contented, and happy.

This brings me to a discussion of the choice of medication versus ECT in treating particular patients with major depression. Let's explore the pros and cons of each approach. Treatment with medication is certainly simpler. Taking a couple of pills or capsules once or twice a day is quick and easy. The main problem with antidepressants is the unavoidable delay between the initiation of treatment and significant improvement in symptoms. A course of ECT more or less requires an inpatient hospital stay, with a trip to the operating room or treatment suite several times a week for two to four weeks and requires general anesthesia for each treatment. Also, the brief periods of disorientation after the treatment can be distressing. I've already mentioned the memory problems; these are minor in the vast majority of cases but troublesome nonetheless. When trying to decide on a treatment course, I like to think of ECT as a kind of surgical procedure; it is not without risk but is clearly indicated in some cases. The decision to proceed with ECT is clear when the depression is life threatening. Patients whose nutritional status is critical need a treatment that is going to work quickly. The desperately suicidal patient is another obvious case. Patients who are distraught, sleepless, and agitated can exhaust themselves, become dehydrated, and even suffer heart attacks or strokes because of their distress. ECT can sometimes bring about significant symptom relief after one or two treatments—that is, in only a few days. When the situation is an emergency, ECT is indicated.

Although there is disagreement on the exact numbers, there is considerable evidence that antidepressant medication simply is not effective in all cases of the depression of affective disorder, and ECT is sometimes the only thing that will work. Earlier I discussed delusions—false beliefs that are very distressing but that the patient cannot be persuaded to abandon. There is some evidence that for patients who have delusional thinking as part of the symptom picture, medication alone will be ineffective and ECT will be necessary. To some extent, this is an academic point; delusional patients are obviously very ill and usually need quick symptom relief, so ECT is a logical treatment choice for them anyway. Finally, ECT should be considered if the patient simply is not responding well to medication.

ECT is not as effective in patients who have very long-term problems with depression. These patients do not respond as well to ECT as do people with more clear-cut episodic illness. If such patients do respond, their symptoms usually return within a few months after the ECT has ended. Sometimes, however, ECT will be given to these patients to provide them with at least some temporary relief from symptoms. If a lengthy depression is threatening to cost them their job, for example, ECT may prevent this from happening and provide more time to find the combination of medications that will keep them from getting depressed again.

To sum up the guidelines for making this decision: Medication will work in the majority of patients, especially those whose symptoms are not too severe. ECT becomes the treatment of choice if an emergency exists, if adequate trials of medication have failed, in elderly patients, for whom it seems to work especially well and quickly, and in pregnant women, for whom it provides a nearly drug-free method of recovery from what can be a life-threatening illness.

## Tests for Mood Disorders

From the moment psychiatrists formulated the idea that some mood problems might have a biological basis, the search was on for a biological marker—something that could be seen or measured in the body to "make the diagnosis" of affective disorder. As we shall see in chapter 4, such a search by one psychiatrist led to one of the most valuable discoveries in the therapy of mood disorders—lithium. Is there some blood test, x-ray, or brain scan that can measure a change in body chemistry in patients having an episode of a mood disorder? Several tests were developed that seemed to hold great promise. Unfortunately, none have proved valid or accurate enough to be of much practical use diagnostically. So, unfortunately, there are no tests for affective disorder—at least not yet.

Unless, of course, one considers a trial of medication to be a test. For many years, psychiatrists were very reluctant to prescribe medication for patients if it wasn't clear that they had a mood disorder. To some extent this was because of a misunderstanding of what mood disorders are. Before the discovery of today's effective medical treatments for mood disorders, almost all treatment for psychiatric disorders focused on psychotherapy, and most theories on their origin involved mechanisms and solutions that could be understood from the psychotherapeutic point of view. Vastly oversimplified, this view is that personality style, ways of coping with adversity and conflict, and the development of psychiatric symptoms are the results of life experiences, especially early childhood experiences. Psychotherapy seeks to make patients aware of how these experiences contribute to their personality and to the symptoms they are suffering. It helps them to grow emotionally, develop new coping skills, and approach adversity in a more mature and effective manner.

Many psychiatrists believed that antidepressants, and all other psychiatric medications for that matter, simply treated symptoms without getting to the "real" cause of the problems, a cause that was essentially psychological—the result of childhood trauma, repressed unpleasant experiences, and other problems the patient would need to "work through" in psychotherapy.

This point of view has fortunately fallen by the wayside. Advancements in neurochemistry clearly indicate that there is a biological basis for affective disorder, and few believe that treatment with medication will "cover up" some deep-rooted underlying problem that will only make itself known in other ways or with other symptoms. There is really no reason not to use available treatments—especially the newer antidepressants, which have almost no dangerous side effects—if there is any chance they may help. Such a trial is at this point the only test for affective disorder available, and it can prevent long periods of unhappiness and perhaps save a great deal of money that might be wasted on other types of treatment.

This is not meant to minimize in any way the necessity of psychotherapy in treating mood disorders. On the contrary, people who are suffering from mood disorders need a tremendous amount of professional support, reassurance, and education. As they get better, most do not need weekly hour-long sessions to discuss their childhood experiences, marital relationships, and so forth, but the vast majority do need frequent visits initially to monitor their symptoms and any side effects, help them adjust to their diagnosis and treatment, and most important, to help them put all these issues into perspective and get on with their lives. Patients, especially those with mood disorders that have been untreated for a long time, may suddenly find relationships strained, develop job dissatisfaction, and have symptoms of anxiety. Change is always painful, and even getting well is a change and can take some adjusting to. "If only I had done something about this sooner" is a comment I often hear. I'll be discussing these issues in more detail later (see "Psychotherapy," under "Who Can Help" in chapter 7).

# CHAPTER 4

# Bipolar Disorder

## What Is Bipolar Disorder?

When I prescribe medication for major depression, my patients some-times ask me, "Do I have bipolar disorder?" Many people have heard this term and are acquainted with the idea that bipolar disorder is an often seri-ous psychiatric illness. I hope the preceding chapters make clear that in some persons depression can be the only symptom of a mood disorder, and that it too is very much a serious illness, requiring medical treatment and respond-ing to medication.

What, then, is bipolar disorder? I'll warn you here that the answer to this question turns out to be rather complicated. But people are complicated creatures, after all, so this shouldn't be too surprising. I think that if you take your time and read this chapter slowly and carefully, perhaps pausing after each section to think about what you've read, you'll come away with a good understanding of this complex disease.

Let me start by reviewing some of what I discussed in the first chapter, specifically the description of good mood. I said that when people are in a good mood they are optimistic, self-assured, and confident. A good mood makes one energetic, ready for new projects and challenges, and perhaps less troubled than usual by a fear of failure. Now imagine an emotional state in which all these qualities of mood are abnormally magnified, and you will begin to understand what the *manic state* is like. *Bipolar disorder,* formerly called *manic-depressive illness,* is a mood disorder in which the affected person has episodes of depression or low mood as well as an abnormal mood that is in some respects the opposite of depression. A case study will illustrate the symptoms of mania:

Dave is a salesman for a large insurance company. He is one of the most successful agents in his district, and the company has led him to believe that when the district manager retires in the next year or so Dave will be offered that position. He is in his early thirties, single, healthy, and fit. He lives in the same town as his parents and is close to his family. In the office Dave has a reputation as a workaholic, a high-energy person who would rather be calling on customers than going to a movie or ballgame. He's well liked by his friends, customers, and colleagues.

It seemed odd, then, when John, the district manager, began to get complaints about Dave from customers. John had recently received two phone calls from policyholders complaining that Dave was badgering them. Dave had called them several times in the same week trying to get them to buy more insurance. One customer was furious because Dave had awakened him at 6:00 a.m., when he had said just the night before that he wasn't interested in more coverage. Dave was a good salesman, and customer relations was his specialty; he had always walked the fine line between persistence and pestering with great skill. Customer complaints about him were simply unknown.

John thought he should drop by Dave's office and pass on the complaints. Perhaps Dave had been pushing himself too hard this past month; some of the paperwork he had turned in was a little sloppy, and Dave was usually very precise in this regard. When John met with Dave he noticed the slightest change in his appearance and manner. Dave's usually meticulously organized desk was covered with papers and folders, and his shirt was wrinkled. Nevertheless, he was his energetic self, perhaps even more energetic than usual.

"You can't blame me for trying harder!" Dave replied cheerily when John mentioned the complaints. "I won't double my sales this year by giving up easily!"

"Double your sales?" John asked, "Dave, you're already the top salesman in the district. Don't burn yourself out."

"Johnny, I have a great feeling about this year. I just know I can double my sales. It's just a matter of persistence, persistence, persistence. As for the 6:00 a.m. call, well, the early bird catches the worm!"

"Okay Dave, I guess I can't be too hard on you for being a good salesman. But I think you need to slow down a little. As I said, you don't want to don't burn yourself out."

"Right."

John had a nagging uneasiness about their meeting, a feeling that something wasn't quite right, that there was something different about Dave. He had an intensity, a driven quality that was more than just his usual energy. And what was this "Johnny" stuff? No one ever called him "Johnny." John's uneasiness was borne out the next week when he got three more customer complaints. One woman said she had felt intimidated by Dave on the phone and had agreed to buy insurance just to keep him from calling back. John went to call Dave into his office for a real meeting this time. Dave's job was in jeopardy if these complaints got to higher levels in the company. He discovered Dave at his desk, which was again covered with papers, files, and notebooks.

"Johnny, I'm working on something that is going to revolutionize the way this company does business. Listen to this!"

Without even waiting to hear why John had come to see him, Dave launched into a description of a scheme for selling insurance over the phone using automatic dialing machines, a scheme that was—well, crazy. It was difficult to interrupt him. John began to tell Dave to forget starting anything new and concentrate on working out his customer relations problems. But Dave only wanted to discuss his new marketing techniques, and their conversation became heated. Dave said, "No wonder you're getting out of the business, Johnny. You're behind the times! You can't deal with the fact that a real innovator like me is going to take your job away from you, triple the sales of this office, and make you look like a fool. District manager is just the beginning—I'm going to run this goddamned company one day."

John had actually said very little. Dave was doing all the talking; in fact, he was hoarse from talking. He got angrier by the minute and finally stormed out of the office. John tried to get him to come back, but Dave was off down the corridor like a shot, and John let him go. He started walking back to his own office. "What's wrong?" he wondered. Was Dave drinking? Using drugs?

There was more. On the way back to his office, John picked up his mail from his secretary. There was a letter from a local bank. Dave had applied for a mortgage in the past week—a mortgage on a $2 million home. On the application he had projected salary and commission of $3 million for the next year. Would John verify that this was possible? Dave had already put $50,000 down on the house. "God," thought John. "He must have put down all his savings and cashed in his IRA to do this."

I'll interrupt the story here, not because Dave's manic episode has reached its most severe state, but because the essential features of mania are well illustrated at this point. As you can see, the idea that people in the manic state are simply happy while those in the depressive state are sad is not entirely accurate. As with the depression of affective disorder, the manic state of affective disorder can be defined as an abnormal change in mood, with certain accompanying peculiarities of the mood state and a change in vegetative functions such as sleep and energy level (see table 4.1). As with depression, the manic state often starts insidiously, in many cases with a minor elevation of mood. The person becomes mildly elated, optimistic, and confident. As the clinical course goes on, this "overconfidence" becomes worse, and the most striking quality of the elated mood state can be grandiosity. This can be understood as an exaggeration of the self-confidence that is usually part of a good mood. Manic people can believe they are more talented, more intelligent, more wealthy, more everything than others. This can worsen to the point where they become delusional—convinced of ideas that are impossible. In the full-blown state patients can, for example, believe they have been elected to some high political office, that they have been appointed by God for a religious mission, or even that they are God. They may become convinced that they are on the verge of great scientific discoveries, that they have developed a new economic theory that will wipe out poverty, or that they have solved the great mysteries of the universe. Some become convinced that religious revelations have been made to them. Spending sprees are common, and patients sometimes borrow large sums of money or run up huge credit card bills.

The mood of the manic state has been described as expansive, and manic patients sometimes show what has been called *pressured socialization*—seeking out people, getting involved with new organizations (or even starting new ones), and talking to everyone in sight in a pressured, driven way. Also, their mood has been described as "infectious," especially in the early stages of an episode, meaning that just being around a manic person requires a great deal of energy and may even seem to boost one's own energy level.

Hypersexual behavior is also seen: the sex drive is heightened. Manic patients may start extramarital affairs, seek out prostitutes, or otherwise lose their inhibitions and engage in sexual activity that is unusual for them.

The euphoria of the manic state is often short-lived, and mania can quickly become very unpleasant. Some people with bipolar disorder don't get particularly euphoric at all but instead develop severe irritability. Their energy level is boosted to the point where they feel pressured, driven, tense, and very uncomfortable, becoming enraged at the smallest perceived slight. Their thoughts race, their minds so speeded up that they can't talk fast enough to express them, and speech can become incoherent.

TABLE 4.1 Common Symptoms of the Manic State

Elevated Mood
    Pervasive, expansive, infectious quality
    Overconfidence, grandiosity (can become the basis for delusional thinking)
    Sudden preoccupation with success, wealth, power, fame
    Irritability, angry outbursts, paranoid feelings
    Pressured socialization
    Spending sprees, foolish investments
Vegetative Signs
    Decreased need for sleep
    Appetite disturbance
    High energy, pressured speech, racing thoughts, hypersexual behavior

Paranoia—an unwarranted suspiciousness and the false belief that one is being persecuted—may be seen. Usually the paranoia can be understood as arising out of the grandiose mood; that is, it is mood congruent. Patients may believe their phone line is tapped because their phone calls are so important. They may feel that others are jealous of their special talents or great wealth or are trying to get at them because of their discoveries or religious powers.

Before medications were available to end the manic state, mania had a significant mortality rate. Patients exhausted themselves and simply collapsed, dead from a heart attack, cerebral hemorrhage, or dehydration. Mania is *not* pleasant.

Another abnormal mood state sometimes seen in bipolar disorder is called a *mixed affective state.* This mood has qualities of both major depression and the manic state. Usually the irritability and the driven, hyperactive energy level of mania are present, but the emotional quality is that of depression, with feelings of hopelessness and even impending doom. Separating out this mood state from mania may be artificial, since, as I state above, most of the feelings seen in the manic state are not pleasant. Some experts consider mixed affective state simply a severe form of mania, but others consider it distinct from mania and depression.

The manic state of affective disorder is obviously an abnormal mental condition. It usually seems to arise out of nowhere, and the person is so changed that it is easy to conclude that something is very wrong. Mania cannot be mistaken for a normal mood state except in its earliest stages. Therefore, the disease concept—the idea that some change in brain chemistry has occurred—is easy to invoke, as John did in wondering if Dave was on drugs. Let me emphasize here that the manic state is not just "getting carried away" or overenthusiastic about something; it is not in any way self-induced.

The manic state, like the major depressive syndrome, is an expression of a change in brain functioning.

Many patients who develop a manic state have had a prior episode of the depression of affective disorder. In some cases a single episode of bipolar disorder can have a *triphasic* character—that is, there are three phases to the episode. Often there is a brief period of depression that is not very severe and lasts only a few weeks or even a few days. The mood suddenly swings into a manic state that may last for several weeks, and finally depression sets in again for several weeks more. This swinging of the mood from one extreme to the other is the most striking characteristic of this form of affective disorder and led to the name given it at the turn of the century, *manic-depressive psychosis.* Today it is called *bipolar disorder.* By the way, most experts believe that affective disorder characterized by manic episodes only does not exist. Though many more people suffer from major depression than from bipolar disorder, the illness is far from rare. Most studies estimate prevalence rates at about 1 percent of the population.

## The Hypomanic Syndrome

In 1881, a German psychiatrist named Emanuel Mendel published a book about the manic state and in it proposed that another term be used for states of mild euphoria and hyperactivity which did not progress to full blown mania. He called this condition *hypomania.* (The prefix *hypo-* comes from a Greek word meaning "below" or "under.") Hypomania can be thought of as consisting of the symptoms that are present at the beginning of a manic episode: the elated mood, increased energy level, rapid thinking and speaking, and sometimes a bit of the irritability.

It has become clear that many persons with forms of bipolar disorder never develop full-blown mania but instead have periods of hypomania. This is one of the reasons why the term "manic-depressive illness" was abandoned. Many individuals never develop full-blown mania but nevertheless experience abnormal mood states in two different "directions" or *poles;* hence the term "bipolar disorder."

Some individuals with bipolar disorder have hypomanic periods that are quite mild, so mild in fact, that they and those around them (and sometimes even their psychiatrists) don't recognize them as abnormal mood states. After all, these symptoms don't sound so bad, do they? More energy than usual, less need for sleep, euphoria. Couldn't everyone use a few days like this now and then?

Although persons in the hypomanic state do not have the severe mental disorganization of mania and are by definition not agitated and frenzied to the point of violence toward themselves or others, hypomania can nevertheless have unpleasant and sometimes dangerous consequences. Feelings of increased confidence can lead to foolish investments in real estate (like Dave's multimillion dollar house) or in the stock market; patients can squander personal resources on grandiose and risky business ventures. Increased sexual feelings can lead to extramarital affairs or promiscuity—actions that can be life threatening in the age of HIV disease. The irritability of hypomania can lead to arguments and disagreements with family, colleagues, or neighbors that can sour relationships, sometimes irreparably.

Persons with even mild hypomania can quit a good job in a burst of overconfidence or irritability, withdraw a life's savings for a "get rich quick" scheme, or simply start driving their car too fast: all behaviors with potentially devastating consequences.

Words like "seductive" and "addictive" are frequently applied to the hypomanic syndrome; because the individual in a hypomanic state feels so good, they seldom seek treatment.

## Another Duality

In chapter 2, I discussed the classification of depression and introduced two terms formerly used: *endogenous depression* and *reactive depression*. I now want to discuss two other terms you may come across that have been used to classify depression: *unipolar depression,* referring to mood disorders characterized by episodes of depression alone, and *bipolar depression,* for mood disorders characterized by both episodes of depression and episodes of the manic state in the same person. Because the term *bipolar depression* is a bit self-contradictory, I prefer to use the term *depression of bipolar disorder*. Because there are several mood disorders characterized by depression only, I will continue to use the terms that I introduced previously: *major depressive disorder* and *dysthymic disorder*.

Let me pause a moment to make a very important point about severe depression seen in mood disorders. The symptoms of depression in people with bipolar disorder are in many respects identical to the symptoms of those who have major depressive disorder (persons who only experience episodes of depression). There are a few subtle differences: the depressive symptoms seen in bipolar disorder tend to be more severe, and patients with bipolar disorder who become depressed often are more slowed down or "retarded" than patients with unipolar depression. However, differentiating between unipolar depression and bipolar disorder in depressed patients experiencing their first episode of illness is very difficult.

At first glance it may even seem arbitrary to separate out patients who have only depressions from those who have both depressive and manic episodes. However, when this separation is made and the groups are compared, there are important differences that warrant this distinction. There are differences between the two groups in the age at which the first episode occurs, with bipolar disorder often beginning earlier than major depressive disorder. Major depressive disorder is more common than bipolar disorder. Major depressive disorder is much more common in women, whereas bipolar disorder is equally common in men and women. Family histories are also usually different: persons who are having a major depressive episode are more likely to turn out to have bipolar disorder (that is, to develop manic or hypomanic symptoms at some future time) if there are other people with bipolar disorder in their family. People with only major depressive disorder in their family are far less likely to have bipolar disorder. Some experts recommend treating a person with a major depressive episode for bipolar disorder if they have a family history of bipolar disorder.

I've already mentioned the subtle differences between the symptoms of depression sometimes observed. There are also differences in the treatment of these two types of mood disorders, as we shall see later. All of these differences are so consistently observed that this is taken as compelling evidence that major depression and bipolar disorder are two distinct, though clearly related, mood disorders.

So what is the answer? "Do I have bipolar disorder?" asks my patient about to start treatment for a major depressive episode. Like many diagnostic issues in psychiatry, the answer is often unclear in an individual patient, especially in a younger person having their first episode of severe depression. If the patient has had an episode of mania or hypomania in the past, then their diagnosis is bipolar disorder. If the patient knows that other members of their family have bipolar disorder, there is a higher likelihood that they will turn out to have it as well. If none of these conditions hold true, then the diagnosis of major depressive disorder is appropriate, but it must always be somewhat tentative, especially in a young person.

## "Mood Swings" and Cyclothymia

In chapter 2, I told you that the depression of affective disorder can vary considerably in severity. The question naturally arises, then, Can bipolar disorder also exist in more severe and less severe forms? As the discussion in the previous section on hypomania makes clear, the answer is yes. Another case history will illustrate.

---

Tom, a thirty-year-old architect, made an appointment to see me after he had picked up a brochure on depression given out by the local community mental health center staff at a health fair in a suburban shopping mall. As he took a seat, he pulled out the little brochure and showed it to me. "This describes me perfectly!" he said, flipping through the pages. I noticed he had taken a yellow highlighter and marked the booklet as if it were a textbook. "I've known there was something wrong with me for years, but I didn't know what. Now I've discovered it! I have major depression."

Tom was an intense young man. He spoke quickly, concisely; listening to him reminded me of the way people read telegrams in old movies. "It started in college." Stop. "I should have seen a psychiatrist back then." Stop. "I'm sure this medication can help." Stop.

Tom clearly described episodes of clinical depression. He experienced periods of several days almost every month when he had such a low energy level that he stayed in bed all weekend and sometimes even took time off from work. Sometimes he seemed to lose all interest in both work and play. He would stop going to the YMCA after work and get really down on himself, feeling fat, lazy, and good for nothing. He never really thought of these episodes as depression, usually shrugging them off afterward as "a virus I just couldn't shake" or "cold or cloudy weather that just gets me down."

I asked Tom, "Do you ever have other mood changes that you can't explain? Like feeling really good for a time for no particular reason, or really irritable?"

"Well, I definitely get more irritable at times. Some days when I get up in the morning I know it's going to be one of those days when everybody better just steer clear of me."

"You find your temper is really short some days?" I asked.

"O-o-oh yes. This is embarrassing, but I guess I need to tell you these things. One morning last week I was late getting to the bus stop, and the bus was pulling away. The driver wouldn't stop for me. I completely lost it. I was running down the street yelling and screaming. That was the worst it's ever gotten. I got this brochure just in time."

Depressed people don't go running after buses yelling and screaming. This was not simply depression.

"When you have these short-tempered days, do you notice you have more energy than usual?"

"I guess you could say that. A nervous energy. I get that way too sometimes, especially if I haven't gotten enough sleep. I can rip through my drafting work and get a lot of routine things done that I've fallen behind on. I've stayed at the drafting table fifteen, twenty hours straight. It's very compulsive though; I certainly can't do anything that's at all creative."

Tom had never sought help for his mood changes; it had never even occurred to him that he might have a problem that could be helped with medication. Yet in talking to him about his past, it became clear that unpredictable mood changes had been interfering with his happiness and productivity for many years. Since college he had had recurrent changes in mood and energy level lasting several days to several weeks. The changes had become severe enough in the past two years to cause him to lose time at work when he was depressed and to do embarrassing and foolish things when he was, as he called it, "nervous." He had broken up with a girlfriend because during one of his "hyper" states he had said something she felt insulted by and she wouldn't forgive him. Yet the mood swings had never become terribly severe. Because they were not extreme and because they always went away in a few days or weeks at the most, he could rationalize the symptoms as being caused by some outside agent or event: a cold virus, a tight deadline at work, losing the car keys, or even the old cliché about getting up on the wrong side of the bed.

Tom was suffering from *cyclothymia*. *Thymos* is a Greek word meaning mind, but it has come to be used as a root in psychiatry referring to mood. (Remember, dysthymia refers to depressed mood, *dys-* meaning bad.) The prefix *cyclo-* means just what you'd think: cycling.

Cyclothymia can be thought of as a less severe form of bipolar disorder. The depressive periods are not serious enough to be called major depressive episodes, and the manic-like states are not extreme enough to be called mania. It may appear arbitrary to consider cyclothymia a separate disorder from bipolar disorder. I agree, and so do many experts in the field of mood disorders. Although it is clear that many people who are said to have cyclothymia never go on to develop a full-blown major depressive or manic episode, the same treatments are effective for both.

## Is There a Spectrum of Mood Disorders?

The word *spectrum* is often used to talk about the colors of a rainbow. In a rainbow, the green band of color blends into the yellowish-green, then into greenish-yellow, then yellow, almost imperceptibly. A similar term is *continuum*. If a continuous series of things blend into each other so gradually and seamlessly that it is impossible to say where one becomes the next, those things are said to exist "on a continuum." For the purposes of treatment, it is often useful to think of a spectrum or continuum of mood disorders, with mood disorders characterized by only depression existing on one end of a continuum and bipolar disorder characterized by severe depressions and also by episodes of full-blown mania at the other.

This leads me to another discussion about the classification of bipolar disorders: you may have read about *bipolar I* and *bipolar II* disorders. Simply put, bipolar I patients have a clear history of both major depressive episodes and manic episodes, whereas bipolar II patients have major depressive episodes and only hypomanic symptoms.

Also, if you look at the end of the section on bipolar disorders in the *Diagnostic and Statistical Manual of the American Psychiatric Association*, you will see a category titled "Bipolar Disorder Not Otherwise Specified" (also called simply "Bipolar NOS"). This odd category exists because the developers of the *DSM* recognized that there are patients who seem to have *some* kind of bipolar disorder, but who don't meet the diagnostic criteria for bipolar I, bipolar II, or cyclothymia. Psychiatrists have long recognized that there are many forms of bipolar disorder. For many years, clinicians have described various types of "soft" bipolar disorders, mostly patients who came to be treated for depression, whose illness seemed related to bipolar disorder. Terms like *pseudo-unipolar depression* and *bipolar III* have been coined to describe various types of severe depressions that have some features of bipolar disorder but do not fall into traditional categories for bipolar diagnoses. Very often, these describe patients who have had a long history of depressive symptoms but who have very mild and/or very brief periods of hypomania. Some also have very brief and mild periods of mixed symptoms: agitation, irritability, and "rages" which, because they are so short-lived, can be overlooked or explained away. This concept of "soft" bipolar disorder is an important one; I will return to it after I discuss treatments for bipolar disorder.

## The Chemistry of Bipolar Disorder

What can neurochemistry tell us about bipolar disorder? Are there any findings that will help us understand the relation between bipolar disorder and major depression? Unfortunately, the neurochemistry of bipolar disorder is just as obscure as that of major depression.

Remember that the antidepressants were found almost by trial and error to be helpful in the treatment of depression; the discovery of the usefulness of the medications used to treat bipolar disorder was also mostly due to a series of lucky accidents. We've discovered over the years how to use these medications effectively and safely, but the biological basis of bipolar disorder is also only beginning to become clearer. As we will see in the next section, one medication is often used to treat both the depressed and the manic phases of bipolar disorder. How can this be? How can one medication treat such different clinical states? An even more basic question is: How can one illness have two completely opposite sets of symptoms? The answer may be that the basic defect in bipolar disorder, like in major depressive disorder, involves *neuroplasticity*. As I mentioned earlier, this refers to the ability of brain cells to react and reshape their structure and their functioning, perhaps "tuning" to certain levels of signaling in various brain centers that control mood and modulate our emotional responses to stresses, losses, and challenges. When you think about it this way, it's not so surprising that a problem in how these brain systems work could lead to a whole variety of abnormal mood states, including depression as well as manic, hypomanic, and mixed states.

## The Treatment of Bipolar Disorder
### MOOD-STABILIZING MEDICATIONS

The definition of *mood-stabilizing medications* is somewhat controversial, but since the term is used so commonly, it's best that I use it too. A definition that I think is very useful is to call any medication that has *both* anti-manic and antidepressant effect a mood-stabilizing medication. The first and still one of the most important of these is also a name that you have probably come across.

### Lithium

"The Three Princes of Serendip" is a Persian fairy tale about finding valuable objects by chance on a journey toward another goal. No innovation in modern psychiatry so parallels this story as does the discovery of the therapeutic effects of lithium on the symptoms of bipolar disorder.

For hundreds, perhaps thousands, of years, Europeans have traveled to various cities and towns where natural mineral springs occur to "take the waters." One of the first such towns to become popular has lent its name to all that have followed. Spa is a mountain hamlet in Belgium, about thirty miles from the German border. Spa, the city of Bath in England, and many other cities with such natural springs drew visitors because of the water's reputed healing properties, and several developed into health resorts. All kinds of therapeutic effects were ascribed to various spring waters, which were bathed in, drunk, used in massages, and formulated into elixirs, teas, ointments, and muds. As medical science grew more sophisticated in the nineteenth century, it was slowly realized that many of the illnesses the therapeutic waters were said to ameliorate were those that were chronic but somewhat variable in their course. Illnesses like arthritis and emphysema, for example, tend to cause symptoms for many years but show spontaneous periods of remission, usually followed by relapse. The "therapeutic" effect of spa waters began to look more and more like the result of rest, good food, lots of attention and pampering, and a bit of good timing. Nevertheless, chemists began sampling the spring waters to see what was in them.

One of the chemicals they found was *lithium*. Lithium is an element, a single kind of atom that is chemically similar to sodium, with which it shares many characteristics. In valiant attempts to duplicate and possibly enhance the effects of spa waters, lithium was administered to patients with epilepsy, diabetes, and gout. Although results were disappointing, as a result of this work, lithium was formulated into compounds suitable for medical use. But because they seemed to lack any therapeutic effects, these lithium compounds were put on the shelf and forgotten.

In the 1940s the biology of salt and water balance in the body was being investigated. Researchers discovered that restricting salt intake was beneficial in certain medical problems where the body was impaired in its ability to get rid of excess salt and water—conditions such as congestive heart failure, where water can build up in the lungs with fatal results. (Table salt consists of a sodium ion and a chlorine ion chemically bound together to form the compound sodium chloride; it is the sodium ion that is crucial to water balance in the body.) But low-sodium diets are extremely unpalatable, and it was (and still is) difficult to get patients to stick to them. The search was on for a salt substitute to flavor low-sodium foods.

Lithium was pulled off the shelf, and various lithium compounds were tried as salt substitutes. The results were disastrous; lithium was found to be toxic in surprisingly small concentrations. Even worse, patients with impaired sodium excretion also were impaired in their lithium excretion and were thus set up for lithium poisoning. Deaths were reported. Lithium was put back up on the shelf—way back in the corner of the top shelf!

In 1949, John Cade, an Australian psychiatrist, was investigating the manic state. Specifically, he was looking for a biological marker, some abnormal chemical level or measurable change in biological functioning that characterized the disorder. Cade analyzed the urine of manic patients hoping to find some "toxin" that might possibly lead to a test or even a new treatment. Cade was especially interested in a group of compounds called *urates* that are by-products of protein digestion found in urine. For his work, Cade needed to be able to dissolve the urate compounds easily in water. It turns out that they dissolve most easily when combined with lithium. You can think of this fact as the first gift from the Persian princes of Serendip.

In the course of his investigations, Cade injected lithium urate into laboratory guinea pigs, and he noticed that the animals became lethargic. Further experiments revealed that it was the lithium, not the urate, that induced the lethargy, and Cade at first thought he had discovered a new sedative. This erroneous conclusion was the second serendipitous event. Cade decided to administer lithium preparations to several patients who were chronically agitated. The effect on patients with mania was dramatic. Here is one case report from Cade's original paper:

> CASE I—W.B., a male aged fifty-one years, who had been in a state of chronic manic excitement for five years, restless, dirty, destructive, mischievous and interfering, had long been regarded as the most troublesome patient in the ward. His response was highly gratifying. From the start of treatment on March 29, 1948, with lithium citrate he steadily settled down and in three weeks was enjoying the unaccustomed surrounding of the convalescent ward. As he had been ill so long and confined to a "chronic ward," he found normal surroundings and liberty of movement strange at first. He remained perfectly well and left the hospital on indefinite leave with instructions to take a dose of lithium carbonate, five grains, twice a day. He was soon back working at his old job. However, he became more lackadaisical about his medicine and finally ceased taking it. His relatives reported that he had not taken any for at least six weeks prior to his readmission on January 30, 1949 and was becoming steadily more irritable and erratic. On readmission to the hospital he was at once started on lithium carbonate, ten grains three times a day, and in a fortnight had again settled down to normal. He is now (February 28, 1949) ready to return to home and work.

Dr. Cade had treated ten manic patients with lithium, and all ten had shown the same dramatic improvement. Now, reporting a therapeutic use for lithium in Cade's day was a little like reporting a beneficial effect for Agent Orange would be today. Lithium had such a bad reputation that it was years before Cade's results were noticed.

It would take a decade of perseverance from a psychiatrist half a world away, Morgans Schou of Denmark, for lithium to be accepted as a standard treatment for mood disorders. Schou had read Cade's paper and started to prescribe lithium to his patients. He very quickly became convinced of lithium's efficacy in treating bipolar disorder, and in 1954 he published a landmark study, "The Treatment of Manic Psychoses by the Administration of Lithium Salts," which described how giving lithium would make the racing thoughts, agitation, and hyperactivity of the manic state gradually disappear. Schou also discovered that if the lithium was stopped, the patient's symptoms returned "unless the manic phase had spontaneously subsided in the meantime."

In 1967 another paper indicated an even more valuable use for this new medication. The paper was called "Lithium as a Prophylactic Agent," and Dr. Schou was a coauthor. *Prophylactic* can be defined as *preventive,* and this paper showed that continuing lithium even after the resolution of manic symptoms could prevent repeat episodes of either the manic state *or* depression. Lithium was found to have a specific action against bipolar disorder; it treated the acute symptoms and in many cases prevented symptoms from coming back for as long as the patient took it.

The prophylactic effect of lithium was at first strongly resisted. An article titled "Prophylactic Lithium, Another Therapeutic Myth?" appeared in a leading British medical journal the very next year. As further investigation was done, however, this effect was verified again and again. Studies showed that lithium also successfully treats depressive episodes in patients with bipolar disorder and major depressive episodes in patients who had never had mania—patients with major depressive disorder. Although it was not until 1970 that lithium became widely used in the United States, it has remained a very important drug in the treatment of mood disorders.

Unlike the antidepressants, which can be effective at a relatively wide range of doses and blood levels, lithium is most effective when a particular level is reached in the body. Because lithium can be toxic at levels not much higher than the level at which it is therapeutic, regular blood tests are required to make sure the patient is getting enough to be effective but not so much as to risk toxicity. It usually takes several weeks to find the dose necessary to attain a blood level in the therapeutic range. Sometimes, when the patient is having severe symptoms and the psychiatrist wants to get to the therapeutic level of lithium as soon as possible, the tests may be repeated several times a week. After the correct dose is ascertained, regular blood tests are still necessary because changes in body weight, the addition of medicines for other problems, and many other factors can affect the lithium level.

The therapeutic range for lithium was determined through clinical trials in which blood tests were always done twelve hours after the last dose of the medication. For this reason, it is important that when a blood test is necessary patients try to be in the laboratory twelve hours after their latest dose of medication. Since most people take a bedtime dose at about 11:00 p.m., it's usually relatively easy to put one's a.m. dose in a pocket or purse instead of taking it and to drop by the clinic or laboratory in late morning for the blood test, taking the "skipped" morning dose on the way out. This timing is very important; a blood test taken too long or short a time after the last dose will give inaccurate information, leading to erroneous changes in dosage.

Lithium has a number of side effects that are more uncomfortable than dangerous. Because lithium is so closely related to sodium, the body handles it much the same way, through the kidneys. Starting on lithium is similar to raising salt intake; many patients notice an increase in thirst and urination. Some people, especially women, experience water retention that causes puffy fingers or ankles. The body seems to adjust quickly to the new salt/water balance, though, and this problem often subsides. It is very important

TABLE 4.2 Side Effects of Lithium

Short Term (Temporary)
    Increased thirst and urination
    Water retention (especially in women)
Ongoing
    Gastrointestinal tract irritation (nausea, diarrhea; often treatable)
    Birth defect potential
    Tremor (dose related and also treatable)
    Concentration and memory problems (dose related)
Long Term
    Kidney problems (urine concentration problems causing excessive thirst
        and urination)
    Thyroid problems

not to start on a diuretic medication while taking lithium. (Diuretics, also commonly known as "water pills," increase urine production and are used to treat high blood pressure and other medical problems.) Diuretics change the way the kidneys excrete sodium (and therefore lithium), and some can cause lithium toxicity. Patients taking lithium can use diuretics, but the dose may require adjustment; this should reinforce the need to tell *all* doctors about *all* the medication one is taking.

Lithium is somewhat irritating to the stomach and digestive tract, and some patients have nausea or diarrhea when they start taking it. The nausea can usually be avoided by taking the medication immediately before or after meals so that there is food in the stomach. Also, there are slow-release forms of lithium that may help with the gastrointestinal side effects.

Another common side effect is a slight tremor or shaking, especially of the hands. This is more of a problem at higher doses, and tremor can get worse with anxiety or nervousness, or sometimes when lithium is taken with certain other medications. Cutting back on caffeine is often helpful in treating this side effect, and there are medications called beta-blockers that can lessen it. In my experience, this is rarely necessary. Some patients report that when they are taking lithium their concentration and memory are not as efficient as usual, and there is some evidence that initiative and speed of performance on some psychological tests are dulled. These effects are dose related; that is, they subside if the lithium dose is lowered.

Lithium can cause other more serious side effect problems in patients who take it for extended periods. Taking lithium for a long time, usually many years, can affect the urine concentrating function of the kidneys and also can suppress thyroid gland functioning. Because of these potential side

TABLE 4.3 Symptoms of Lithium Toxicity

Fatigue and lethargy
Clouded thinking and impaired concentration
Severe nausea and vomiting
Dizziness
Muscle weakness
Slurred speech
Unsteady walk

effects, blood tests are done every year or so to be sure no such problems are beginning to occur. Many people can take lithium for years at a time with no problems at all, but persons taking lithium should be on the lookout for changes in bladder habits (for example, waking up to urinate more often at night) and for symptoms of thyroid problems (unexplained changes in body weight, changes in their tolerance of hot or cold weather, changes in energy level or the texture of their hair and skin). Lithium has been associated with cardiac birth defects. Women in their childbearing years are often advised to practice birth control while taking lithium.

Because toxic levels are so close to therapeutic levels, patients taking lithium must be familiar with the symptoms of lithium poisoning. The most common and earliest signs are the symptoms experienced by Cade's guinea pigs—lethargy and fatigue. Dizziness, muscle weakness, slurred speech, and an unsteady walk are signs of advancing toxicity and warrant a trip to the emergency room. Those taking lithium should be careful not to get dehydrated in hot weather, since this concentrates the lithium in their bodies. Patients sometimes ask if they should drink extra water or take salt tablets. This is really unnecessary because the body has a natural mechanism to make sure it has enough water: the thirst reflex. I tell my patients to drink when they are thirsty and maybe drink a bit extra for good measure, especially in hot weather. More than this is not necessary.

All these blood tests, toxicity, birth defects—it may seem that lithium is a lot of trouble. The patients who benefit from it will tell you differently. For those with bipolar disorder, the benefit is obvious. These patients' changes of mood and behavior can be so serious that they must be hospitalized. Sometimes the episodes can recur every few years or even more often. A medication that can treat and thus shorten an episode of bipolar disorder and prevent future episodes makes the difference between a normal life and spending years in a hospital, as happened to many patients with bipolar disorder before there were effective medications.

Patients with less severe mood swings can also benefit from lithium therapy. "My life is predictable for the first time in years," one of my patients with cyclothymia told me. "Before I started taking lithium, I never knew how I would feel when I got up in the morning. It was impossible to plan anything. Vacations had to be canceled because I'd wake up so depressed on the day we were to leave." Another said to me several months after starting lithium, "I feel like I always thought I was supposed to but never could. My husband told me that if I were any more normal he wouldn't know how to act around me anymore." It's often only after lithium therapy begins that patients and their families realize that for years the rhythm of their lives had danced to the syncopated beat of unpredictable mood swings.

## ANTICONVULSANT MOOD-STABILIZING MEDICATIONS

After the introduction in the 1960s of a new drug called carbamazepine for the control of epilepsy, several reports appeared indicating that for epilepsy patients who also had mood problems, carbamazepine not only controlled their seizures well but also improved their psychiatric symptoms. It was a small step, then, to test carbamazepine in patients with mood problems who did not suffer from epilepsy. Japanese clinicians looking for an alternative to lithium, which was not approved for use in Japan until years after it was available in the United States, did much of this early work. In 1980, a study appeared in the *American Journal of Psychiatry* titled "Carbamazepine in Manic-Depressive Illness: A New Treatment," and the race was on to refine the use of this medication in mood disorders and define the group or groups of patients that it helped most. As more new drugs for the treatment of epilepsy were developed, they too were tested in patients with mood disorders. Many of them have also been found to be helpful in treating bipolar disorder and major depressive disorder. In the sections that follow, I'll discuss these medications in more detail.

### Valproate (Depakote, Depakote SR, Depakene)

The development of valproate (brand names include Depakote and Depakene) for the treatment of mood disorders is another convoluted study in serendipity. Valproic acid is a carbon compound similar to a number of others that are found in animal fats and vegetable oils—a fatty acid. It was first synthesized in 1882 and used as an organic solvent for many years for a variety of purposes. (Remember that a solvent is a liquid that other substances easily dissolve into.) Many decades ago, pharmacists used it as a solvent for bismuth salts, which were used to treat stomach and skin disorders.

In the early 1960s, scientists looking for treatments for epilepsy were working with a group of new pharmaceutical compounds that appeared promising but that were difficult to dissolve. (Is this beginning to sound familiar?) They discovered that valproic acid was an effective solvent for the compounds they were testing and started using it to dissolve drugs for animal experimentation. As they tested the various new pharmaceuticals, they seemed to obtain confusing results—until someone realized that it didn't matter *which* of the new pharmaceuticals were used. *Any* of them dissolved in valproic acid were found to be effective in stopping epileptic seizure activity. It soon became obvious that it was the valproic acid that was stopping the seizures, not what was dissolved in it. By 1978, valproate was approved by the Food and Drug Administration for use in treating epilepsy.

In the 1960s, there were some reports that valproate might be helpful in mood disorders, and throughout the late 1960s and early 1970s a French psychiatrist named Pierre Lambert published a series of papers about using it to treat bipolar disorders. In the mid-1980s, several studies by American psychiatrists appeared, and ten years later, valproate had become firmly established as an effective anti-manic medication.

In reading about this medication, you may become confused by the many names it goes by: valproate, valproic acid, divalproex sodium, not to mention the brand names Depakote, Depakote SR, and Depakene. Many chemicals, numerous medications included, consist of two parts called ions, one positively charged and the other negatively charged. When the two parts exist together as a *compound,* the charges cancel each other out and the system is stable. Valproate is actually the name of an ion. When it is associated with a hydrogen atom, the result is valproic acid. In combination with a sodium ion, it becomes sodium valproate. Depakote is a preparation manufactured by Abbott Laboratories consisting of a stable combination of sodium valproate and valproic acid that is called divalproex sodium. Lastly, Depakene is Abbott's brand name for their valproic acid preparation.

Valproate's therapeutic action in mood disorders is not well understood, but it also appears to enhance neuronal plasticity. Valproate is well established as being effective in the treatment of acute mania. Its effectiveness in the treatment of acute depressive episodes of bipolar disorder has been less impressive in the research literature, but I think most experienced psychiatrists will agree that some patients do indeed derive important antidepressant effects from it. Valproate does not seem to be terribly effective in treating major depressive disorder. There are several studies that show that valproate is helpful in cyclothymia, bipolar II, and "soft" bipolar disorders and that lower doses and lower blood levels are required for these than in the treatment of bipolar I.

Like lithium, valproate can be measured in the bloodstream. As with lithium, blood for valproate levels should be drawn twelve hours after the last dose of medication.

Valproate has a milder side effect profile than lithium and is not nearly as toxic in overdose. Side effects that are common as a patient starts taking the medication include stomach upset and some sleepiness. These problems usually go away quickly. Increased appetite and weight gain are not unusual. Some patients report hair loss, usually temporary, which resolves even more quickly with anti-dandruff shampoos containing the mineral selenium.

Several cases of severe liver problems have been reported in patients taking valproate, but these have occurred almost exclusively in children taking the drug for control of epilepsy, most of whom had other medical problems and were taking several different medications. A 1989 review article states that no fatalities from liver problems caused by valproate had ever been reported in patients over the age of ten who were taking only valproate. Just to be on the safe side, however, a blood test that can detect liver inflammation is done on patients taking valproate for the first time and is repeated at appropriate intervals while they are taking it. Since valproate also, rarely, causes a drop in blood counts, a complete blood count is usually done as well. Again, these are very rare problems and when they do occur, they develop slowly and usually during the first six months of therapy. Thus, they can be picked up with routine blood tests; nevertheless, patients on valproate should be on the lookout for signs of liver or blood count problems, which include unusual bleeding and bruising, jaundice (yellowing of the eyes and skin), fever, and water retention.

Valproate has been associated with birth defects such as spina bifida, and women in their childbearing years should practice birth control while taking valproate.

## Carbamazepine (Tegretol, Equitro, Epitol)

Despite the fact that carbamazepine has been used for bipolar disorder for several decades, there is much less research data on its efficacy in this illness than there is for other medications such as lithium and valproate. This gap is slowly being filled, however, and newer studies have appeared prompted by the development of a sustained release preparation of carbamazepine.

Like the other mood-stabilizing medications, carbamazepine can be measured in the bloodstream and blood levels used to adjust the dose. Unfortunately, not much work has been done on blood levels in bipolar patients, so the therapeutic range used for the treatment of epilepsy is usually the target psychiatrists aim for in their patients.

Carbamazepine is metabolized in the liver and, like some other drugs, it causes the liver to increase the level of the enzymes that metabolize it. This means that the longer a person takes carbamazepine the better the liver gets at getting rid of it. So after a few weeks, the blood levels may go down and the dose may need to be increased. This increase in liver enzymes can also affect other medications that the patient might be taking, including certain tranquilizers, certain antidepressants, other epilepsy medications, and some hormones. The change in hormonal levels is very important for women who are on birth control. Some birth control medications that use very low hormone levels lose their effectiveness if taken with carbamazepine. It is very important that all physicians involved in a person's care know when carbamazepine has been started so that dosage adjustments can be made.

Carbamazepine can cause the sort of general side effects that many medications affecting the brain can cause: sleepiness, light-headedness, and some initial nausea. These problems tend to be short-lived and dose-related.

As with valproate, there have been rare cases of liver problems, so blood tests for liver inflammation are routinely done. There have been a few reports of dangerous changes in blood counts, so blood cell counts are also done, especially in the first several weeks of therapy. Some cases of a rare but dangerous skin reaction called Stevens-Johnson syndrome have occurred. Although all these problems are very rare, patients should be on the watch for the development of a rash, jaundice, water retention, bleeding or bruising, or signs of infection.

## Oxcarbazepine (Trileptal)

As its name suggests, oxcarbazepine is similar to carbamazepine. It is also used to treat epilepsy and it seems to work similarly to—but has several advantages over—carbamazepine. It is not associated with the blood count problems that can be caused by carbamazepine, and it does not cause the changes in liver enzymes that affect the metabolism of other drugs. This makes it significantly easier to take, with less need for monitoring blood tests and changes in dosage. Much of the earlier work on oxcarbazepine in bipolar disorder was done in Europe, and studies done by German investigators in the mid-1980s suggested it was as beneficial as carbamazepine for mania. More recently American clinicians have also made favorable reports on its safety and efficacy.

Many clinicians have been reluctant to prescribe oxcarbazepine's parent compound, carbamazepine, because of the possibility of severe adverse reactions. Since these problems are much less significant with oxcarbazepine, we will probably see it prescribed more often and studied more closely.

## Lamotrigine (Lamictal)

This is a rather new anticonvulsant medication that is used to treat bipolar disorder. The most important aspect of its profile is lamotrigine's effectiveness in the depression of bipolar disorder. Its use in treating major depressive disorder is growing as well. Blood levels are not routinely ordered for lamotrigine because of its low toxicity and because therapeutic effects have not been correlated with a particular blood level range.

In contrast to the other mood stabilizers, lamotrigine has a very low side effect burden. It can cause some initial nausea or gastrointestinal upset and the sorts of side effects that many medications affecting the brain can cause: sleepiness, light-headedness or dizziness, headache. At higher doses, some patients complain of concentration problems similar to those often reported by patients taking lithium. In my experience, lowering the dose usually takes care of this problem.

The most serious problems that have been reported from lamotrigine are very dangerous types of allergic skin rashes called Stevens-Johnson syndrome and toxic epidermal necrosis (TED). These problems were reported early on, when the drug was being given to patients with epilepsy, and research to see which patients were at highest risk of these reactions determined that patients who started lamotrigine at high doses and children were more likely to develop a serious rash. Subsequently, the drug's manufacturer recommended against prescribing the drug to children except under special circumstances and also changed the dosing recommendations for adults. Now patients start lamotrigine at a very low dose and gradually increase it over a period of weeks. This means that it may take five weeks or more to get to the usual therapeutic dose of 200–400 mg/day (even longer if the patient is already on a drug, such as valproate, that raises lamotrigine levels in the body, in which case they must increase their dose even more slowly). Since these recommendations were put into effect, however, the numbers of people developing serious rashes from lamotrigine has dropped dramatically. In clinical trials in which the drug was prescribed to several thousand patients for the treatment of bipolar disorder, none of the patients developed a serious rash.

Many individuals develop skin reactions to medications (and to lots of other things, as well), so it's important when starting lamotrigine to take precautions against developing a rash from another source. If a rash develops with an unknown cause, the patient might be told to stop lamotrigine unnecessarily, just in case it is the source, perhaps missing out on a medication that might be very effective for him. For this reason, patients starting on lamotrigine should consider following the protocol developed at Stanford University to prevent skin rashes.

## OTHER ANTICONVULSANT MOOD STABILIZERS

A number of other anticonvulsant agents show promise for the treatment of bipolar disorder. For the most part the promise of these medications is based on a few case reports of a therapeutic effect. In some cases, they are medications in the same class as other pharmaceuticals already shown to be helpful.

Gabapentin is another anticonvulsant that may be a mood stabilizer in some patients. As with the other anti-seizure medications, reports of benefi-

TABLE 4.4 The Stanford Protocol for Patients Starting Lamotrigine

Do not start lamotrigine within 2 weeks of any rash, viral infection, vaccination
During first 3 months of treatment, avoid new:
   Medicines, foods
   Cosmetics, conditioners, deodorants
   Detergents, fabric softeners
During first 3 months of treatment, avoid
   Poison ivy/oak, sunburn

cial effects on mood disorder symptoms in patients who were taking it for epilepsy were the first indications that it might be useful for bipolar disorder. Then several reports appeared that supported this use. However, in several well-designed studies, gabapentin was no more effective than placebo in treating symptoms of bipolar disorder. Because of these conflicting data, it's difficult to say for sure exactly how gabapentin should fit into the treatment of mood disorders.

Case reports and small studies suggest that topiramate (Topamax) may be an effective treatment for bipolar disorder. There have been reports of topiramate helping with both the depressed and manic phases of bipolar disorder, but there have also been reports of the medication making depression worse and triggering mania and mixed states. The side effect profile of topiramate is favorable—the most serious difficulties are attention and concentration problems that become troublesome at higher doses. Topiramate has a common side effect that, for once, is usually considered an advantage: weight loss. Patients vary in this response, but most lose several pounds and some a significant amount of weight. If topiramate turns out to be a useful medication for bipolar disorder, it will be a welcome addition to our list. However, the final word on efficacy and safety is not yet in.

Tiagabine and zonisamide are other antiepilepsy drugs that have attracted the interest of clinical researchers on bipolar disorder. Ongoing research may result in these drugs also being introduced as mood-stabilizing medications.

### ANTIDEPRESSANTS AND BIPOLAR DISORDER

In Roland Kuhn's original paper on the use of imipramine in depression, he noted that "in individuals who are predisposed, it may give rise to a somewhat manic-like or even manic state." He did not comment on, and probably did not realize, what this predisposition was but only reassured readers that imipramine was not a "euphoriant" and did not lead to addiction. We now know that the "predisposed" individuals Kuhn noted had bipolar disorder.

It is very clear now that antidepressants can precipitate a manic episode in persons with bipolar disorder. That they do not do so in everyone with mood disorders seems to indicate another fundamental difference between major depressive disorder and bipolar disorder. It appears that not everyone with a mood disorder has the "chemistry" necessary to become manic, but for those who do, antidepressants can induce a manic state. For many years this fact was noted but did not much affect how antidepressants were used. People with symptoms of major depression were treated with antidepressants, and if they later turned out to have bipolar disorder, it was thought that they could just be switched to lithium and everything would be set right. To sort out whether people with symptoms of the depression of affective disorder as their first episodes of illness had major depression or were in the depressed phase of bipolar disorder was thought to be more or less an academic exercise. There is some evidence now, however, that patients with bipolar disorder who take antidepressants can develop manic states that are more difficult to treat, and it has even been suggested that in some people antidepressants precipitate a switch to a more severe "rapid-cycling" bipolar illness, and they may have more frequent episodes of illness. This last point is quite controversial, but a number of studies have shown that antidepressants can destabilize the mood in predisposed persons for many weeks.

Clearly, then, it seems prudent to avoid starting antidepressants in depressed patients who may have bipolar disorder. How is it possible to tell if the patient may have bipolar disorder if they've never had a manic episode? As I mentioned earlier, one clue is a family history of bipolar disorder; this form of affective disorder seems to run from one generation to the next and between closely related persons. Often a history of hypomania precedes the first severe episode of bipolar disorder, even if that episode is a major depression, so it is important for the psychiatrist to ask carefully about possible prior mild episodes and important for the patient to thoughtfully consider the possibility that unexplained periods of higher than usual energy and elevated mood, however pleasant when they occur, might represent indications of a bipolar disorder.

## OTHER TREATMENTS FOR BIPOLAR DISORDER
### Antipsychotic Medications

Severe mania is a dangerous condition; as I stated earlier, it used to have a significant mortality rate. Some manic patients can be highly aggressive and even violent. Like suicidal depression, it is truly a psychiatric emergency. In many cases, antipsychotics are used to treat the acute manic symptoms and are extremely effective. Additionally, the newer antipsychotic medications (the atypical antipsychotics) are being increasingly used for the longer-term treatment of bipolar disorder, as there is mounting evidence that these medications also help to prevent the return of symptoms. The development of this group of medications has been a real breakthrough in the treatment of bipolar disorder, and their use is likely to grow as we become more experienced with them.

### Electroconvulsive Therapy

Before antipsychotics and lithium were known, ECT was used to treat mania. It is still used for this purpose in some patients, and it may work even faster than antipsychotic medication while producing the same specific effect as lithium on all manic symptoms—the best of both worlds. Some experts in the field of affective disorder now feel that ECT is underutilized as a treatment for acute mania, and it may become more widely used for this purpose in the future. I find it fascinating that both ECT—a treatment that causes seizures—and anticonvulsants used to prevent seizures can be effective treatments for the manic state. No one knows why this should be. It only serves to remind us how mysterious and complicated an illness affective disorder is.

## Length of Treatment in Bipolar Disorders

The issue of how long to take medication is much more difficult to address for bipolar disorder than for major depression. In major depression, since the periods of remission can be much longer than the periods of relapse, it generally makes sense to recommend that patients take their antidepressant for the usual length of time of a major depressive episode, six to eighteen months. (See chapter 3 for a more complete discussion of this issue.)

In bipolar disorder, however, episodes of illness generally occur much more often—every several years, yearly, or even several times a year. In addition, there is some evidence that episodes are more frequent as one gets older. At one time it was recommended that, in treating the first episode of the manic state, lithium be prescribed only for several months and then discontinued. The field has been moving further and further away from this for many years now, and toward the recommendation that patients be treated indefinitely. Why?

Clearly, a patient who is having relapses several times a year will want to take medication continuously. But how about the person who has had only two episodes, say five years apart? Should someone take medication continuously for a problem that may not come back for five more years? The key word in that sentence is "may." Although some patients have a course of illness with regular cycles, many do not.

As we have gained experience in diagnosing and treating bipolar disorder, it has become clear that the benefits of treatment far outweigh the risks for most patients. Once a clear diagnosis of bipolar disorder has been made, medication is now continued more or less indefinitely. It is very clear that the most effective action one can take to prevent an episode of bipolar disorder is to take medication. Whether preventing an episode is worth taking the medication, having any necessary blood tests, putting up with possible side effects, and so forth, is a very personal decision. What is important is that it be an informed decision, made after careful consideration of the available facts.

Some of the most severely impaired and psychiatrically handicapped persons I have ever come in contact with were a few patients I saw during my training who did not take their diagnosis of bipolar disorder seriously. They would stop taking their medication almost as soon as they recovered from an episode of illness. I would be called to see them in the emergency room again and again over a period of years and could tell from their medical records that many psychiatric staff members before me had also seen them again and again. I would read through their charts and find that as episode after episode of mania occurred, their employers, their friends, and sometimes even their families had lost patience and just dropped out of their lives. I saw women whose adult children would not even visit them in the hospital. In the worst cases, even the hospital staff retreated into a sort of cynicism, treating the patients almost as naughty children when they got ill again, the whole treatment effort seeming to be a waste of time. Fortunately such cases are rare.

I don't relate this story to frighten anyone—certainly not to intimidate anyone into meekly following doctor's orders without question. Rather, I want to make the point that manic episodes have consequences and that sometimes the consequences of an episode are impossible to predict. People with bipolar disorder who choose not to take medication to prevent further episodes of illness place themselves at risk. They may or may not recognize the return of symptoms in time to start treatment soon enough to abort the episode. Remember that the first symptoms of a manic episode may not be unpleasant, and it may be very difficult indeed to start back on medication when you're feeling *better* than usual. By the time the "feeling good" stage of mania starts to change into the dysphoric stage, the episode is well on its way and hospitalization may be required to bring the symptoms under control. At that point several weeks of inpatient treatment may be needed.

Instead of asking why they should continue taking medication, patients with bipolar disorder should probably ask themselves, "Why not?"

One of the known facts about bipolar disorder is the tendency for the symptoms of the illness to come back again and again. Medication allows the patient to control the illness rather than the other way around. (More on this

TABLE 4.5 Indicators of Possible "Soft" Bipolar Disorder

Family history of bipolar disorder
Hypomania or mixed symptoms caused by treatment with antidepressants
A history of a very rapid response (in 1–2 days) to an antidepressant medication
History of mixed symptoms, even if brief and mild: "rages," unpredictable periods
   of irritability
Increased mood cycling on antidepressants

issue will be discussed in the section "Relapse," under "Living with a Mood Disorder" in chapter 7.)

## Treating "Soft" Bipolar Disorders

I hope that the discussion of bipolar spectrum illnesses made it clear that attempts to separate people into two categories, as having either bipolar or "unipolar" depressive disorders, don't always work very well. There are certainly individuals whose illness is "very bipolar" (involving a history of major depression and of full-blown manic episodes) and individuals whose illness is "not very bipolar at all" (with a history of only depressive symptoms, no family history of bipolar disorder, and no symptoms whatsoever of hypomanic or mixed states, not even symptoms lasting only a few hours).

However, many patients with difficult-to-control symptoms of depression have an illness that is "just a little bipolar." Perhaps they have "rages": uncharacteristic and unexpected periods of irritability and agitation that last only an hour or two. Or perhaps they had periods of weeks or months of increased energy, overactivity, less need for sleep and a change in confidence level and risk-taking behaviors early in the course of their illness that have disappeared as they grew older. Often these patients have a therapeutic response to antidepressant medications that only lasts a year or two, or they have a partial response to one antidepressant after another but remain ill. Some of the indicators of a "soft" bipolar disorder are listed in the table.

It's clear that treating "somewhat bipolar" illnesses needs to include the medications that are used to treat full-blown bipolar illnesses: lithium and other mood stabilizers. In my experience, patients who have one of these soft bipolar disorders are often not recognized as such and end up on high doses of antidepressants, sometimes taking several antidepressants simultaneously but remaining depressed for long periods. Although the antidepressants may keep them from slipping into the worst depths of incapacitating depression, they also frequently seem to cause their moods to become more unstable, with more very uncomfortable periods of irritability and agitation (which can be thought of as mini-mixed-states). Sometimes these periods cause them to resort to uncharacteristic behaviors in an effort to cope: substance abuse, self-injurious "cutting" behaviors. These problems, in turn, may result in them being given a diagnosis of a personality disorder.

Changing the focus of medication treatment from antidepressants to a regimen based on a mood stabilizer often helps these patients do significantly better. They may continue to need an antidepressant (often at a lower dose), but recognizing the "bipolarity" of their illness can be a giant step toward improved control of their symptoms.

# PART II

# VARIATIONS, CAUSES, AND CONNECTIONS

# CHAPTER 5

# Variations of the Mood Disorders

THE MOOD DISORDERS, ESPECIALLY MAJOR DEPRESSION, HAVE MANY SYMP-
toms besides change in mood. I've discussed many of these in the chapters
on depression and bipolar disorder. Changes in appetite and sleep, energy,
activity level, and concentration are some of these symptoms, and in some
people they may dominate the clinical picture or at least be so prominent
that other types of illnesses can be mistakenly diagnosed. This chapter will
deal with some subtypes of affective disorder that are especially likely to be
called something else, "explained away," or missed altogether by the affected
person, family members, and even doctors.

Mood disorders commonly fluctuate in relation to other biological events
such as the menstrual cycle and childbirth, can be associated with cerebrovascular accidents (commonly known as stroke), and can be affected by the
change of the seasons. Mood disorders in young people and in the elderly
have some special characteristics as well, and there are relationships between
depression and chronic pain and between depression and panic attacks.

## Major Depression in the Elderly

"Your mother has Alzheimer's disease. It's an incurable, deteriorating
disease that causes progressive loss of thinking capacity. I suggest you start
investigating nursing homes." Can a more terrible pronouncement be imagined? To see a loved one withering away, mind and body gradually failing

until death is a welcome release? And yet there is another illness that can mimic all the symptoms of Alzheimer's disease. It is major depression—and as you know by now, major depression is easily treatable.

---

Pearl was sixty-eight years old, a retired executive secretary who worked for a large retailer. She had been referred to me by her internist, who told me she was showing memory loss and other signs of intellectual deterioration. "She's really taken this hard. So has the family. I'm going to send them all over to your office for some counseling."

Pearl and her two daughters came into my office and sat down. "We need your advice, Doctor. We want to know what we can do for Mother—how best to help her."

Pearl sat in the middle of my small sofa between her two daughters. Both daughters sat on the edge of the cushion, their knees pointing toward the center and almost touching their mother's. One daughter held her mother's hand and looked over at her while the other watched me as she spoke. They reminded me of a triptych by some Renaissance painter, only instead of a Madonna or crucified Christ as the center panel, this altarpiece was dominated by the figure of Despair.

Pearl was a handsome, almost stately, woman. One would be tempted to call her robust, but her posture and expression radiated anything but health. Her skin was pale, almost sallow, her hands were crossed in her lap like useless, heavy things, and her shoulders drooped. Her eyes were downcast, her brow furrowed, her mouth fixed in a deep frown. She sat motionless.

"How did your mother's difficulties begin?" I asked.

"Mother always hosts a big family dinner the first night of Passover, and since Daddy passed away I've helped her with some of the cooking. I went over a few weeks ahead to start planning and found her like this." She looked forlornly at her mother.

"Can you tell me what was different?"

She turned back to me with a look of surprise, as if to say, "What's the matter with you? Can't you see how terrible she looks?" I tried to respond to this unstated question. "I want to know exactly what changes have occurred so I can know how best to help your mother and you."

"Well, she was sitting in her apartment with the lights out and the television on, but she wasn't even aware of what she was watching. She looked like she was in a daze, just staring. Just like this." She looked at Pearl again and then said, "I asked her, 'Mother, weren't you expecting me? Don't you remember that I was coming over to start getting ready for Passover?' 'I can't remember anything anymore,' she said. 'I've forgotten all the recipes anyway.' Doctor," her voice lowered almost to a whisper, "sometimes she doesn't even know what day it is."

"Mrs. Feldman, tell me about your memory problems."

"My memory is completely gone, Doctor," said Pearl, not even looking up from the floor. "I don't see how you can help me; I'll never be the same again."

"Mother, Dr. Leeds is your medical doctor. He is going to help with your memory. This doctor will help you with your depression."

I began asking Pearl some questions to test her memory and thinking. "I'm going to say the names of three ordinary objects for you, Mrs. Feldman. I want you to remember them for a few moments, and later I'll ask you to repeat them."

"I'll try."

I named the objects and then asked, "Can you subtract seven from one hundred for me? Then subtract seven from that number, and keep subtracting sevens until I tell you to stop."

"I can't. I just can't think clearly. My mind's a blank."

"I want you to try."

She sighed deeply. "Ninety-three." She was silent. The quiet daughters looked away, pained. "That's all. That's all I can do."

"Okay. That's hard, isn't it? Don't be discouraged. Can you remember those three objects?"

Pearl's brow became even more furrowed; her glance wandered about the room as if searching for the answers printed on the diplomas on the wall or the spines of the books on the shelves. Then she looked down at the floor again. "I can't remember. I told you my memory was gone."

"How has your mood been, Mrs. Feldman?"

"Terrible. How would you feel if you couldn't think, couldn't remember?"

"How has your sleeping been?"

"I toss and turn all night; I can't rest. I'm losing my mind, aren't I, Doctor? That's why Dr. Leeds sent me over here, isn't it? I should be put away, just put away in a nursing home."

"No, no, Mrs. Feldman, you don't need to worry about that," I replied. I leaned over and took her hand, "I'm confident that we're going to get you better."

I asked Pearl to step into the waiting room so I could talk to her daughters alone for a moment. "I want to put your mother into the hospital so we can be more aggressive in treating her depression."

"Well, if you think it's a good idea, Doctor. Can't you do some counseling or prescribe medication for her as an outpatient, though? Mother is frightened of hospitals. She could stay with one of us until she's feeling better."

"Your mother may be a very good candidate for electroconvulsive treatments for her depression, and she would need to be in the hospital for that."

"Shock treatments! Doctor, my mother's not crazy!"

I saw I had a lot of educating to do, but I knew they would thank me in the end.

---

The collection of symptoms and findings typical of Alzheimer's disease is actually seen in many different conditions. Memory loss, loss of the ability to concentrate, disorientation—for example, not knowing what day it is—these are all symptoms of the psychiatric syndrome known as dementia. The patient with dementia is perfectly alert but experiences a decline in all intellectual functions. Dementia is usually progressive and often irreversible. But not always.

Dementia can be seen in a number of brain diseases such as Parkinson's disease or repeated strokes; even brain injury from an automobile accident can cause the syndrome. One of the commonest causes of dementia in the elderly is Alzheimer's disease, now thought to be caused by the degeneration of a single brain center.

As the field of geriatric medicine has developed, it has become clear that many conditions that had often been dismissed as normal concomitants of aging are not normal at all, but instead are due to disease processes. It has also become clear that many of these diseases are treatable, making it all the more important that the physician look for them in evaluating the elderly patient.

As the field of geriatric psychiatry developed, the term *pseudo-dementia of depression* came to be used to describe a condition often seen in elderly persons suffering from major depression. It was noted that depressed elderly people often have a decline in intellectual functioning that looks exactly like dementia. In fact, in more and more articles in the professional journals the "pseudo" is being dropped and the memory problems, confusion, and concentration problems are being called simply the dementia syndrome of depression.

Often the decline in memory has qualities that specifically indicate the dementia syndrome of depression rather than dementia from another cause. Patients with this syndrome are usually extremely distressed by their deficits in intellectual functioning. This is in contrast to the picture usually seen in patients with Alzheimer's disease, who are sometimes unaware of their memory problems in the early stages and often attempt to make light of them or cover them up. Depressed patients, on the other hand, seem to dwell on their memory problems and, like Pearl, see every missed answer as confirmation of their "hopeless" condition.

ECT seems to be particularly effective in the elderly. It works quickly, and it also has a diagnostic use. If an elderly person shows symptoms of dementia and also of major depression, a single ECT treatment can sometimes sort out the diagnosis. Remember, I said earlier that people with brain injury were especially prone to prolonged confusion following ECT treatments. If someone has Alzheimer's disease, ECT will make the confusion much worse (temporarily); in those with the dementia syndrome of depression, ECT will make it better.

The need to make this differentiation is, I hope, obvious. If the diagnosis of major depression is missed, there is the risk that the elderly patient will be written off as suffering from an incurable disease and simply sent to a nursing home.

Major depression seems to present a slightly different symptom picture in the elderly. The dementia syndrome of depression is one such variation. Another prominent feature in older individuals is *hypochondriasis,* a preoccupation with physical symptoms that sometimes grows into the conviction that one is suffering from some terrible illness. More often, the patient just seems to have one minor physical complaint after another for which no serious underlying cause can be found. Patients report physical symptoms such as vague pains, nausea, tiredness, or simply feeling sick. Of course, anyone who has physical symptoms should be evaluated for physical causes. But an older person who complains of many vague physical symptoms for which little or no basis can be found and who seems chronically upset and unhappy should be evaluated for major depression.

I have had patients referred to me by doctors who say they have given them "the million-dollar workup" for their symptoms. Having done every conceivable diagnostic procedure—some very expensive and even dangerous—the doctors make a referral to a psychiatrist as a last resort. How much time, money, and suffering might be saved by considering the diagnosis of major depression earlier on?

Another issue in evaluating depression in the elderly is the tendency to assume that depression is an expected part of growing old. Persons over sixty or so are often beset by losses. Spouses, siblings, and friends may die, sometimes one after another in a short period. There is often loss associated with illness and physical incapacitation. These losses inevitably lead to some depression. But as in any grieving process, the change in mood should be short-lived; there is resolution and acceptance as time passes. Losses do not make one lose interest in living to one's fullest capacity. It is certainly not normal for an elderly person to be chronically depressed.

## Mood Disorders in Children and Adolescents

Although both major depression and bipolar disorder usually first manifest themselves in the young adult years, younger people can suffer from mood disorders as well. As has often happened in psychiatry, the understanding of mood disorders in children was long hampered by misconceptions based on theory rather than on fact. For many years it was believed that children were too psychologically immature to experience true depression. As a more empirical approach to psychiatric problems replaced those rooted in theory, it has become clear that children do indeed get depressed. Mood disorders seem to be less common in children, especially younger ones, and thus risk for developing them does appear to increase with age.

### MAJOR DEPRESSION IN CHILDREN AND ADOLESCENTS

Children who are depressed often show the same symptoms as adults. Children may be tearful and look quite sad, or they may be irritable or petulant. They can have the same changes in self-attitude as adults do, can feel guilty or responsible for having caused trouble, and can show the same low self-esteem and self-reproach. Loss of interest in usually pleasurable activities, low energy and fatigue, and poor concentration can also be seen in children. The vegetative signs, of course, are often present: poor sleep and loss of appetite with weight change. The same uncomfortable bodily sensations that plague adults can lead to complaints of "tummy aches," and headaches are common too.

Children, especially young children, do not have the verbal skills to describe a concept as subtle as mood, so the changes in behavior caused by their unhappiness and vegetative symptoms can sometimes be the only clue to the onset of a major depressive episode. For example, they may become listless and lose interest in school or play. Children who are depressed may suddenly revert to behaviors they had outgrown. For example, children who have been toilet trained for months or even years may begin to wet themselves again. Others may resume sucking their thumbs. Sometimes children who are depressed develop phobias or unwarranted fears; they may suddenly show fear of animals, be afraid of the dark, or refuse to go to school.

Adolescents, of course, get depressed too. Like old age, adolescence is a time of life when symptoms of depression are often explained away as being so common as to be normal. Again, this is simply not the case.

Like young children, depressed adolescents can have a hard time expressing emotional distress verbally, and behavioral changes may be their most prominent symptoms. They may express their uncomfortable feelings through angry, destructive behavior rather than lethargy and listlessness, and sudden aggression (a behavior that has sometimes been said to represent a "depressive equivalent") in a formerly compliant teenager may signal the onset of depression. Adolescents can also show the same symptoms as depressed adults. The boy who suddenly loses interest in bodybuilding or the girl who doesn't bother with her hair anymore may be showing the decreased sense of self-worth and even hopelessness that are typical symptoms of a depressive disorder. I will discuss drug and alcohol abuse and mood disorders in a later section. Here it is enough to say that the onset of chemical dependency can be a symptom of major depression. I suppose the key word in much of this is "change." Affective disorder is episodic in its course. Any change in activity level, dropping grades, or loss of interest in friends, dating, sports, and so forth may indicate that a change in mood is occurring, and that change may be due to major depression.

Because mood is a concept that adolescents and especially children may be unfamiliar with, they may not complain of feeling depressed, and it often is what others notice about their behavior that signals something is wrong. Because of this, young people with major depression are especially liable to be misdiagnosed. Young children who show a lot of fearfulness may be mislabeled as suffering from a phobia or another anxiety disorder. Those who are listless and uninterested in school may be considered learning disabled or be diagnosed as having attention deficit / hyperactivity disorder (ADHD). The worst type of misdiagnosis, of course, is when they are called "lazy" or "troublemakers" at school or at home. As I stated above, teens may show predominantly behavioral problems and thus be labeled delinquent. Some studies have suggested that many children and adolescents who refuse to attend school are actually depressed.

There is a link between eating disorders, including anorexia nervosa, and mood disorders. In anorexia nervosa, which is most common in adolescent girls, patients stop eating, lose a tremendous amount of weight, and seem intent on starving themselves. Research indicates that many of these patients have major depression, and treatments for major depression are often very helpful for these patients.

## BIPOLAR DISORDER IN CHILDREN AND ADOLESCENTS

Bipolar disorder has been documented in children and adolescents. As with major depression, it is more common in older age groups and seems much less prevalent in children than in adults. Some studies indicate that the appearance of manic symptoms at a young age indicates a severe form of the illness with a worse prognosis. These children often have a strong family history of a mood disorder, especially bipolar disorder. As in major depression, the symptoms of the manic state in children are very similar to those seen in adults, but the behavioral changes can be the most prominent.

As you might expect, children with manic or hypomanic moods can look very much like children with attention deficit/hyperactivity disorder (ADHD). In both problems the child cannot sit still and is extremely talkative, disruptive at school, and always getting into trouble at home. Important differentiating characteristics between these two disorders include the cyclic nature of the change in activity level and the typical changes of mood in bipolar disorders. Differentiating between these two problems is quite difficult, however, and the relationship between the disorders is poorly understood. There is some evidence that mood disorders in younger persons are more complex and more difficult to treat than in adults. They nearly always require the subspecialty care of a child psychiatrist.

## SUICIDAL BEHAVIOR IN CHILDREN AND ADOLESCENTS

Perhaps no other psychiatric problem has received as much attention in the media, in schools, and among mental health professionals in recent years as adolescent suicide. The frightening truth is that self-destructive behavior among young people has truly increased; the suicide rate for persons between the ages of ten and twenty-four has risen more than 200 percent since 1960. Suicide is the third leading cause of death in those under twenty-five; almost one-quarter of all adolescent mortality is due to suicide, and two-thirds of all suicides occur in the twenty- to twenty-four-year-old age group.

The reasons for these frightening numbers are the subject of great debate, which I will not attempt to summarize here. The points I wish to drive home are that suicide is most often seen in people suffering from a mood disorder; that children and adolescents suffer from mood disorders; and that, *as a group,* adolescents attempt and complete suicide at a significantly higher rate than adults. This means that the adolescent with a mood disorder is doubly at risk, and that it is therefore even more vital that mood disorders be recognized and treated in this age group.

Late adolescence is a time of many emotional changes, when separation from parents and family and a struggle for emotional autonomy reaches its height. Sexuality issues and sexual feelings may conflict with parental and societal expectations. It is a time when the comforting social structure of high school is about to end and the need for financial self-sufficiency begins. For these reasons late adolescence can strain one's ability to cope to its limit. It is *not,* however, a time when it is "normal" to be depressed or to have suicidal thoughts. The emergence of symptoms of depression should never be brushed off simply because they occur in an adolescent. On the contrary, as the statistics above indicate, in adolescents depressive symptoms should be looked at even more seriously, and measures to get the adolescent evaluated for major depression should be taken without delay. It is also important to remember that adolescents sometimes "mask" their depression with aggressive, destructive behavior and substance abuse.

## ANTIDEPRESSANTS AND SUICIDAL BEHAVIOR IN CHILDREN AND ADOLESCENTS

Another issue that has received much in the way of media attention is concern about reports that taking antidepressants can cause individuals, especially adolescents, who had not been suicidal to become so. The issue is quite complex and deserves some extra discussion.

To some extent, the issue has been recognized for many years. It has long been known that the period when a person is just beginning to get better from depression can be an especially dangerous time. People who are severely depressed are often so emotionally shut down and so lacking in energy and initiative that they pose little risk of self-harm. It is only when they begin to get slightly better that their feelings (still very depressed feelings) begin to awaken and they have the energy to act on suicidal thoughts. Years ago, when the only available antidepressant medications were the toxic tricyclic antidepressants, physicians were acutely aware of this phenomenon. Physicians knew about the risk of fatal overdose with these medications and took pains to be very careful about monitoring patients closely during the first weeks of treatment. Also, because of the significant side effect burden of these medications, patients were seen frequently to make the necessary dosage adjustments and for coaching and support to help them take the medication until it started to work and the side effect problems faded.

When the SSRI antidepressant medications became available in the late 1980s, several factors conspired to lessen the degree of monitoring by physicians. The fact that these are essentially non-toxic medications is an important one. Also, the side effect problems are much reduced and there is less need to make dose adjustments. These factors meant that many more people were prescribed medication for depression, including people whose depression was less severe. More antidepressants were prescribed by non-psychiatrists such as family physicians. Many more prescriptions for antidepressants were being written, and there was less vigilance for the potential problems with prescribing them, including the fact that the person beginning to emerge from depression can be at higher risk for self-destructive behaviors.

Another explanation has to do with the tendency of antidepressants to cause problems for individuals with bipolar disorder. As I discussed previously, these drugs can precipitate very uncomfortable agitated, overenergized, but still depressed mood states in some persons with bipolar mood disorders. During these mixed states, patients are very vulnerable to self-destructive behaviors. Again, careful diagnosis and monitoring as the patient starts on antidepressants is called for.

Also, as more individuals, and more young people, were prescribed SSRIs, it also became apparent that in addition to the problems I've already discussed, there are indeed a very few patients who do not appear to have bipolar disorder, but who nevertheless develop uncomfortable agitated states on SSRIs. In some patients, this seems to be due to severe anxiety, but these problems are not well understood.

In response to the concerns raised, the Food and Drug Administration instructed the pharmaceutical companies making SSRIs to add warnings and advice to the labeling for these drugs that patients should be closely monitored when they are prescribed them. Who can argue with this? Although there were some who called for these drugs to be taken off the market and not prescribed for anyone, cooler heads prevailed, and this fortunately didn't happen. Although the process by which all of this came about was sometimes portrayed in the media as a controversy, there's not very much controversial in recommending that patients with a life-threatening illness—depression—should see the doctor frequently, especially when they start on a new medication that has the potential, however small, to cause serious problems.

## Mood Disorders in Women

There may be disputes among the scientists who do research on mood disorders, but all agree that major depression is more common among women than among men—about twice as common. At one time it was thought that it only *seemed* that more women than men had depression because women were more willing to come for treatment and therefore more were counted in studies that surveyed patients at mental health clinics. If women were more willing to come for treatment than men, it might appear that more women suffered from major depression if one simply counted the relative numbers of men and women who came to the clinic.

Several later studies on the prevalence of psychiatric problems have attempted to avoid this problem (called *ascertainment bias* by statisticians) by interviewing representative samples of very large groups of people—whole cities in fact—rather than looking at hospital charts or interviewing patients visiting mental health clinics. People in the community were picked at random and interviewed, and psychiatric diagnoses were made. These studies, designed to be free of ascertainment bias, seem to bear out the older ones and to verify that depression is indeed more common in females than in males. (Bipolar disorder, remember, is found equally often in males and females.) Is there something different about depression in women that explains this finding?

## POSTPARTUM DEPRESSION

"Postpartum" refers to the time after giving birth, and mood problems during this period are extremely common. For many years, all kinds of "psychiatric" problems were described in women who had recently given birth. Most of these problems were actually periods of disorientation and delirium that probably had medical causes such as dehydration, blood loss, infections, and other problems that have largely disappeared with modern obstetrical techniques. Nevertheless, mood changes do occur in the postpartum period that do not seem to have anything to do with the trauma of labor and delivery.

The range of symptom types is wide, and the range of severity is even wider. In one study, over 90 percent of the women interviewed reported crying spells they could not explain, perhaps the mildest form of the disorder. A smaller number reported mood changes that were persistent and caused some disturbance in their functioning, and a very small percentage had serious, debilitating mood changes that could last months.

Immediately after the baby is born there is often a period of euphoria—a very good mood—and then a period of depression that starts two to five days after the birth. The depression may be limited to brief crying spells for only a day or two ("the baby blues"), but in some women, the full major depressive syndrome may appear. The guilty qualities of the mood change may be prominent; often this takes the form of concerns about the baby's health. ("The baby cries too much; I must have done something wrong during my pregnancy; I didn't take good care of myself.") Women sometimes feel they don't love the baby enough. They may feel some resentment at the prospect of so many new responsibilities, and so they question their commitment and love. ("I should enjoy changing diapers; if I don't that must mean I'm going to be a bad mother.")

The biological factors that have been implicated in this problem are, as you might suspect, hormonal. During pregnancy, the body produces high levels of various hormones to maintain the blood supply of the uterus and support the baby developing inside. These are the "female" steroids. During the delivery of the baby there is significant pain, blood loss, and other physical stress, and then the "stress" steroids such as cortisol are produced. Some have speculated that the high levels of these steroids cause the euphoria seen immediately after birth, and that when these levels drop, a "steroid withdrawal" causes the mood change. It may be that in most women this change is quickly compensated for as the body recovers from pregnancy and birth, and so "the baby blues" are mild and transient. In some women, however, the hormonal changes may precipitate a chain of events that produces the change in brain chemistry causing the symptoms of major depression.

An even smaller number of women develop severe psychotic symptoms with these mood changes, a syndrome that has been called *postpartum psychosis*. It is thought that this more serious illness is related to bipolar disorder.

It is also clear that women with bipolar disorder are at extremely high risk of developing a manic episode in the postpartum period and need to be closely monitored during this time, especially if they have decided to stop taking medications during pregnancy.

## PREMENSTRUAL MOOD DISORDERS AND "PMS"

A 1984 paper in the *American Journal of Psychiatry* noted, "Despite 50 years of study, relatively little is known about the relationship of menstruation and mood disorders."* Fortunately, in more recent years, research has helped to increase our understanding of this relationship, and I think it's fair to say that most experts agree on some facts. Nevertheless, we are far from a consensus on a description of signs and symptoms of the disorder, let alone on the mechanisms and treatment of *premenstrual syndrome (PMS)*.

It is quite clear that many women experience a variety of physical and emotional symptoms starting about five days before the onset of menstruation and continuing for about two days after their menstrual flow starts. Those who do not have these symptoms during the rest of the month have been said to have premenstrual syndrome.

Defining premenstrual syndrome has perhaps been the most difficult aspect of the issue. Studies that have set out to define the syndrome vary greatly depending on the research interest of the investigator. Psychologists and psychiatrists have tended to study emotional symptoms, and gynecologists have focused on physical ones. Endocrinologists have concentrated on hormone levels. All claim to be looking at women with "PMS," but whether they are studying the same or different groups of patients is sometimes difficult to ascertain. Some studies do not differentiate between symptoms that occur only during the premenstrual period and symptoms that are present most of the month but get worse premenstrually.

The common symptoms that usually are considered to represent PMS are mood changes, including depression or irritability, and several physical symptoms, including water retention and consequent weight gain, appetite disturbance (often an increase in appetite with "carbohydrate craving"), sleep changes (usually insomnia), and tiredness and impaired concentra-

---

* D. R. Rubinow et al., "Premenstrual syndromes: Overview from a methodological perspective," *American Journal of Psychiatry* 141 (1984): 163–72.

tion. Many other symptoms have in one study or another been thought to be part of the syndrome; a total of 150 symptoms have been considered to vary with the menstrual cycle.

The crucial question in investigating this problem is this: Is there a discrete group of women who share certain symptoms during the premenstrual period and not at other times? There are enough reasonably well-designed studies suggesting a tentative yes to this question that the American Psychiatric Association has added a diagnostic category to an appendix of the *DSM* that lists "conditions in need of further study."

The menstrual cycle is characterized by the rhythmic rise and fall of several hormones, primarily estrogen and progesterone, the female sex steroids. Do women with premenstrual exacerbation of mood disorders have some hormonal imbalance? It has not been possible to demonstrate abnormal hormone levels in women with premenstrual mood symptoms, and attempts to treat premenstrual symptoms (psychological and physical) by manipulating hormone levels have been uniformly disappointing. The best evidence implicates the sudden *change* in hormone levels rather than absolute amounts, and it appears that some women, probably because of genetic factors, react to these normal hormone fluctuations with mood symptoms.

One very practical conclusion to be drawn from this confusing set of facts is that some women who have mood problems premenstrually may in fact suffer from affective disorder, specifically major depression, and may get relief when treated with antidepressants. Some women may have mild symptoms of depression all the time that they ignore, learn to live with, or consider normal. When their mood gets much worse during the premenstrual period, however, it may interfere with their functioning. This group may label themselves as having "PMS" and see a gynecologist. If the gynecologist is adept enough to diagnose a mood disorder and suggest antidepressant medication or refer them to a psychiatrist, they will get relief. Premenstrual mood variation in patients who are being treated for major depression can cause an episodic worsening of symptoms that is confusing to both patient and doctor. Another case study will illustrate this problem.

---

Mary had been successfully treated for a major depressive episode, but the premenstrual exacerbation of her depression caused a lot of confusion. When she first came to my office, Mary's symptoms were severe. They had started abruptly after a few nights of sleeplessness and took the form of severe anxiety, fearfulness, and even dread. Mary's powerful feelings of impending catastrophe made her desperate and were severe enough to cause her to be suicidal, so she was admitted to the hospital. I immediately started Mary on an antidepressant, and because she was so distressed, I added a small dose of an atypical anti-psychotic medication.

The first confusing event was the almost complete resolution of her severe symptoms after only a few days of taking the medication. Patients who turn out to have bipolar disorder sometimes get symptom relief from antidepressants in significantly less time than the more usual two to four weeks, so this was definitely a concern. Mary went home after only a few days and came back for a follow-up appointment the next week. When I saw her she was looking so much better and was in such good spirits that I completely stopped her antipsychotic medication.

About ten days later I got a call from Mary's husband, who said she was sleepless again and had started to become fearful and seemed paranoid. Since the only change had been discontinuing the antipsychotic, I told her to start taking it again. The medication helped Mary get to sleep, and in a day or two she was much better again.

Mary and her husband were glad the antipsychotic was helping, but I was worried—perhaps Mary had bipolar disorder. That might account for her rapid recovery in the hospital and her sudden deterioration after the antipsychotic medication was stopped.

I saw Mary the next week, and she again seemed to be doing extremely well. I questioned her closely about her symptoms, looking for any hint of a history of hypomanic or mixed symptoms. There were none. How could I account for the unusual pattern of symptoms? I told her to keep taking the antipsychotic medication for now.

I saw Mary several more times and tapered off her antipsychotic dose a little. The antidepressant that Mary was taking was imipramine, one of the pharmaceuticals used to treat depression that can be measured in the bloodstream. To see if the drug level might shed some light on the issue, I had Mary get a blood test for the antidepressant level.

At the next appointment Mary said, "You know, I still get those fearful thoughts and sleepless nights every once in a while. But I just take a few extra tranquilizers and I'm okay. I've noticed that it's always right before my period. Do you think I have PMS?"

As Mary was saying this, I picked up the lab slip with her antidepressant level from my desk. Her level was in the therapeutic range, but just barely so. "Do you remember if you were about to get your period when you first got sick, before you were admitted to the hospital?" I asked. "Yes," she replied. "In fact, I think it started the day after I was admitted."

I asked a few more questions, and the pattern quickly emerged.

Mary did indeed have major depression, but her mood was strikingly affected by the hormonal changes in the premenstrual period. Her sudden "recovery" in the hospital was probably a spontaneous improvement related to coming out of the premenstrual hormonal state. Her abrupt "relapse" was not caused by discontinuing the antipsychotic but was a premenstrual exacerbation of her major depression. She was taking enough antidepressant to get good symptom control during most of the monthly cycle, but the added stress of the premenstrual changes "overpowered" the effects of the medication and caused a breakthrough of symptoms. The barely therapeutic lab result supported this reasoning. We raised the dose of antidepressant to get her more solidly into the therapeutic range, and her symptoms were completely controlled.

---

In this section I've highlighted two important facts about major depression in women: the disorder occurs more frequently in women than men, and the symptoms of major depression seem to be precipitated or exacerbated in some women during times of dramatic hormonal events—the premenstrual period and the postpartum period (and possibly the menopausal period as well). The conclusion seems almost inevitable that there must be some link between the female hormonal system and the neurochemistry of depression. The nature of this link remains a mystery. Perhaps being female is necessary for the expression of certain genes for mood disorders (as being male is necessary for the expression of some forms of baldness). Perhaps a particular hormonal state that only women can have confers an added vulnerability to major depression.

Is PMS just an exacerbation of major depression or a separate entity? The American Psychiatric Association is still gathering data, and *late luteal phase dysphoric disorder* may yet find its way into the *DSM*—if enough research shows that it's possible to accurately and consistently describe a homogeneous group of symptoms that occur only during this phase of the menstrual cycle.

## Depression and Stroke

Few medical problems appear as suddenly or cause such devastating impairment as cerebrovascular accident. The common name for this problem, stroke, is derived from these qualities, since the victim is often "struck down" as if by a bolt of lightning, going from health and normal functioning to paralysis and often unconsciousness in minutes or even seconds. A stroke occurs when the blood supply to part of the brain is suddenly cut off. This can happen for a variety of reasons, but the most common is blockage in a blood vessel, usually a blood clot caused by the same kind of circulatory disease—atherosclerosis—that causes heart attack. The brain cannot function for even a short time without the oxygen blood carries to it, and the part of the brain affected immediately ceases to work. If the blood supply is not restored in a very few minutes, brain cells die.

The symptoms of stroke vary with the size of the blood vessel affected. If a tiny branch vessel is blocked, the symptoms may be minor; if one of the major vessels is blocked, there can be paralysis of an entire side of the body. Depending on which part of the brain is affected, speech is often impaired, either because the brain area coordinating the muscles of speech is damaged or because the language area of the brain is affected.

It is no wonder that patients who have had a stroke become depressed. Within minutes one can change from a well-coordinated athlete or musician into a profoundly handicapped invalid—speech slurred, one arm hanging useless, leg and foot dragging in a shuffle. For many years the high frequency of depression in stroke patients was dismissed as understandable in light of their impairment. As psychiatry became more interested in the diagnosis of affective disorder, however, some interesting facts were noted. Most striking was that a much larger number of stroke patients than expected seemed to develop not the expected reactive or psychological form of depression, but the full-blown major depressive syndrome. Some seemed to experience a major depressive episode simultaneously with the other stroke symptoms; in a sense, they seemed to be depressed as soon as they regained consciousness. Also, these depressed patients got better with the usual treatments for major depression, antidepressant medication and ECT. Moreover, if they did not receive medical treatment for depression, their mood symptoms lasted six months to a year, just the time a major depressive episode would be expected to last. When a group of patients who had had strokes was compared with a group of patients with equally disabling injuries that did not involve the brain, the stroke patients were found to be more frequently and more severely depressed. When the psychiatric symptoms of severely depressed stroke patients were compared with those of patients with major depression in a psychiatric hospital, the types of symptoms were almost identical. Further studies have shown that nearly half of patients who have strokes develop symptoms of major depression within two years.

The almost inevitable conclusion is that when the brain is injured in a cerebrovascular accident, the same process is often set in motion that causes the symptoms of major depression. The symptoms, the time course of the untreated illness, and the response to treatment are identical. In effect, the stroke produces the syndrome of major depression in every way, presumably in patients who would not otherwise show such symptoms.

These findings have tremendous importance for stroke patients, their families, and their physicians. When a person who has had a stroke becomes depressed, it is imperative that the diagnosis of post-stroke major depressive syndrome be considered and that the patient be treated appropriately. Many of the impairments caused by stroke—muscle weakness and loss of coordination, for example—need to be treated with physical therapy and sometimes more specialized rehabilitation such as speech therapy. These treatments require tremendous motivation and commitment from the patient. Patients who are depressed will not have the emotional resources necessary to participate in their rehabilitation. They may, in fact, feel so hopeless that they do not believe any recovery of function is possible and so refuse rehabilitation therapy. They may simply want to lie in bed, yet if this is allowed, already weakened muscles can waste away, and sometimes severe muscle and joint degeneration called contracture can develop, making physical therapy painful and more difficult. The lethargic, bedridden, partially paralyzed person is prone to chronic medical problems such as bedsores, and even life-threatening medical problems can supervene—pneumonia and phlebitis, for example. (Phlebitis is the formation of a blood clot in an inflamed vein, usually the large veins of the legs. Such clots can break loose and travel through the blood vessels to the brain, causing another stroke, or sometimes to the lungs, causing an often fatal cardiovascular collapse.)

Stroke victims who show symptoms of depression should not be dismissed as simply discouraged by their new infirmity or demoralized at their loss of health. Major depression may occur in as many as 50 percent of stroke patients. What a tragedy if the mood symptoms are ignored or considered untreatable and the patient dies from complications of inactivity! Just as the symptoms of major depression are often dismissed as normal in the elderly and in adolescents, it is not difficult to explain away depression in a stroke patient. An appropriate course of treatment, however, either with antidepressant medication or with ECT, can speed recovery from the physical impairments of stroke by restoring a normal mood state so that the patient can participate in rehabilitative treatments.

Aside from the clinical implications discussed above, the recognition that stroke can cause major depression has been significant for neuroscientists interested in the biological basis of mood disorders. Much of what we know about the nervous system was discovered by studying people who had suffered brain damage from strokes as well as other illnesses and injuries. By carefully cataloging the pattern of symptoms and signs seen following an injury and then carefully observing the exact location and extent of damage to the brain after the victim's eventual death, it was possible to "map out" many areas of the brain and their functions.

The most elementary discovery was that the muscles on one side of the body are controlled by the opposite side of the brain. For example, a blood vessel blockage that damages the left side of the brain will cause paralysis on the right side of the body. By correlating the site of injury in the brain with the operation disrupted when that injury occurs, many brain functions have been localized. Most muscle movements, bodily sensations, vision, hearing, and even more complicated activities such as some language operations have been found to have well-defined locations. With the development of sophisticated imaging techniques, damaged areas of the brain can be mapped in living patients in a painless, non-invasive way, without the need to wait for postmortem examination. These techniques have aided clinical research and accelerated the acquisition of knowledge about the organization of the brain.

Has the study of stroke patients with depression allowed localization of a "mood center" in the brain? Not quite yet, but there have been some intriguing findings that may offer hints. First, patients who have had strokes involving the left side of the brain develop depression more frequently and are more severely depressed than patients who have "right-sided" strokes. Second, the closer the damage is to the front of the brain on the left side, the more severe the depression.

Animal experiments have shown that damage near the front of the brain on one side only will produce a widespread depletion of neurotransmitters in the brain. A single damaged area seems to affect the balance of neurotransmitters throughout many brain areas. Cutting a power line as it enters an office building will make all the lights in the building go out, whereas cutting a smaller cable inside may knock out only the lights on one floor. Similarly, there seems to be a "cable" of nerve fibers that passes through the front of the brain on one side and then fans out, traveling to many areas of the brain. Such a system might be responsible for setting a tone or level of chemical activity necessary for efficient brain functioning.

A manic episode following brain injury is a much rarer event, the incidence being a small fraction of that of post-stroke depression. Nevertheless, studies have shown that patients who develop manic symptoms following brain injury often show damage to the right side of the surface of the brain and to specific deeper structures. Many of those studied had a family history of mood disorder or had had an episode of major depression or mania themselves. The findings are therefore more difficult to interpret, but they suggest that right-sided brain structures may also be involved in regulating mood.

## Depression and Pain

Like the symptom of depression, pain is a universal human experience. As we have seen, depression can sometimes widen and deepen to include a whole collection of other symptoms that severely impair the sufferer and form a "syndrome" that takes on a life of its own and needs specific medical treatment. The same seems to be true for pain, and the term *chronic pain syndrome* describes a comparable collection of pain-related symptoms.

Chronic low-back pain is the commonest such syndrome, although chronic headache is a widespread problem as well. It's difficult to define a chronic pain syndrome with precision. Victims complain of long-standing and constant pain that is poorly explained by medical findings and seems to interfere with normal functioning out of proportion to the findings.

Notice I said *poorly* explained and interfering *out of proportion* to the findings. Chronic pain syndrome does not refer to pain that seems to be totally psychological; usually these patients have real medical problems or pathology—for example, arthritis in the lumbar (lower back) or cervical (neck) spine or a history of pelvic infections or surgery that can cause chronic discomfort. What distinguishes them is that their complaints of pain and the handicapping effects of their pain are much greater than in other patients who seem to have the same medical histories and the same amount of pathology. They request more pain medication, they cannot attend to jobs or housework, and they complain that their pain prevents them from sleeping properly. They lose interest in sex and lose weight. They are irritable and can't enjoy anything.

These patients had been thought to have more severe symptoms for a variety of reasons. The vague concept of low pain threshold was invoked. They were thought to suffer from personality problems; perhaps they were "addictive personalities" and were exaggerating symptoms to get narcotics from their doctors. They were sometimes thought to be malingering, hoping for disability insurance payments. All too often they were simply called "crocks" and ignored. I hope that by now, however, this collection of symptoms is very familiar to you; it includes many of the same ones that together characterize major depression. In the 1970s, when special hospital units were beginning to be set up for patients, usually addicted to pain medications such as narcotics, who had debilitating pain not well explained by medical findings, the treatment teams included medical doctors, surgeons (often neurosurgeons, who most often do back operations), anesthesiologists (who in effect are the specialists in pain relief), and also psychiatrists. The psychiatrists noticed that many of the pain patients had all the symptoms of major depression. In studying this group further, they noted that their family histories included a higher-than-expected prevalence of alcohol problems and depression. (Further discussion of the relation of alcohol abuse to mood disorders and the genetics of mood disorders will be found in the next chapter.) As you might expect, trials of antidepressant medications on these patients sometimes produced dramatic results; not only did the symptoms of depression get better, but the pain was somewhat relieved as well.

Pain can be a symptom of major depression. Headaches and vague abdominal pains are common, but other types of pain are seen as well—indeed, as many kinds of pain as there are body parts and organs. In some people who have major depression, pain is prominent; in fact, they may attribute their other symptoms—weight loss, insomnia, and so forth—to the pain. They may even attribute their depressed mood to their pain, and this can lead to problems, especially if their doctor is "a guy with a hammer." Perhaps you've heard the old saying, "If you're a guy with a hammer, everything looks like a nail." It's possible for some doctors, particularly specialists, to focus only on their specialty and to miss a more general problem such as depression.

On the other hand, I've known of patients who have become very angry, even stormed out of the office, when their medical doctor suggested a psychiatric consultation. Several times a year I'll get a phone call from one of my medical colleagues with an "emergency" patient with headaches or some other pain symptom who has seen doctor after doctor without receiving relief of the pain or an explanation of its source and who is now "very depressed and desperate." I promise to see the person the very same day, after usual office hours if necessary, only to get a phone call later canceling the appointment. The idea of seeing a psychiatrist is just too threatening for some people.

I think several factors conspire to cause these doubly unhappy outcomes. The first is the simplistic view that all human experiences can be divided into those of the mind and those of the body (a division that has been called the *Cartesian dichotomy,* after the French philosopher who first proposed it) and that these two "realms" do not affect one another. The hypothetical wall dividing these realms has been crumbling stone by stone, but it is still a high one. The term coined to express the relationship, *psychosomatic,* has come to be almost pejorative, implying, "It's all in your head."

Although we have come to accept that chronic tension can worsen peptic ulcers and that "type-A personalities" may have early heart attacks, for many people, the idea that depression can worsen and perhaps even cause pain is still so foreign that it prevents them from getting the treatment they need. The second and perhaps more important factor is the stigma associated with "mental illness." This is so important that I will discuss it in some detail in a later section (see "Stigma," under "Living with a Mood Disorder" in chapter 7).

Another clearly understood fact about pain and depression is that pain from existing medical problems can be exacerbated by depression. Symptoms of arthritis, back problems, and some of the painful complications of chronic medical conditions such as the nerve pain called *neuropathy* seen in diabetes can get much worse. Pain that was being adequately controlled with medication no longer responds. This problem is especially difficult to diagnose correctly, since both doctor and patient can easily assume that the original problem is worsening when in fact a second problem—depression—has arisen.

## FIBROMYALGIA

*Fibromyalgia* is a poorly understood and difficult to treat medical condition characterized by pain of the soft fibrous tissues in the body: the muscles, ligaments, and tendons. Patients with fibromyalgia often say that they ache all over and that their muscles feel sore, as if they have been overworked. Sometimes the muscles twitch and burn. Patients with fibromyalgia are troubled by a variety of other uncomfortable symptoms that include fatigue, sleep disturbances (often reporting that their sleep is not refreshing), chronic headaches, and trouble with concentration and memory. More women than men are afflicted with fibromyalgia and it can occur at any age.

Fibromyalgia is diagnosed clinically; that is, no biological markers, such as abnormalities in a blood test, x-ray, or scan, have been found to be reliably present in all sufferers. The clinical finding of painful tenderness at eleven of eighteen points on the body (called *tender points*) that cluster around the neck, shoulder, chest, hip, knee, and elbow areas is used to make a diagnosis of fibromyalgia. Although more than seventy-five other tender points have been found in patients, they are not used for diagnostic purposes.

You have probably already noticed that many of these symptoms are the same as those seen in major depression. The similarities don't end there. Sleep studies have shown that most patients with the disorder fall asleep without much trouble, but that their deep-level (or stage 4) sleep is constantly interrupted by bursts of brain activity similar to that seen during waking. As you'll see in the next chapter, this is very similar to the sleep abnormalities seen in people with severe depression. Some biochemical similarities have been found as well. The neurotransmitters serotonin and norepinephrine may be involved, as well as an important neuronal molecule called *substance P* that has also been implicated in the biology of depression.

One of the most important treatments for fibromyalgia is the prescription of antidepressant medications. But antidepressants alone rarely bring about complete relief, and it is fairly clear that fibromyalgia is not simply a form of depression.

The nature of the relationship between mood disorders and fibromyalgia is a subject of debate, but most experts agree that a relationship exists. I often tell my patients who suffer from fibromyalgia that it may be the body's reaction to chronic, long-term anxiety and depression. Or perhaps the biological factors that are involved in depression also trigger the syndrome of fibromyalgia in people who have genetic susceptibility.

## MIND AND BODY

Over the years, I have tried many ways to explain to my patients the associations and connections between physical symptoms and psychiatric symptoms. Some have enough medical sophistication to discuss such things as the autonomic nervous system, adrenaline surges, and so forth. But there's a rather simple statement that aptly sums up these complicated theoretical problems: "The brain *is* connected to the rest of the body." As medical scientists grow more familiar with the complexities of the body, the connections become more and more evident.

One of the first breakthroughs, and perhaps the most startling, linking the experience of pain with the chemistry of the brain was the discovery of opiate receptors in certain areas of the nervous system. An opiate is a substance derived from the opium poppy, and various related drugs manufactured from this plant are collectively referred to as narcotics (from the Greek *narkotikos,* meaning "benumbing"). Opiate or narcotic compounds include opium, morphine, codeine, heroin, and many others. The valuable medical use of these substances is their *analgesic* (pain-relieving) quality; they also can produce a state of euphoria, and it is this effect that accounts for their widespread abuse. Opiates were of course well known for centuries before the discovery of neurotransmitters, but as pharmaceutical researchers worked to produce safer and more effective pain medications from opium, they discovered new substances with some interesting properties that indicated that opiates might mimic a chemical produced by the brain that is involved in the experience of pain. They found that a slight alteration in the chemical structure of an effective analgesic could cause it to block the effect of other narcotics (accounting for the name of these compounds: *narcotic antagonists*). This result would make sense only if there were receptors for opiates in the nervous system. If such a receptor worked like other known neurotransmitter receptors, a chemical that mimicked the neurotransmitter very closely in structure would also mimic its function (like a copy of a key good enough to open a lock). Another substance that is close but not an exact match in chemical structure might block the original drug's effects (like a key copy that fits into the keyhole but won't turn, yet prevents the door from being opened even by a key that fits).

As neuroscience techniques advanced, the receptors were found in various parts of the brain and spinal cord. Why were they there? Why should the brain have receptors for poppy compounds? The answer, of course, is that the poppy compounds mimic some substance naturally produced in the brain that is involved in the perception of pain. Some of these substances have been isolated from brain preparations and have been called *endorphins* (from *endo-*, meaning "within," and *morphine,* the name of one of the compounds derived from poppies).

An interesting point about the opiate receptors of the nervous system is that they are found not only in brain and spinal cord areas that are known to transmit pain impulses but in other areas of the brain as well. Some of these other brain areas are in the limbic system, which seems to be intimately involved in the experience of mood.

Knowledge of narcotic drugs and opiate receptors has thus revealed another of what must be many direct connections between major depression and chronic pain. Narcotics cause euphoria—which is definitely a mood change—and there are opiate receptors in the limbic system of the brain, which seems to be involved in mood and mood disorders.

Throughout this book I have emphasized again and again that psychological symptoms, symptoms that affect mental processes, and experiences such as abnormal changes in mood can be caused by changes in the *biological* functioning of the body and require medical treatment. In this chapter I have explained that a causal relationship extends in the opposite direction as well. Depression, a condition primarily affecting the mental experience of mood, can cause and exacerbate pain, and psychiatric treatment often can play an important role in pain relief.

## Seasonal Affective Disorder

In every culture and religion, for as long as humans have recorded their rituals and religious observances, there have been celebrations and rites to mark the end of the short days of winter and the beginning of spring. The Roman Saturnalia, Christmas, Hanukkah, and other holidays cluster around the winter solstice, December 22, the shortest day of the year. Some ancient civilizations built monumental astronomical observatories to calculate solar eclipses and the biannual solstices and equinoxes. The darkening of the sun seen during an eclipse caused terror and great apprehension among these peoples, and the solstice marking the sun's return was calculated and celebrated by structures such as Stonehenge, the temple of the pharaoh Ramses at Abu-Simbel, and the pyramid observatories of the Incas and Aztecs.

Many species of animals are driven by powerful inner forces attuned to the changes of the seasons, which bring about changes in behavior. Seasonally determined migrations of birds and sea mammals and hibernation in bears and other land mammals are familiar examples. The scientific field that studies these phenomena is called *chronobiology* (from *chronos*, the Greek word for "time"), which you may have noticed is a recurring theme in the discussion of affective disorder throughout this book. We have talked about how symptoms of mood disorders relate to the twenty-four-hour cycle of the earth's rotation on its axis or, more simply put, the day/night cycle: early-morning awakening and diurnal mood variation are symptoms of major depression. In the next chapter I will discuss how manipulating the sleep cycle affects mood and affective disorder. Earlier in this chapter I discussed the relationship between affective disorder and the monthly (lunar) menstrual cycle. Perhaps it is not surprising, then, that there is also a relation between affective disorder and the twelve-month cycle, the annual cycle of the seasons.

As with many other mood abnormalities, seasonal variation in mood in some people was noted over and over in the psychiatric research literature before being recognized as a variant of affective disorder. In one of the first textbooks of modern psychiatry, the groundbreaking *Manic-Depressive Illness and Paranoia* by the great German psychiatrist Emil Kraepelin, this variation is described. The seventeenth-century English clergyman and poet George Herbert noticed it as well and wrote, "Every mile is two in winter." The increase of depressive symptoms in the winter months has practically become folklore; the "winter blues" and "cabin fever" are commonly accepted concepts.

It been now been recognized through careful, systematic study that some people with mood disorders get depressed in the fall and winter and have normal moods (or sometimes periods of hypomania) in the spring and summer. Because of the seasonal cycle of the illness, this has been called *seasonal affective disorder (SAD)*.

Let me make it clear that the depression of SAD is a major depressive episode in all clinical respects: sustained lowering of mood, changes in appetite and sleep, feelings of guilt and self-blame, hopelessness—in short, the whole syndrome of depression. A patient is defined as suffering from SAD when for at least two consecutive years there has been a regular relation between the onset of the abnormal change in mood and a particular time of year. The most common form of the illness is depression in winter and normal mood (or with brief periods of elation or hypomania) in summer, but the reverse pattern has also been described—depression in summer and normal mood (or hypomania) in winter.

Although the depression of SAD meets all the diagnostic criteria for major depression, several mood symptoms seem to be more common in SAD. As in major depression of any type, people with SAD have changes in appetite and sleep patterns. The SAD patient, however, almost always has an *increase* in sleep; complaints of chronic winter fatigue are very common. Also, an increase in appetite is more usual than a decrease, and SAD patients often gain weight every winter. Many with SAD report craving sweets and other carbohydrates.

Besides the remarkable seasonal rhythm of SAD, the treatment of the disorder is truly amazing. An effective treatment for SAD is exposure to bright light. This novel treatment was based on the observation that those who regularly got depressed in the winter would see their depressions lift within days if they traveled south—especially far south, near the equator. Patients who lived at different latitudes had winter depressions that were longer and more severe the farther from the equator they lived. How could this variation be explained? In these days of air conditioning and central heating it seemed unlikely that temperature changes could account for it, so research psychiatrists began to investigate another factor: light.

Alaska's long winter nights and summer days are familiar to most Americans from elementary-school geography. Near the poles of the earth, the seasonal variation in length of daylight is most pronounced. At the geographical poles, there is almost six months of darkness in winter; as one moves south, the hours of daylight on a particular winter day increase. At the equator, seasonal variation in daylight hours is minimal, and the days are longer all year round. Once the connection between mood and light was recognized in some patients, it became clear that any change in the duration of their exposure to light could bring about changes in mood. A prolonged period of cloudiness or a change in light intensity at work could also trigger a deterioration in mood in some people.

In 1982, researchers at the National Institute of Mental Health published a paper* describing how exposing a depressed patient to bright light (about ten times the brightness of ordinary room light) alleviated symptoms of depression.

Flower growers regularly manipulate the length of daylight and nighttime darkness to produce desired biological events. Anyone who puts a poinsettia plant or a Christmas cactus in a dark closet each evening in the fall to coax it into bloom for the holiday season is performing just such a manipulation. Many other species of plants flower only in response to very precise proportions of light hours and dark hours (called a *photoperiod*).

Biologists discovered years ago that seasonally determined variations of animal behaviors such as migration and hibernation were also determined not by temperature changes, but by photoperiod. Once this was discovered, the search was on for a hormone or other substance that was triggered by changes in photoperiod. Soon it was discovered that the secretion of *mela-*

---

* A. J. Lewy et al., "Bright artificial light treatment of a manic-depressive patient with a seasonal mood cycle," *American Journal of Psychiatry* 139 (1982): 1496–8.

*tonin,* a hormone produced by the pineal gland, was strongly influenced by photoperiod. The function of the *pineal gland,* a cone-shaped body about the size of grape seed buried deep in the convolutions of the brain, had for many years been a mystery. Centuries ago it was thought that perhaps this gland was the seat of the soul. It was even postulated that the pineal body was a vestigial third eye. These concepts fell into disfavor rather early in the history of scientific medicine, yet no function was found for the organ until 1917, when it was discovered that preparations made from the pineal body of the cow caused changes in pigmentation in tadpoles. In 1958 the chemical (hormone) that caused these changes was isolated and called melatonin, from *melanin,* the name of the dark skin pigment found in many animals, including man. The pineal gland secretes this pigment-regulating hormone, but its function remained obscure and little more than a curiosity. Some thought that the secretion of melatonin in humans was an evolutionary holdover; animals like the Arctic hare, which changes its color from earthy brown to snow white from season to season, had an adaptive use for such a regulatory mechanism, but no such phenomenon could be observed in humans.

Evidence has accumulated over the years, however, that suggests that the pineal body, though perhaps not the seat of the human soul, may be the seat of our internal clock. Through a complicated series of neural connections, the pineal gland receives input from the eyes and secrets melatonin in cycles over a twenty-four-hour period, more at night and less during the day. Manipulating the light/dark cycle in the research laboratory can affect this cycle, as does seasonal variation of photoperiod.

As we trace the connections of the pineal body to other parts of the brain and nervous system, we encounter some very interesting relationships. In addition to the connections to the eyes, the pineal body is known to have connections to the adrenal glands, which secrete cortisol in a diurnal pattern. The pineal gland and the adrenal glands share connections with a division of the nervous system called the sympathetic nervous system, in which epinephrine and norepinephrine are important neurotransmitters.

The treatment of SAD with light is still being refined. Patients in the original study were exposed to special fluorescent bulbs that reproduce closely the wavelength characteristics of sunlight. Whether ordinary artificial light is sufficient to produce the same results is not known. We know that the light must be five to ten times brighter than ordinary room light, about the same brightness as one sees looking out a window on a sunny spring day. Patients sit a few feet from a bank of lights and can read, sew, or do paperwork. They must keep their eyes open and are instructed to glance directly into the light for a few seconds every minute or so. A SAD patient treated with light notices an improvement within three or four days. Remember that antidepressant medications take two weeks at the very least to show results, and even ECT often takes a week or more. The significance of this finding is unknown; it may mean that SAD symptoms are brought about by a different mechanism that responds more quickly to manipulation.

Why are some people's mood disorders so closely related to photoperiod? Since we understand so little about human chronobiology—or about the mood disorders, for that matter—we don't know. It is intriguing to speculate that since so many people talk about hating winter, complain of "cabin fever," and experience "spring fever," SAD may be widespread indeed. It's clear that further study of SAD will greatly clarify the biology of mood disorders.

## Schizoaffective Disorder

An older version of the *DSM* (the *DSM-III-R*) called schizoaffective disorder "one of the most confusing and controversial concepts" in the classification of psychiatric illnesses. As you might guess from the word *schizoaffective*, the term is used to describe a disorder that has symptoms of both schizophrenia and affective disorder.

The symptoms of schizophrenia include prominent auditory hallucinations ("hearing voices"), delusional thinking, and sometimes bizarre thought-control experiences in which patients are convinced that some outside force is controlling their thoughts, putting thoughts into their heads, or removing their thoughts. There are other symptoms as well, none of which are often seen in mood disorders. In contrast with the symptoms of mood disorders, patients with schizophrenia usually experience little change in their mood state. In fact, mood appears to flatten out and the patient seems emotionally empty—not able to feel any emotions, either elation or depression.

The diagnosis of schizoaffective disorder has been applied to patients who have both marked changes in mood and bizarre hallucinations and thought disruptions. The category has no treatment implications; that is, there is no specific treatment for schizoaffective disorder, and most patients who are diagnosed with this illness are treated with antipsychotic medication (the drugs used for schizophrenia), medications used for affective disorder, or a combination of both.

Some psychiatric research indicates that schizoaffective disorder is a totally separate illness, neither a mood disorder nor schizophrenia. It has even been called "the third psychosis." But it seems that for every study claiming to show that schizoaffective disorder is separate, there is one claiming that patients with this disorder can always be categorized as having either schizophrenia or a mood disorder and that schizoaffective disorder does not really exist as a distinct disease entity. Many experts believe schizoaffective disorder is a misleading term that has been applied to patients with severe bipolar disorder who develop bizarre symptoms when they get sick but who respond to treatments for affective disorder.

However, it is clear that there are some patients whose illness definitely seems to combine two disorders: patients with the kind of bizarre delusions common in schizophrenia that seem to have nothing to do with an abnormal mood, but who also have very clear-cut episodes of depression and mania. A diagnosis of schizoaffective disorder is in many ways more serious than that of bipolar disorder, as this illness shares some of the features of schizophrenia and some of the treatment challenges of that illness. Delusions and hallucinations may respond only incompletely to medication treatment, and more severe (and sometimes progressive) social and occupational impairment is not uncommon. If a diagnosis of schizoaffective disorder is being considered, it is very important for psychiatrists to be extra careful in reviewing the symptoms and course of illness in order to make the correct diagnosis.

## Panic Attacks and Mood Disorders

Lisa was an interior designer who had worked for a large architectural firm for fifteen years. She was forty-eight but looked much younger, a well-dressed, composed woman. She had been attending a furniture show in High Point, North Carolina, when she had her first panic attack.

"Dr. Knox said the quickest way for me to get rid of these attacks was to come right to you, so here I am. I don't want to have these things happen to me again, *not one more time.* I'll do anything."

"Tell me about these attacks."

"I literally thought I was dying. I was walking down the aisle at the show and these terrific Italian lamps had caught my eye when I suddenly noticed that my heart was beginning to pound.

"'Too much coffee, my dear,' I thought, and I started to look for the ladies' room to throw a little cold water on my face. Well, the show was in this huge new exposition center for the first time this year, and I didn't know where the ladies' room was. I was heading for the information booth when it really hit me. My heart started pounding so hard my chest ached, and I was sure I was having a heart attack; I was dripping with sweat; my head was spinning, I couldn't breathe, my vision was going blank. I saw a chair and sat down. Well, it turned out to be an eighty-thousand-dollar *antique,* so in a flash I was surrounded by security guards, and all these people were pulling at me to get out of the chair. What a nightmare! Someone, God bless him, said, 'I think she's sick,' so they laid me out on the floor, called an ambulance, and whisked me off to the hospital.

"Well, this cute paramedic was with me in the ambulance and he had a really calm and reassuring way about him. I was feeling better by the time I got to the hospital, and I remember thinking, 'Well, dear, this wasn't the big one after all; you've only had a *teensy* heart attack.' When they told me they couldn't find anything, I didn't know whether to laugh or cry. I was in Dr. Knox's office the next morning, and she introduced me to the term *panic attack*. So am I going crazy or what?"

"Do you think you are?" I asked. "Sometimes people with panic attacks feel like they're losing touch with reality."

"I thought it was one of those near-death experiences—you know, where people feel like they're outside their bodies, looking down on the scene as if it wasn't real."

Lisa was describing the experience of "de-realization" or "depersonalization," a feeling that what's happening isn't real or that one is disconnected from the world for a moment and a very common symptom of panic attacks.

She had all the symptoms of panic disorder, and the first attack at the furniture show represented what is known as the "herald" attack, which, like a trumpeter, announces the onset of the disorder. This first attack usually strikes without warning and takes patients completely by surprise while they are involved in some ordinary activity. The herald attack may even awaken them from sleep.

Lisa's internist had already prescribed an effective antianxiety medication (also called an anxiolytic medication), and she had had no recurrence of the panic symptoms in several days. Like many people who have had a panic attack, however, Lisa couldn't forget how frightening the first attack had been, and she kept worrying about having another. She started to feel anxious whenever she thought about attending a trade show or some other large gathering of people, especially in an unfamiliar place. She had even rushed through her grocery shopping the day before because of her worry. Lisa was having what psychiatrists call *anticipatory anxiety,* feelings of anxiety that are triggered by the thought of having another panic attack.

"I told Dr. Knox I was fine on my new medication, but she said I should come to see you at least once to find out if this Klonopin is the right stuff for me. I'm not going to get hooked on this, am I?"

It was becoming clear that Lisa's business-as-usual attitude was a bit of a facade and that she had been and still was very frightened by her experience. Part of her coming to see a psychiatrist was to get a second opinion about her symptoms, which she had a hard time be-lieving were not signs of a very serious medical or psychiatric prob-lem. Her flippant "Am I going crazy?" expressed her real fear, and she needed more reassurance from an expert in "craziness." Her internist was astute enough to pick this up, but she realized it would be easier to get Lisa to see a psychiatrist if she made the referral as though *she* wanted reassurance about the choice of medication.

I explained to Lisa that panic disorder is more of a biological than a psychological problem and that some people seem to have an inborn tendency toward the disorder. The herald attack certainly can be trig-gered by a period of stress, too much caffeine, lack of sleep, or a com-bination of many factors, but once it occurs it seems to turn on the tendency for more attacks. Dr. Knox's choice of medication was what I might have prescribed for her, and I told her she could be confident that Dr. Knox could treat her effectively. "You will get better from this," I told her.

We had a discussion of what was happening in her life that might have triggered the attack. Her mother had died the previous month after a bout with stomach cancer. Lisa's eyes filled for a moment, but she blinked back the tears. "Don't get me started on my mother; it's a long and not very pleasant story."

Lisa had not gotten along with her mother for a long time. Her mother had had a drinking problem, and some of Lisa's childhood memories included telling lies to friends who wondered why their house was so dirty. She never endured physical or even verbal abuse, but she had been embarrassed again and again by her mother's isolation and withdrawal as she drank away the lonely afternoons in the suburbs.

"Neil says that's why I became a furniture and lamp person; I'm still obsessed with the 'house beautiful' I never lived in."

Lisa and her mother had grown further and further apart after Lisa married, and when her husband Neil was offered a job far away from Lisa's native Oregon, he took it. Lisa's mother had been diag-nosed with stomach cancer only the previous summer. Lisa had made one trip back to see her mother before she died; their meeting had been strained but polite. Lisa was home with Neil when her sister called from Oregon with the news of her mother's death. Lisa didn't attend the funeral.

"You probably think that's disgraceful, but I didn't want to be a hypocrite. I had written my mother out of my life years ago, and Madeline and the rest of the family had too. I've been feeling bad about the way things turned out, but I wasn't the one who let my kids make dinner for my husband when they were six and five."

Lisa couldn't control the tears this time and took a tissue from the table in front of her.

We talked a bit more about her mother, and I suggested she might get some benefit out of coming a few more times to talk and resolve her feelings.

"I'm doing better with all that, really. I was getting over it very well until these panic attack things started, and since I've been taking my little blue pills I haven't had any more attacks. I feel much better since I've talked to you; I understand these things a lot better now. I'll stick with Dr. Knox. Thanks for seeing me."

About two weeks later I got a phone call from Lisa. She had had another panic attack—not as bad as the first, but she considered it quite a setback and was worried that her symptoms were getting worse. I saw her again in the office.

"These have got to stop. I had my period last week, and my nerves were a mess. I'm better now, but last week I completely lost it with Neil. I stayed in bed a whole day because I was so tired and upset. I can't keep taking pills the rest of my life every time I have my period, either!"

Like many people with anxiety, Lisa was reluctant to take her antianxiety medication regularly, so we talked about another medication approach to the treatment of panic disorder. "Antidepressants? But I'm not depressed, I'm a nervous wreck!"

"We don't quite understand why antidepressants help with panic disorder, but they do," I told her.

---

It was discovered in the 1960s that some patients with severe anxiety symptoms got better when they were treated with antidepressants. As the symptom response was investigated more thoroughly, the concept of panic disorder as a special kind of anxiety problem emerged. In patients who had discrete attacks of paralyzing anxiety separated by periods of much less anxiety or even none, the attacks seemed to be prevented by these antidepressants. Even if they were starting to have anticipatory anxiety, preventing full-blown panic attacks let them go longer without an attack, and the anticipatory anxiety gradually faded.

---

I explained to Lisa that an antidepressant would prevent further attacks but that we would have to start her off with a small dose and gradually raise it until her symptoms responded. Unfortunately, Lisa did not tolerate her medication very well at first. For several weeks she tried to take it, but felt groggy much of the time. Even a small dose seemed to prevent the worst of the attacks, though, so I encouraged her to lower the dose and continue taking the antianxiety medication for now.

I told Lisa I wanted to see her in a week to assess her progress and talk about raising her medication dose, but as before, Lisa was reluctant to see me regularly and preferred to keep in touch by phone and make an appointment only if she "needed to come in." About a month later, Lisa was back in my office.

"I'm sorry to be bothering you again, but I'm just not getting any better. I've been really thinking about myself, and I've come to the conclusion that I'm just as bad off as when I first came to see you."

Lisa had the manner of a prodigal child coming to beg forgiveness and start again on the right foot. She told me she felt tense all the time and was irritable and cross at home. Her appetite was up and down, and she had gained weight in the past month.

"I told you I was getting better as far as my mother was concerned. That's not true. I wake up every morning completely ashamed of myself for not having been there when she died. That part might even be getting worse; I've burst into tears at dinner twice this week for no reason."

To look at her casually, one would not suspect that Lisa was having so many symptoms, but as I looked more closely I saw her stiff posture. She was almost over-composed, and her effort to appear calm became apparent.

It became clear to me that Lisa's panic symptoms were not the whole problem. She was having a major depressive episode. She did not present the typical picture—her mood was more tense and miserable than sad—but she had vegetative symptoms and a change in self-attitude, and even her premenstrual exacerbation of symptoms was consistent with a mood disorder. Perhaps most significant, when I told her I wanted to start a different antidepressant and not give up so easily this time, she agreed. "I think you're right; depression really might have been the problem all along."

We started a different antidepressant and got up to a therapeutic dose in a week. In two weeks, there was no question that the diagnosis of a mood disorder was the correct one.

"Now I realize why I didn't take enough of the little blue pills. I knew they weren't doing the job."

"Can you explain that to me a bit more?"

"Well, they did stop the attacks, and they made me calmer, but I realize now that I was having these bad feelings all the time that they just weren't helping with. Sometimes I began to wonder if they weren't making things worse. When my sleep started getting bad, I thought maybe I was getting dependent on them. I remember thinking, 'This is great; I'm not only a neurotic mess, I'm turning into a drug addict too.' Whatever this new stuff does, though, it's the right way to go. I haven't felt this good in months."

"Are you taking any Klonopin now?"

"I haven't needed any for three days now. I'm sleeping well, and I've lost two pounds. I'm a new woman."

---

The relation between major depression and panic disorder is not entirely clear, but that there *is* a relationship cannot be denied. Study after study has found that patients with severe anxiety symptoms, especially panic symptoms, often also have a history of major depression. Sometimes the panic attacks occur only during the episode of depression, sometimes the two problems seem to arise independently and follow separate courses. Genetic links have also been made; that is, people with panic attacks have been found to have a higher than expected number of relatives who suffer from major depression. Whether panic disorder and major depression are two variants of the same disorder—two sides of the same coin—is unknown. As we learn more and more about the biochemistry of both of these disorders, perhaps their relationship will become clearer. In the meantime, it is important to remember that panic attacks can, in some people at least, be the first sign of the onset of a major depressive episode. Affective disorder, as we have seen, can take many forms and appear to be many different things.

Let me make a few more comments about Lisa and the problems she had in getting the right treatment. Because so many types of information are needed to make a psychiatric diagnosis, it can rarely be done in just one visit. There are always pitfalls for those who make snap judgments about diagnostic issues and are too quick to toss out information as irrelevant. Just as the psychiatrist must have an open mind whenever a new patient walks in the door, the patient needs to have an open mind as well.

Suppose when Lisa went to Dr. Knox she had her blood pressure taken and got a reading of 150/90. She might have said, "Lisa, this is a little worrisome. I want to see you in two weeks so I can check this again. This may be the beginning of high blood pressure, so I want to follow up on it and not just ignore it."

Lisa most likely would have said, "Absolutely, Dr. Knox. I'll see you next week." She probably wouldn't have said, "Don't be silly. I'm too healthy to have high blood pressure. It must have been something I ate. I'll call for an appointment if I start to feel bad."

And yet that was exactly Lisa's attitude toward her psychiatric treatment. After her first visit she did not want to come back to discuss her feelings about her mother's death and explore why she had been so strongly yet unexpectedly affected by it. Later, when her symptoms were barely controlled on her medications, she did not want to make regular appointments but preferred to call if she got worse (as she did).

Because mood disorders (and many other psychiatric problems as well) are often very slow to develop and slow to respond to treatment, and because little guidance is available from the laboratory or x-ray department, it's vital that the patient faithfully come in for the only objective examination available to record progress or regression: the meeting with the doctor to review symptoms. If Lisa had come in weekly or even biweekly, it probably would have become clear to me much sooner that she needed to be aggressively treated for depression. She would have felt better sooner and in the long run would have saved herself the money she probably thought she was saving by having fewer appointments. I was hesitant to be too aggressive in switching medications because I was afraid Lisa wouldn't agree to the frequent follow-up visits she would need for me to assess progress, look for side effects, and make the necessary medication switches and dosage changes. Lisa was reluctant, and I was reluctant. What way is this to attack a health problem and get the symptoms under control as quickly as possible? Mood disorders are as serious as any other medical condition and need to be taken just as seriously. Their often slower pace is no excuse not to be vigorous in their treatment.

Lisa's case is typical in another way too. She could not take the first antidepressant but responded well to the second. This is another reason for the patient to be in close contact with the doctor and report side effects as soon as possible. There's no use waiting until the next appointment to announce, "I haven't taken the medication for a week. It made my mouth too dry." Believe me, the doctor is as interested as patients are in their progress and wants them to get better as soon as possible. I'll discuss these issues in more detail in chapter 7.

# Causal Factors and Associations

## The Heredity of Mood Disorders

A question that always comes up in a discussion of mood disorders is the issue of heredity. It has been recognized for many years that mood disorders run in families, and patients are usually concerned about the chances of passing the disorder on to their offspring.

A brief discussion of the principles of genetics—the scientific study of the inheritance of biological attributes—will be useful here. The patterns and rules of inheritance in living things were first formulated by Gregor Mendel, an Austrian monk and botanist. Before Mendel's work in the late nineteenth century, many thought that the traits of one parent were somehow simply blended with the traits of the other so that any one characteristic in offspring would be intermediate between those of the two parents. Mendel discovered that this was not always true. In elegantly planned and executed experiments with plants—mostly peas—carried out in his monastery garden over many years, Mendel elucidated the basic principles of inheritance. He found, for example, that crossing a pea plant that produced green peas with a plant that produced yellow ones did not produce plants with yellow-green peas (that is, an intermediate form). He found instead that *all* the seeds formed by the cross grew green peas. Crossing these offspring seeds, he found that three-quarters of the second-generation seeds produced green peas, and one-quarter produced yellow peas; again, there were no intermediate forms. He concluded that each parent contributed something that determined pea color, and that these "somethings" were distributed to each offspring (in this case, seeds). Most important was his discovery that, although there was some interaction between them, there was no blending of traits. The seeds or offspring got either a green inheritance or a yellow; there were no in-betweens. These "somethings" are now called *genes,* and can be thought of as the units of inheritance.

Some traits seem to be determined almost completely by one gene, like the color trait in garden peas. As in the peas, knowing the pattern of these traits in the parents can permit very precise predictions about the likelihood of the offspring inheriting a particular trait. It can often be reliably predicted that 50 percent or 25 percent (or some other simple proportion) of offspring will inherit the trait. These simple inheritance patterns are called Mendelian patterns in tribute to their discoverer.

Many human traits follow Mendelian patterns; blood types are a familiar example. Knowing both parents' blood types lets us make rather definite predictions about the blood types of their children. This is the reason blood testing can sometimes validate or invalidate paternity claims. Some human diseases seem to be passed on by a single gene that follows Mendelian patterns. Huntington's disease, the degenerative brain disease that killed folksinger Woody Guthrie, is an example. The children of those with Huntington's disease have a 50 percent chance of developing the disease, and those that do develop it have a 50 percent chance of passing it on to each of their children. The percentages are crisp, precise, and reliable.

Most human traits, however, seem to be determined by many genes that often interact with one another, a pattern that has been called *complex inheritance.* Height is a good example. There are so many genes involved, and so many other factors (diet, sickness, injury, and so forth) that can affect height, that predictions become very difficult to make. Tall parents have a greater chance of producing tall children than short parents do, but how many children will be taller than average and how tall they will be is almost impossible to say.

It turns out that many, perhaps most, common illnesses (high blood pressure and adult-onset diabetes are good examples), also have complex inheritance; many genes are involved in causing them, and these genetic factors interact with environmental factors (diet, body weight, amount of exercise one gets) to determine who will be affected by the illness and how severe their problem will be. With the development of gene-mapping techniques and extensive studies of families affected by mood disorders, we have learned that these illnesses also have complex inheritance. Thus, mood disorders seem to fall into the category of inherited traits for which only rough estimates can be made about the chances of inheriting the illness.

Studies of twins have shed much light on the genetics of mood disorders. In identical (monozygotic) twins, which develop from the same fertilized egg and have exactly the same genes, there is a nearly 80 percent *concordance rate* for bipolar disorder, meaning that if one twin has bipolar disorder, there is an 80 percent chance that the other twin will have it too. Twin studies looking at major depression find high concordance rates, too, but not as high as in bipolar disorder. If only one gene were involved, and if there were no environmental contribution, one would expect a 100 percent concordance rate for these disorders in identical twins. These studies indicate that there is a strong genetic influence in the development of mood disorders, especially bipolar disorder, but that there are also other as yet undiscovered influences that are important in determining whether a particular individual will develop a mood disorder.

People who have a first-degree relative (parent, sibling, or child) with major depressive disorder are one-and-a-half to three times more likely than the general population to have the disorder, on the order of 10 percent for males and double that percentage for females. The hereditary occurrence of bipolar disorder is even more striking, with the risk of developing bipolar disorder if a first-degree relative is affected more than five times that seen in the general population: on the order of 6 percent.* These numbers rise if more than one relative is affected; for example, the chances that a child of two parents with bipolar disorder will also be affected with the illness rises to over 30 percent.

## Alcohol and Drug Abuse and Mood Disorders

A distinction still tends to be made between alcohol abuse and addiction and the abuse of and addiction to other drugs such as narcotics, cocaine, and the barbiturate sedatives. Many argue that the distinction is arbitrary and that whether one abuses alcohol or another drug has more to do with social and economic factors than with anything else. I'm going to lump the two problems together and call them both "chemical dependency." All theoretical considerations aside, at least two relationships between affective disorder and chemical dependency are very clear: chemical dependency can cause symptoms of mood disorders, and mood disorders can look like simple chemical dependency. This can make diagnosis very difficult. Another case history will illustrate:

* These risk estimates are from Steven Molden, "Psychiatric Genetic Counseling." In *Washington University Adult Psychiatry,* ed. Samuel Guze (St. Louis: Mosby, 1997).

I was asked to consult in the care of a patient who had been admitted to the "detox" unit of a general hospital, his second detoxification admission in a month. George was a fifty-five-year-old comptroller for a manufacturing company who was admitted following several months of heavy alcohol use.

George was an alcoholic by just about anyone's standards. Like many men who develop alcohol problems, George had started drinking when he was a teenager. He grew up in a small town in the South and dropped out of high school to work at a gas station just after turning sixteen. At first his drinking was not that abnormal, though it seemed to be a frequent pastime. Saturday night was the time to be with his buddies and tie one on. And Friday called for a few beers to mark the end of the workweek. By the time George turned twenty, the drinking that began on Friday would continue through to Saturday night without much of a break. Soon George discovered that Mondays were a lot easier to face if he just got the week started with a beer. His drinking was a sort of joke at the gas station and even around town, where he became something of the town drunk. George started to have a harder time laughing along, however, as the years went by and he was still pumping gas at age twenty-eight. That year his alcohol use seemed to accelerate dramatically; he got into fights and spent a few nights in jail every couple of months. Then George lost his job.

This last event seemed to shock him into taking stock of his situation as he hadn't for years. He remembered the great plans he had made as an adolescent—plans to learn auto mechanics, run his own service station, even own a chain of stations someday. But the years between those days and today seemed to have slipped away. He felt like Rip van Winkle, awakening at age twenty-eight to find himself no more ready to face the future than he had been at sixteen. No job, no skills, no money, and only one friend—the bottle.

George entered an alcoholism treatment center in another town and began turning his life around. He discovered Alcoholics Anonymous. He went back to pumping gas but also got his high school equivalency certificate. He took some business courses at the community college, and found a job as a bookkeeper. He went to college at night to become an accountant and then landed a "real job" as an accountant. He married and had children. He attended AA meetings every week for years and maintained total sobriety—not a single drink in nearly thirty years. He lost the desire to drink, and he gradually dropped out of AA.

When I met George, however, he was a very sad-looking man. He sat in his darkened hospital room smoking a cigarette. His face was like a mask, grim, weary. "I don't know what to tell you; I don't know how to talk to a psychiatrist. Maybe you should just ask me some questions," he said in a monotone. It was as if talking to a psychiatrist marked a new low point in his life. "Wasn't it bad enough to be a drunk? Now they think I'm crazy," he seemed to be thinking.

"Tell me about your slip," I said. Alcoholics Anonymous refers to an alcoholic's relapse into drinking as a "slip." The word implies something temporary, almost beyond the person's control. It was a word George would be familiar with and would show that I wasn't judging or criticizing him.

"I started feeling it come on a year ago. I should have started back with my meetings, but I didn't. Maybe none of this would have happened. I started having trouble at work. I couldn't concentrate; I was paranoid."

"What do you mean by that?" I asked.

"I got worried that I was making mistakes on the ledgers without realizing it. I would check and double check everything to be sure it was right. I felt sure that the company wanted to get rid of me and that the president was watching my performance, gathering evidence of my incompetence so he could fire me."

"How much were you drinking at that time?"

"That was before I started drinking."

This didn't quite make sense to me. "Why did you think the company wanted to get rid of you?" I asked.

"I was sure they knew about me." George looked straight at me. He seemed to be steeling himself for the inevitable next question.

"What were you sure they knew about you?"

"That I'm an alcoholic."

This was not an answer I was expecting.

"I thought you said you were still sober then."

"An alcoholic is an alcoholic forever," George said, as if he were reading a death sentence.

Months before he started drinking again, George had started worrying that his somewhat disreputable past was beginning to come to light on the job where he had been a valued and productive employee for over ten years. He had been sober for so long, and had not attended AA for so long, that he simply didn't mention it as a problem when he was hired. He had had a stable work history as an accountant for years; the remote past simply didn't figure in his hiring, and his past life as "town drunk" (even this was an overstatement) was long ago and far away. As I questioned him more closely, the symptoms of major depression came tumbling out one after another. Early morning awakening, weight loss, feelings of shame and guilt. George became convinced that his employer would "find out sooner or later anyway," so he began drinking. It was not long before the dependency syndrome became full-blown, with missed work, drinking to get started in the morning, hidden bottles at home.

His wife got him to check into a detox unit of the hospital, and he seemed to make something of a turnaround. He had gone back to work but still felt tremendously insecure and had difficulty getting his work done with his usual effectiveness. He lasted only a month before he went to a bar one evening and got drunk, then called a cab and had himself driven back to the hospital. He was again admitted, but he had uncontrollable crying spells for the first two days of his hospital stay, and so his doctor ordered psychiatric consultation. I made the diagnosis of major depression complicated by alcoholism.

---

Did major depression cause George's alcoholism? Unfortunately, I don't think we know enough about either mood disorders or alcoholism to answer this question. It is clear that some people with mood disorders will begin drinking more than usual or using other substances that induce euphoria because these chemicals temporarily relieve some of the uncomfortable feelings mood disorders cause. In depression, the slight boost in mood and feeling of relaxation caused by the rise of the alcohol level in the bloodstream may help for a while with the tension, anxiety, and pervasive gloom of the illness. The term often used to describe this is *self-medication*. Persons in the manic state may also use drugs to intensify their "high." Some of these people do not suffer from chemical dependency, and when their mood disorder is properly treated they return to abstinence from drugs and more normal use of alcohol.

Nevertheless, it is clear that some people are prone to chemical dependency (which I'll continue to characterize as loss of normal behavioral restraint in the "search for the high"), and that if these people try to "treat" their mood problems with drugs or alcohol, another chain of events is set in motion that quickly causes their lives to fall apart.

I think George is one of these people. He is an alcoholic, or rather was a recovering or sober alcoholic for many years until he started to develop symptoms of major depression. Affective disorder was the banana peel he slipped on. If he had not gotten depressed he might not have started drinking again. He would almost certainly have stayed sober after the first detox admission given the success of treatment many years before. George's case shows how intolerable the symptoms of the depression can be. They can overcome even the best intentions and the strongest of wills.

When I made my diagnosis of George's problem, I ignored one of my own cautions to medical students and psychiatric residents: diagnosis of a psychiatric problem is very difficult to make reliably in a substance abuser whose chemical dependency is still active. Studies indicate that between one-quarter and two-thirds of drinking alcoholics have symptoms of depression severe enough to significantly impair their everyday functioning beyond the damage caused by their intoxication and "hangovers." It is certain that not all of these people have affective disorder, even though many of them have enough symptoms of major depression that an antidepressant would certainly be prescribed by most physicians. The most effective treatment for these "secondary" depressions, however, is abstinence from alcohol. There is usually a complete resolution of the depression within several days or, at most, weeks after they stop drinking.

Several factors made me bend my rule in George's case: he had become depressed before he started drinking, and he had remained depressed even after the first detox admission.

Abuse of other drugs can also mimic the symptoms of affective disorder. Chronic marijuana abuse can cause a tired, lethargic state with low motivation that can look a lot like affective disorder. Most of the sedatives, sleeping pills, antianxiety medications, and other "downers" can cause depression in some people, sometimes even at therapeutic doses. Amphetamines ("speed") and ecstasy and other "club drugs" can cause severe mood problems. These drugs are potent stimulants and produce a hyperalert, high-energy state characterized by a sense of well-being and physical robustness. But they tend to cause severe depression when people stop taking them. Cocaine abusers often suffer a comparable crash after a binge. These states look *exactly* like major depressive episodes and have caused suicides.

Phencyclidine or PCP ("flakes," "angel dust") was developed as an anesthetic but produced severe psychiatric side effects during clinical trials and was never introduced for that purpose. It is used by abusers to produce hallucinatory experiences and euphoria. Many extremely violent reactions to this drug occur, some of which can be prolonged. One of the possible reactions is what has been called *symptomatic mania,* a mental state that is indistinguishable from mania and requires treatment with lithium. I once treated a young man in whom PCP had produced a state that could only be described as religious ecstasy and that disappeared on treatment with lithium. Most PCP psychoses are not nearly so pleasant, and suicide and grotesque murders have been reported as a result of them in every city where PCP abuse has been at all prevalent.

What conclusions should we draw about the relation between affective disorder and drug and alcohol abuse? Drugs, especially alcohol, can mimic many of the symptoms of mood disorders. Some patients who abuse substances will be able to stop doing so when an underlying mood disorder is treated, without specialized treatment for chemical dependency. However, the term "self-medication" has probably been overused, and many of these patients are better thought of as having two disorders—a mood disorder *and* chemical dependency.

I tell these patients that mood disorders and substance abuse disorders feed on each other and that *both* disorders need treatment: treating either one will not make the other simply go away.

## Medical Causes of Mood Disorders

Just as many conditions can cause a symptom like shortness of breath or chest pain, many different conditions can cause the collection of symptoms that form the clinical pictures of the mood disorders. Various diseases, medications, poisonous substances, and infectious agents can cause the same set of biological changes in the brain. Both major depression and the manic state can be mimicked by several medical problems.

Formerly, when a patient had all the symptoms of a mood disorder but it was discovered that an underlying disease or medication was the cause, they were said to have an *organic* mood syndrome. Two of these words are familiar to you by now: *mood* and *syndrome,* a collection of symptoms and signs of illness that frequently occur together and are recognizable as a unique clinical entity with a limited number of causes. *Organic* is an older term in psychiatry that has fallen out of favor. The dictionary defines organic as "of or arising from a bodily organ." It was useful when psychiatry made a clear distinction between psychological disorders, which were "of the mind," and organic disorders, which were "of the body," but you can see, I hope, why it is a problematic term now. Depression was considered of the body if it was caused by a tumor, infection, hormone imbalance, or other pathological condition that could be seen on an x-ray or measured with a blood test. Now that we know that major depression and bipolar disorders are associated with changes in brain functioning and are therefore just as "organic" as any other disease, the term *organic mood syndrome* could be applied to these illnesses as well.

Now these problems are described in a much more accurate way: when a major depression or manic state is caused by a poison, medication, or some underlying alteration in biological function of an organ other than the brain, the patient is said to suffer from a mood disorder *secondary to* that disorder. Thus, a patient with major depression symptoms caused by adrenal gland disease would be said to suffer from a mood disorder secondary to adrenal disease. I'll separate these types of causes of mood symptoms into several categories and describe each in turn.

## MEDICATIONS AND OTHER CHEMICAL SUBSTANCES

Many medications can cause mood syndromes; in fact, we have already heard about two. Remember from chapter 1 that the observation that reserpine—the antihypertensive (high blood pressure) medication—causes symptoms of major depression practically started the biological revolution in psychiatry when it was also noted to deplete the neurotransmitter norepinephrine in nerve cells. The tendency to trigger symptoms of major depression is shared by a number of drugs used to treat high blood pressure.

In the section of chapter 3 titled "Complicated Depression," I told you about a patient who developed a serious depression while taking a steroid medication. This large group of medications can cause severe mood symptoms. The word *steroid* refers to a chemical structure shared by many hormones, including the sex hormones. The term *steroid medication,* however, usually refers to preparations and derivatives of *cortisol,* the steroid hormone secreted by the adrenal glands. Because they are potent anti-inflammatory agents, the steroids have many uses in medicine; in fact, when the first steroids became available they seemed to be miracle drugs because they are helpful in so many chronic inflammatory diseases that at the time had few effective treatments. Diseases of the joints such as rheumatoid arthritis, inflammatory diseases of the blood vessels such as lupus erythematosus and polyarteritis, bowel diseases such as ulcerative colitis and Crohn's disease, lung diseases such as chronic bronchitis, emphysema, and asthma—the list goes on and on. Steroids are also used in chemotherapy for some cancers of the blood cells and immune system.

Steroids can cause mood changes in either direction—that is, they can cause either depression or euphoria. In fact, they often cause both in a particular pattern. When first started on a steroid, the patient may experience a hypomanic state: high energy, euphoria, decreased need for sleep, and so forth. This lasts a few days, until there is a gradual slipping away of these good feelings and depression sets in. The depression can range in severity from mild to severe.

Another class of medications related to the steroids are oral contraceptives. The female sex hormones are very closely related to cortisol and technically should be designated steroids, though they are not usually called that. They form the constituents of all oral contraceptives and can certainly cause mood problems, usually depression.

Another set of medications that frequently cause mood symptoms are the sedatives, often used to treat anxiety symptoms (anxiolytic medications) and to induce sleep (hypnotic medications). Older, now obsolete sedatives were especially likely to cause depression. These include the barbiturates (Nembutal, Seconal, and others), meprobamate (Miltown, Equanil), ethchlorvynol (Placidyl), and methaqualone (Quaaludes). Even the safer, more effective medications that replaced them—drugs in the benzodiazepine class—can cause depression in some people. These medications include diazepam (Valium), clonazepam (Klonopin), alprazolam (Xanax), and others.

There are a few poisons that can cause mood disorders. They usually cause many other problems and quickly make themselves known with other symptoms, but if the patient is exposed to low levels over a long period, depression may be the only symptom for quite a while, leading to diagnostic confusion.

One poisonous substance that can cause depression, and to which long-term low-level exposure is not rare, is lead. Painters who inhale lead from paint dust or burning old paint can be exposed to toxic levels and show all the symptoms of major depression: low mood, fatigue, irritability, loss of interest in sex, and so on. In a study of thirty men exposed to lead and evaluated at an occupational medicine clinic, most complained of depression, among other symptoms, and several reported that depressed mood was their most severe symptom. One patient had complete resolution of his depression when treated with a lead-removing medication but had a full relapse when he resumed scraping and sanding paint without a face mask.*

## HORMONAL PROBLEMS

In the previous section I noted that steroid medications can cause mood problems, so it should come as no surprise that medical problems that affect the amount of steroids the adrenal glands produce can also cause mood disorders. Tumors of the adrenals can sometimes cause them to secrete hormones in abnormally large amounts, producing essentially the same result as taking steroid medication. Though it may seem paradoxical, a deficiency of steroid hormones can also cause mood symptoms. This can occur when adrenal gland tissue is destroyed by tumor or infection. Sometimes the adrenal glands seem to shrivel up for no apparent reason, a condition known as Addison's disease. A lack of the hormones secreted by the adrenals can produce generalized weakness, loss of appetite, weight loss, and other symptoms that can mimic major depression.

Mood seems to be even more closely tied to the thyroid system. The details of the link between the thyroid hormones and mood are not entirely clear, but several facts are pretty much proved. Hypothyroidism can clearly

* R. S. Shottenfield and M. R. Cullen, "Organic affective illness associated with lead intoxication," *American Journal of Psychiatry* 141 (1984): 1423–6.

cause all the symptoms of major depression. Patients can experience slowed thinking, a decreased energy level, and memory problems in addition to depressed mood, which is sometimes of suicidal proportions.

In some people who suffer depressive symptoms that seem to be caused by thyroid malfunction, laboratory tests of thyroid function appear normal. These patients get better when they are treated with thyroid hormones, even though their test results do not indicate thyroid problems. Sometimes a depression that responds incompletely to the usual treatment with antidepressants can become fully responsive if a small amount of thyroid hormone is added to the antidepressant. Whether these patients suffer from some subtle deficiency of thyroid hormone incapable of being measured or whether they have a variant of major depression that is more dependent on thyroid hormones for its expression remains to be seen.

I'll pause here for a moment to say that the connections between these two hormonal systems, adrenal and thyroid, seem to be very important in the development of the symptoms of affective disorder. I've already mentioned that the pattern of secretion of the adrenal hormones is disrupted in some people with major depression (see "Tests for Mood Disorders" in chapter 3), and that too much or too little of the adrenal steroid hormones, which may be caused by adrenal gland disease, can mimic all the symptoms of hypomania and depression.

Too little of the thyroid hormones can mimic the symptoms of depression, and sometimes extra thyroid hormones must be added to antidepressants to completely relieve symptoms. Without going into unnecessary detail, let me state that the activity of both the adrenals and the thyroid glands is regulated by the pituitary gland at the base of the brain, and that the pituitary in turn receives hormonal and possibly neural input from a part of the brain called the hypothalamus. As with the pineal body, melatonin, and light and their effects on mood (see "Seasonal Affective Disorder" in chapter 5), the facts about the thyroid and adrenal glands, the effect of their hormones on mood, and their connections to the brain offer some tantalizing room for speculation about the nature and ultimate causes of the mood disorders and will no doubt shed much light on the search for causes and better treatments.

A rare hormonal problem that can cause mood changes is disease of the parathyroid. The parathyroid glands control the level of calcium in the bloodstream, and it is the abnormal calcium level that seems to cause the mood problems. Too much calcium can cause depression; too little causes a severe anxiety state that can also look like major depression of the more "agitated" type.

## OTHER NERVOUS SYSTEM DISEASES

Several other illnesses can include prominent mood disturbances as part of their symptom picture. First, there are several illnesses that also affect the brain and cause degeneration of particular centers. Patients with Parkinson's disease, a slowly degenerative movement disorder, can sometimes have episodes of major depression in the course of their illness, and in Huntington's disease, a devastating degenerative disorder that affects movement and causes dementia, a mood episode may be the first symptom. In Huntington's disease there is usually a family history of the illness, which is a tip-off to the diagnosis of the underlying disorder.

Multiple sclerosis, a puzzling nervous system disease in which there is spotty, unpredictable destruction of neural tissue, can cause mood changes either early in the disease or late in its course.

Very rarely, brain tumors can present as mood disturbances alone; like the other illnesses, they do not remain "silent" for long, and soon other symptoms like seizures and paralysis occur and point to the underlying disorder.

## INFECTIONS

A whole range of infections have been implicated as possibly causing mood disturbances, especially depression. Depression associated with tuberculosis has been known for many years, but since this illness has fortunately become rare in this country, so has the associated depression. There is an association between certain viral infections and depression as well. Patients with hepatitis, a viral infection of the liver, and with mononucleosis, an often lengthy viral infection that causes profound fatigue, often complain of depression. Patients with HIV can develop either major depression or manic symptoms.

## OTHER CONDITIONS

An association has long been reported between abdominal malignancies, especially cancer of the pancreas, and major depression. The mechanism for this is completely unknown, but complaints of depression for several months before the other symptoms of the disease emerge have been observed too often to be explained simply as a coincidence.

Vitamin deficiencies can cause depression, but true vitamin deficiencies are rare and have many associated symptoms, so the misdiagnosis of affective disorder in such cases would be unlikely.

One has only to scan psychiatric journals for a few months to read reports associating the symptoms of mood disorders with what can seem like every drug, poison, and disease known to medicine. What does it all mean? For the neuroscientist, every association may be another piece in the puzzle of affective disorder, but for practicing psychiatrists and their patients, the picture can be very confusing. If so many diseases, deficiencies, and metabolic disturbances can mimic mood disorders, how much testing for underlying disease should be done? Can we distill some practical guidelines on the diagnosis and treatment of mood disorders from all the data on associated conditions?

Perhaps the first point to make is that mood disorders, especially major depression, are very common. Thus sheer numerical probability makes it likely that a diagnosis of affective disorder in a person with the symptoms of that disorder is correct. (There's an old folk-saying in medicine: "If you hear the sound of hoof beats, don't look for zebras.")

Second, it is rare for mood change and other symptoms of a mood disorder to be the *only* signs of a serious underlying illness. People with thyroid problems have changes in pulse rate, body weight, and skin texture. Those with high steroid levels have alterations in the distribution of body fat and other symptoms. People with infections run fevers. The list goes on and on. Even if the mood change is at first the only symptom, the others will follow in time, and the diagnosis will become clear.

Third, a mood disorder that is caused by another underlying illness often will not respond well to the usual treatments. Antidepressants or lithium will not "cover up" symptoms and allow an undiagnosed medical problem to worsen. If the problem is not affective disorder, treatments for affective disorder tend not to produce good results.

A caveat here, though: the development of a mood syndrome from one of these medical causes sometimes indicates that the individual has a vulnerability (probably genetic) to mood disorders and may develop a "primary" or "independent" mood disorder at some point. You will recall from the discussion of the genetics of mood disorders that environmental factors as well as genetic factors are important in causing them. In some patients, the first episode (or, more often, the first *severe* episode) of a mood disorder can be triggered by one of these medical factors, but the symptoms go on long after the trigger occurs. I once treated a patient who developed terrible anxiety and agitation after taking steroids for only a few days for a serious case of poison ivy. The symptoms went on for weeks, long after the steroids had been stopped, and resolved only after the patient started taking psychotropic medication. On close questioning, it turned out that this patient had a relative with bipolar disorder and had gone through a period of more than mild postpartum depression that had been called "baby blues" and never treated. These facts indicated that the patient probably had a genetic vulnerability to develop mood symptoms. Although the symptoms became significant only after certain hormonal triggers, I advised this patient to be on the lookout for mood symptoms as time went on and to seek psychiatric treatment again sooner rather than later should they develop.

It is simply not sound practice to try to track down every possible medical cause of mood disturbances before starting treatment, especially since the treatment of mood disorders is so benign and effective. If all the patients who had depression symptoms were given a total body MRI scan, had every hormone measured, were tested for lead, arsenic, and mercury, and were otherwise evaluated for every medical condition associated with mood changes, not only would they lose a lot of blood, have gallons of urine collected, and be exposed to unnecessary radiation (not to mention get a huge bill), it would be months before they got any treatment.

## Sleep and Depression

Just as the relationships observed between light and mood (in seasonal affective disorder) and between stroke and depression have taught neuroscientists a great deal about mood disorders, study of the relationship between sleep and mood disorders has led to a better understanding of both the normal experience of sleep and the abnormal experiences of patients with mood disorders. The study of sleep has even indicated promising treatment approaches.

Serious study of sleep has revealed that it is a very complicated process. It had previously been thought that sleep was simply a time of little or no activity, either physical or mental. Various explanations were offered for the process of dreaming, but the sleeping person seemed to be more or less like a machine that had been turned off, especially as far as mental activity was concerned. The tool that has been used most effectively to investigate sleep is the electroencephalogram or EEG (*electro-* refers to electricity, *encephalo-* to the brain, and *-gram* to a written record). When an EEG is performed, electrodes—pads that can measure small amounts of electricity much as sensitive microphones pick up faint sounds—are placed around the person's scalp. Two are also placed near the temples to measure eye movements. The process and equipment are just like those used in the more familiar electrocardiogram, or EKG.

Unlike the heart, though, which has a relatively simple pattern of electrical activity, the brain produces electrical activity that is monumentally complex. The EEG can gather only vague data about the activity of the brain; as a diagnostic tool, it can pick up a few types of abnormalities like large tumors or seizure activity, but although it is sensitive, it is not very specific in indicating the type of problem present. Because of this specificity problem, interpreting the EEG is tricky. I tell medical students it's like trying to diagnose car trouble by listening to the engine: even an amateur can tell when something is really wrong, but only experts can be specific about the nature of the problem, and even they must usually list several possibilities.

Fortunately, though, although the EEG can reveal little about the type of activity in the brain, it gives a rather good measurement of the *level* of activity, and this is why it has proved so useful in studying sleep. When EEGs were run on sleeping persons throughout the night, it became clear that, far from constituting a simple switch from high brain activity to low, sleep consisted of many stages of different levels of activity, and during some of them the brain seemed just as active as in the waking state. There was consistency in the pattern as well, and the term *sleep architecture* was coined to denote the pattern of brain activity throughout the night.

It's not necessary to go into much detail about sleep architecture, but I do want to mention several stages that are important. After falling asleep, a person passes through lighter and then progressively deeper levels of sleep in which the brain seems to slow down and become quiescent. Other body activities slow too. For example, the heartbeat and blood pressure drop to their lowest levels of the twenty-four-hour day. The process is like a submarine descending to darker, quieter, deeper water. The deepest stage is called *slow wave sleep (SWS)* after the type of EEG waves that characterize it. SWS is thought to be the physically restorative part of sleep; in sleep experiments, people who were awakened every time they entered SWS but were allowed to experience the other stages complained of muscle aches and pains. About an hour into the cycle, the "sleep submarine" starts to rise again, and the EEG indicates brain activity not too different from wakefulness. Nevertheless, the person is still asleep, and in fact this is when dreaming occurs. The eyes can be seen moving beneath closed lids, a characteristic that gives this stage of sleep its name: *rapid eye movement,* or *REM,* sleep. The function of REM sleep is not known. It has been speculated that it is somehow necessary for the development of the memory for the day's events, but this is far from certain. People who are REM deprived become irritable and even agitated.

During the night the level of sleep rises and falls; the length of each cycle and the amount of SWS and REM sleep stay within certain normal ranges in healthy people, who are then said to have normal sleep architecture.

One of the hallmarks of major depression is sleep disturbance, and the EEG reveals that a depressed person's sleep architecture is indeed abnormal in several ways. In depression, less of the time asleep is spent in SWS. Since this is the deep, restorative part of sleep, this change may explain the "restless" quality of the depressed person's sleep. The duration and intensity of REM sleep are greater in depressed people, and they enter the first REM stage sooner after falling asleep, a condition known as "short REM latency."

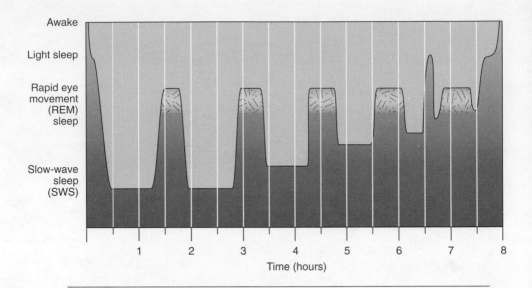

FIGURE 6.1 Normal sleep architecture

When this change in the sleep architecture was first observed and the findings were shown to be relatively consistent, it seemed that a test for major depression might have been discovered. But similar findings were found too often in nondepressed people for the change to be of much use as a diagnostic tool. Nevertheless the findings are consistent enough in enough depressed patients to have caused a great deal of scientific interest in the interrelations between sleep and depression.

Sleep study has led to new treatments for depression, too. After several reports of patients with major depression who had an improvement in mood after being deprived of sleep, studies were done to investigate these reports and replicated the finding: if depressed persons are kept awake all night, their mood is much better the next day. Unfortunately, they have a relapse of their depressed mood as soon as they get some sleep, making sleep deprivation alone an inadequate treatment for depression. However, several studies have shown that medication treatment can often sustain the antidepressant effects of sleep deprivation.

A research group in Italy has reported on their technique of using several alternate nights of sleep deprivation (that is, one night of sleep deprivation followed by a normal night's sleep, repeated several times) in combination with antidepressants and with lithium.* They reported that the antidepres-

* See, for example, F. Benedetti et al., "Dopaminergic augmentation of sleep deprivation effects in bipolar depression," *Psychiatry Research* 104, no. 3 (1999): 239–46.

sant effects of sleep deprivation could be sustained with medication in some patients, indicating that the combination of sleep deprivation and medications may hold the most promise. Studies have shown that sleep deprivation can help with both major depression and bipolar disorder.

It is quite clear that sleep deprivation triggers mania in individuals with bipolar disorder. This has very important implications for patients with this disorder, as it indicates that observing regular bedtimes and avoiding sleep deprivation may help them reduce the risk of an episode of mania.

As with seasonal affective disorder, research indicates that there must be some connection between mood regulation and an internal clock. By manipulating this clock, we may be able to provide relief from symptoms of affective disorder more quickly and perhaps with less medication.

# PART III

# GETTING BETTER

# CHAPTER 7

# Advice for Patients with Mood Disorders and Their Families

In the preceding chapters I have explained what the mood disorders are, how to recognize their symptoms, and how they are treated, as well as describing some of their many variations. Now I shall give what I hope is practical advice to those who have mood disorders and to their families.

First I shall present a guide to getting the proper treatment. Many people seem to feel that seeing a psychiatrist is a desperate last resort when all else fails. I want to persuade you that consulting a psychiatrist for symptoms of depression is as logical as consulting a cardiologist about chest pains or an ophthalmologist about eye problems.

In the section called "Living with a Mood Disorder," I'll address practical issues such as relapse. Since psychotherapy is such an important part of the treatment of mood disorders, I'll spend some time exploring this very special and useful type of treatment.

Sometimes, when symptoms are severe, hospitalization is indicated. Like ECT, this very valuable aspect of the treatment of mood disorders is often feared and resisted because of misconceptions based on outdated ideas. I'll explain what hospitalization in a modern psychiatric unit is like.

Finally, I'll comment on the very real problem of the stigma associated with psychiatric illness and psychiatric treatment.

## Who Can Help? The Mental Health Professionals
### PSYCHIATRISTS AND OTHER PHYSICIANS

The thing that separates psychiatrists from all the other mental health professionals is that a psychiatrist is a medical doctor (M.D.). More precisely, a psychiatrist specializes in the treatment of illnesses whose symptoms involve emotion, behavior, and other disorders of mental functioning. (The word *psychiatrist* comes from *psyche,* "mind," and *iatros,* "physician." Thus, a psychiatrist is a physician of the mind.)

In medical school, psychiatrists learn how to perform a physical examination, deliver babies, treat high blood pressure, look at x-rays, suture lacerations—in short, they become familiar with many, many aspects of health and disease. After an internship that consists of at least several months of caring for patients with general medical problems, psychiatrists enter a training program to learn about the diagnosis and treatment of psychiatric problems. (The training period *after* medical school lasts four years.) Remember that we deal with illnesses whose symptoms mainly concern emotion and behavior. Alzheimer's disease is a good example of a "medical" illness in which the treatment consists of helping to manage behavioral problems and often involves a psychiatrist. Because psychiatrists are physicians, they can prescribe medications, order laboratory tests (such as blood tests and MRI scans), and admit patients to hospitals.

Psychiatrists are like any other doctors in most ways, and the way we do our work is rooted in the same traditions and methods of practice as for doctors in other specialties. We take a medical history, asking about when the symptoms started, the quality of symptoms, associated details, and anything that seems to make the symptoms better or worse. Patients are asked about their family history, which is important because mood problems in relatives make the diagnosis of a mood disorder more likely. We perform the equivalent of a physical exam, called a *mental status exam;* instead of listening to the heart or otherwise examining the workings of the body, we ask patients about their mood and their feelings of anxiety, and often pose a few questions to test memory and concentration. We also try to get to know patients, asking something about their family, their education, work, marriage or "significant other" relationship, and so forth. Some people think that at the first meeting the psychiatrist will want them to talk for hours in deep detail about their childhood, their sexual fantasies, and so forth. Nothing could be further from the truth. Occasionally, I see a new patient who starts off the appointment by saying something like, "I've never talked to a psychiatrist before, so I don't know what you want me to say." It's almost as if they think the psychiatrist uses some special language, or reads minds, or will try to "trick" them into revealing something they are sensitive about.

Like any other doctor, the psychiatrist is interested in helping—that's what patients come to us for!

Some years ago, *family practice* came into being as a separate medical specialty. A family practitioner is a medical doctor whose training emphasizes knowing enough about all branches of medicine to treat most common medical problems competently. In a sense, the family practitioner's specialty is not being too specialized. It may seem that a family practitioner would not be very knowledgeable about mood disorders, but this is not so. Their training readies family practitioners to treat *common* medical problems, and mood disorders are certainly very common. In my experience, among all the medical specialists (other than psychiatrists, of course), family practitioners are the most experienced and competent when it comes to treating patients with psychiatric problems. Doctors who practice general internal medicine are like family practitioners in many ways but are more specialized in the treatment of adult medical problems (as opposed to treating children), and they also have a great deal of experience with mood disorders. Many patients with serious depression can be (and should be) treated by these nonpsychiatric physicians, who will often manage their illness in consultation with a psychiatrist.

## NONPHYSICIAN MENTAL HEALTH PROFESSIONALS

A *psychologist* usually has a Ph.D. degree in psychology from a university. Psychology can be defined as the science of the mind, and thus psychologists do not necessarily treat illness. Some, for example, limit themselves to research or teaching. A *clinical psychologist,* however, provides assessment or treatment of some kind. Some specialize in assessment: administering IQ (intelligence quotient) tests, personality evaluations, and other tests that assess one or another aspect of mental functioning. Others treat patients, mostly by means of psychotherapy.

Although a psychologist who has a Ph.D. can use the title "doctor," psychologists are not medical doctors, and they have not treated medical problems as part of their training. In most places, they cannot prescribe medications, perform physical examinations, or order and interpret laboratory tests. However, momentum is building to give psychologists prescribing privileges. In 2005, the states of Louisiana and New Mexico passed laws allowing psychologists to prescribe medications for psychiatric disorders, and there will probably be more states with similar provisions by the time you read this. These two states require that psychologists complete a course in *psychopharmacology* (the use of medication to treat psychiatric illness).

Although as of this writing only two states have granted these privileges, the requirements for licensure differ substantially between them. New Mexico requires a period of training in patient care under the supervision of a psychiatrist, but Louisiana does not, requiring only the completion of coursework. It remains to be seen which other states enact similar laws and what their requirements will be.

Prescribing privileges for psychologists are intensely controversial, and the issues involved are quite complex. Some argue that there are not enough psychiatrists to treat all the individuals who need medication treatment for psychiatric conditions and that expanding the pool of professionals who can do so is all for the good. Others counter that it is artificial to have one standard of care for the treatment of medical conditions (medical school and postgraduate medical training in patient care) and another for the treatment of psychiatric conditions (a degree in psychology and other training in psychiatric treatment that varies from state to state) and that the overlap between psychiatric and medical illness is so complex that it is not realistic to make distinctions between the two.

There are other health professionals who may treat people with mood disorders. Although in the past *social workers* were mostly involved with social welfare programs, most of them now do much more than, say, help people get food stamps. Schools of social work offer special tracks in counseling or clinical social work, and these programs can prepare excellent psychotherapists. (See "Psychotherapy," later in this chapter to see how this fits into the treatment of mood disorders.) Most social workers who see patients have master's degrees.

Clergy often have training in counseling (sometimes called *pastoral counseling,* as it takes a more spiritual approach to helping), and this usually has included training in recognizing when a congregant might have a psychiatric disorder and need treatment that includes a medical professional.

Nurses can specialize in psychiatric nursing and often see patients in their own practice. Most have also received master's degrees. Because nurses have a medical background, they are perhaps more familiar with the medical model and more comfortable seeing patients who are taking medication. Some nurses, called *nurse practitioners,* can prescribe medication under the direct supervision of a physician. Similarly, *physicians' assistants,* professionals who receive in-depth postgraduate training in treating medical illnesses and prescribing medications, can, under the direct supervision of the psychiatrist, perform some of the more routine aspects of psychiatric care. The practice of nurse practitioners and physicians' assistants might include seeing patients who are doing well on medications, asking about symptoms and side effects, ordering lab tests, and presenting this information to the psychiatrist for review and treatment decisions.

Later in this chapter I will discuss the role of counseling and psychotherapy in the treatment of mood disorders. As will become clear, having an M.D. or even being a psychiatrist does not necessarily make one a skilled psychotherapist, and many nonphysicians are expert at this type of treatment. (By the way, anyone who does psychotherapy is called a psychotherapist; this title implies nothing about training or educational background.)

A word here about the psychoanalyst. It is a common misconception that every psychiatrist is a psychoanalyst—even that anyone who talks to people about their emotional symptoms, trying to figure out the problem and help with it, is "psychoanalyzing" them. A psychoanalyst, however, practices an extremely specialized type of psychotherapy based on the theories of the great psychiatrist Sigmund Freud. Most analysts are medical doctors who completed a residency in psychiatry and then entered a lengthy training period at a psychoanalytic institute, where they studied the theories of Freud and of subsequent practitioners who elaborated upon and developed Freud's theories. This body of knowledge is collectively known as *psychoanalytic theory,* and the type of psychotherapy that follows these principles is called *psychoanalysis* or simply *analysis.* Analysis is a long, very intensive type of treatment in which the patient lies on the famous couch and the analyst sits behind it. Patients in analysis see their therapists three or four times a week for an hour, and the complex task of a very deep, detailed exploration of the patient's entire life experience and personality takes years. Only a minority of psychiatrists are analysts, and most of these have only a few of their patients in analysis. The vast majority of patients who see psychiatrists have sessions not very different from their appointments with their medical doctors.

You can see that the answer to the question "Who can help?" is not a simple one. There is a wide range of knowledgeable people who can help greatly in the treatment of mood disorders. So where does one begin to look for help? Let's limit ourselves here to a discussion of depression, since it is by far the most common mood symptom. Since not all depression is due to a mood disorder, sometimes psychotherapy, counseling, or just good advice may be all that's required to treat the problem. Perhaps rather than trying to answer "Who can help?" it would be more useful to discuss who can best decide on the most appropriate treatment when a person is having depression, mood swings, or other mood problems. I think the answer is clear. The first person to be consulted for evaluation of a possible mood disorder should be an M.D. Some will disagree with me about this, but if you review "Medical Causes of Mood Disorders" in chapter 6, you'll see why I think it is necessary. No matter how well trained and experienced a psychologist, social worker, or even a nurse may be, most simply do not have the familiarity with medical problems that an M.D. does.

Family practitioners and internists will be able to treat less severe mood disorders quite well; they *want* to do so as part of their commitment to providing as much of their patients' care as possible. In fact, since mood disorders are so common, there simply aren't enough psychiatrists to treat all the people who have them. Besides, it's always best if one can receive treatment from the doctor who knows one's history rather than from a new and unfamiliar doctor, even a specialist. Those who have family doctors should see them first. If more specialized care is needed, family practitioners will be able to recommend psychiatrists they have confidence in, and therefore the patient will feel confident, too. If the person with symptoms of a mood disorder does not have a family doctor, there's a lot to be said for seeing a psychiatrist first. After all, psychiatrists see and treat mood disorders much more frequently than other doctors and are the most knowledgeable and experienced experts available.

In the case of bipolar disorder, I recommend seeing a psychiatrist first. The medical treatment of bipolar disorder is usually more complicated than the treatment of depression. Physicians in other specialties will probably have little experience prescribing lithium, for example, and may not know how to manage its side effects as well as a psychiatrist does. Also, of all the medicines for treating mood disorders, those used in bipolar disorder seem to keep changing the fastest. For example, in the past five years or so the use of the anticonvulsant medications in bipolar disorder has dramatically increased. The most up-to-date treatment of bipolar disorder seems to go out of date very quickly, and usually only a psychiatrist has time to monitor the latest information; most other specialists are too busy keeping up with their own rapidly changing specialties.

I have not tried to list national experts in the field of mood disorders, for several reasons. First of all, very few people need a "superdoctor." Most simply need a good psychiatrist who is up to date on the treatment of mood disorders. Second, the "super docs" move around a lot; they may switch from clinical work to spending a year just doing research and not seeing patients, so a list of where they are and which of them is seeing patients quickly becomes obsolete. Instead, I want to give advice on finding a doctor in the community who is right for the patient—advice that will not go out of date as a list of names does.

As in choosing any physician, it is important to pick a psychiatrist the patient feels completely comfortable with. Recommendations from friends, relatives, and, of course, the family doctor are a good way to find a good match. I don't think patients should be made to apologize for preferring, say, a female rather than a male psychiatrist.

If friends and family can't make a referral and there is no family doctor, call the local mental health association, which usually has a list of good psychiatrists. Hospitals often have physician referral services too. If your town has a university with a medical school, there will be a department of psychiatry and often a faculty practice group. Don't be afraid to request a doctor who is male or female. Many psychiatrists also identify themselves as primarily serving African Americans, Hispanics, and other ethnic groups, as being affirmative of gay and lesbian orientation, and so forth. Often a community center has a list of doctors who serve the community, and this can be a resource. We are fortunate in this country to have community mental health centers serving almost every community. Their mandate from state, county, or other municipalities is to provide high-quality mental health care to all who apply for it, regardless of ability to pay. When finances are a problem, this is a valuable resource. The local community mental health center will also usually have a list of private-practice psychiatrists as well and will be glad to make a referral.

As with any medical problem, don't hesitate to get another opinion or to switch doctors if your needs are not being met or if the treating physician doesn't seem responsive enough.

## Living with a Mood Disorder

It is always frightening to be told you have an illness, even one that is treatable. Living with a mood disorder is trying for both sufferers and their families. This section will address some of the problems both groups have in living with a mood disorder.

### RELAPSE

Patients often ask me, "Will I need to take medication the rest of my life?" From the chapters on treatment, you have seen that mood disorders are episodic and that often, especially in major depression, the periods of remission can be long. Even in bipolar disorder there may be months or years between episodes. Yet the onset of an episode can be sudden, sometimes so sudden that there is not enough time to prevent some very uncomfortable symptoms that may persist for days or even weeks before treatment takes effect. Unfortunately there is no test (yet) the sufferer can have done, say, every six months to see if an episode of mood disorder is beginning. Thus, the patient who is not on medication must be vigilant to detect signs of recurrence.

In both major depression and bipolar disorder, sleep disturbance is often the earliest sign. If sleep problems persist more than a few days for no apparent reason, it's a good idea to get in touch with the treating physician. I mentioned in the section on sleep that sleep deprivation is thought to precipitate manic episodes in bipolar disorder. Some experts believe that keeping the biological clock "tuned" by observing regular bedtimes and rising times is extremely important in the control of mood symptoms. "Regularizing" one's life is one way to reduce many types of physical and mental stress and may lessen the chance of relapse.

Energy-level changes can also be an early sign of relapse. Low energy, fatigue, and lack of interest in school or work can be early signs of depression, and increased energy or decreased desire to rest and sleep can herald the onset of hypomania or the manic state. Family members are often the most accurate monitors. Those with mood disorders should resist the temptation to explain away exaggerated changes in mood that their families notice. Just as patients are often the last ones to see improvement after medication is started for depression, they may be the last to realize that an episode of mood disorder is beginning. In patients I have come to know well, I can notice small things like tenseness in the facial muscles and changes in posture that indicate the onset of an episode before the patients realize what is happening. Family members can often pick up these changes even earlier, and they bear listening to—by both the patient and the doctor.

There is a fine line, however, between this type of vigilance and an obsessive scrutiny of the patient's every thought and feeling. It can be very destructive and demoralizing to have someone ask, "Are you taking your medication?" every time one shows disappointment or enthusiasm over something. Having a mood disorder does not mean every change in mood might be abnormal.

Once correctly diagnosed and treated, most people with mood disorders quickly learn to differentiate between normal and abnormal feelings and thoughts. Many of my patients, even before they knew they were having episodes of affective disorder, had names for their episodes: "my gloomy spells," "my hyper days," and so forth. Once they understand the illness and, even more importantly, see the symptoms fade away with treatment, it's not difficult to recognize particular symptoms. As I said earlier, many patients can identify symptoms that are indicators for their episodes. "Whenever I find myself thinking about my grandmother's death and feeling guilty about it, I *know* it's starting," one of my patients once told me. The wife of one of my patients could tell when her husband was starting to have a manic episode by the number of phone calls he made. What is important is to pay serious attention to these symptoms and get the proper medical attention. Just as the heart patient who wants to stay well will never ignore chest pain, and the diabetic patient knows the symptoms of high blood sugar, the mood disorder patient should know the symptoms of relapse and get in touch with the doctor immediately when they occur.

If someone with a mood disorder who is not on medication should be especially vigilant for the appearance of symptoms, why stop taking medication? This is a very personal decision that should be made with great care and after talking at length with the doctor. Many people do not like to take medication, but it is the single most important step one can take to minimize the chance of relapse.

Some people say they resent having to take a medication that "controls" them. This is simply the wrong way to look at it. Antidepressants and lithium can no more control a person with a mood disorder than insulin controls a diabetic. On the contrary, just as diabetics use insulin to control their illness, these medications put patients back in charge of their lives rather than at the mercy of the disease.

## MEDICATION ISSUES

Medication is such an important part of the treatment of mood disorders that, in addition to making some general points about taking medicine, I want to reiterate some things about specific drugs used to treat mood disorders.

First, it is vital that patients be honest with the physician about taking or not taking medication. Some seem afraid to tell their doctors about side effects or to say a medication is not working as they expected. They think their doctors will be disappointed in them or get angry if they complain about their medication. I would much rather get a phone call one week into the treatment from a patient worried about a side effect than see that person at the next appointment and hear, "I only took the medication one day; it made me feel funny, so I stopped it two weeks ago."

The exact timing of taking these drugs is usually not crucial. Almost all the antidepressants build up in the body slowly and are removed slowly. For this reason it is not necessary to take the medicine several times a day; the entire dose can usually be taken at one time. (There are some exceptions to this, so ask your doctor.) This also means that taking these medications at a particular time of day is not usually important, although many of the sedating antidepressants are taken at night to promote sleep. I do not recommend that my patients "double up" if they miss a dose of antidepressant—that is, take twice as much the next day. In fact, to do so may bring on the medication's side effects. For example, one may be very sleepy the next day. Again, because the pace of buildup and removal is so slow, even a whole missed dose won't make a big difference to the level in the body.

Don't forget that the pharmacist is an expert on medication too. If a question comes up, odds are the pharmacist can answer it.

Remember that the amount of medication in the bloodstream rises after one takes a pill or capsule and then falls off until the next dose. It is important that a blood sample for a medication level be taken about twelve hours after the last dose. With most medications, this usually means not taking one's morning dose the day of the test until after the blood has been drawn.

Another point is that feeling back to normal does *not* mean the need for medication is over. Remember, unlike some other illnesses that medication can *cure,* in mood disorders, antidepressants and lithium *treat* the problem. They control the symptoms during the time the "mood system" isn't working correctly, and if they are stopped too soon, the symptoms can come right back. Stopping antidepressant medications or lithium less than six months after starting them places one at very high risk for relapse. Even stopping after less than a year is probably risky. Patients should ask themselves not "Why keep taking it?" but rather "Why *not* keep taking it?" If there aren't good answers to the second question, why take the risk?

Many patients ask if they can drink alcohol while on medication. Most experts are hesitant to absolutely forbid alcohol, and I am too. But if the medication is sedating, alcohol will increase the sedative effect, and one may seem very intoxicated after a relatively small amount of alcohol. For this reason it is important to watch oneself closely and go very slowly when using alcohol for the first time while taking medication. Some drugs, like lithium, have no sedative effect, and the interaction with alcohol is not significant. There is a broader issue concerning alcohol, however. When my patients ask, "How many drinks can I have?" I often retort, "That's like a diabetic asking how many chocolate cupcakes they can eat—the fewer the better!" Remember that alcohol is a destabilizer for the nervous system and seems to have even more of a destabilizing influence on mood.

## PSYCHOTHERAPY

What role does psychotherapy play in the treatment of mood disorders? Before I try to answer this question, it might be useful to talk for a moment about what psychotherapy is. Psychotherapy, defined as simply as possible, is the treatment of emotional problems by psychological means. Counseling, concerned listening, objective advice, education—all these ways of helping can be broadly considered psychotherapy. Psychotherapy is the process of helping people feel better by understanding themselves and learning new approaches to life's problems from a knowledgeable, experienced professional.

Counseling is a rather direct form of therapy that essentially consists of giving advice. A therapist who tends to give advice or make recommendations is also said to be practicing a *directive* form of therapy. Many therapists are taught that giving advice is not therapeutic, because the patient usually has already sought advice from others and knows the path to improvement but lacks the confidence to do the right things to feel better.

Psychotherapy based on the principles of Freud emphasizes the past, especially childhood, and teaches that traumatic or merely difficult experiences in early life can poison many later experiences and relationships because these forgotten traumas linger unresolved in the unconscious mind. Freudian or psychoanalytic therapy emphasizes that patients bring these unconscious memories to every new relationship, including that with the therapist, and that if the therapist is very passive, not injecting any of their own personality into the therapeutic encounter, these memories will cause patients to replay in the therapeutic relationship the fears, false hopes, and unrealistic expectations that cause them to have problems in life. Psychoanalysis is the most intensive form of Freudian psychotherapy.

Psychotherapy that emphasizes the interplay between inner mental experiences, memories, emotions, logic, conscience, and so forth is sometimes called *psychodynamic psychotherapy.*

Most psychotherapy contains elements of both the directive, advice-giving counseling style and also the more passive, analytic style of letting patients do the talking while the therapist points out inconsistent or illogical problem-solving attempts that patients must correct from their own inner resources.

There are nearly as many styles of therapy as there are therapists. These few paragraphs barely scratch the surface, but I think even this briefest of introductions indicates that whatever the style of psychotherapy, directive or analytical, it is an approach to helping patients that is very different from prescribing medication.

It is important to remember that for many years psychotherapy was practically the only approach available for helping persons with mood disorders, and that the biological concepts we now discuss in explaining mood disorders are comparatively recent. As biological theory and interventions such as medication and ECT were developed, there tended to be a division among psychiatrists about the comparative value placed on biological intervention (medication) and psychological intervention (psychotherapy). Psychiatrists considered themselves biologically oriented or dynamically oriented, but usually not both. In fact, not too long ago there was still a bit of name-calling between the two camps. The biologically oriented were said to be "pill pushers" who wrote prescriptions and didn't talk to their patients, and the dynamically oriented were "fuzzy-thinking" wimps who held "touchy-feely" sessions instead of being "real doctors." Fortunately this silly and certainly unproductive polarity has mostly disappeared, and few psychiatrists even talk about "therapeutic orientation" in these terms any longer.

Most patients with major depression or bipolar disorder are reassured when I tell them that they have a medical problem and that medication will make them better, but occasionally patients react to this explanation as if I were not taking their problems seriously. They want to talk about the issues that are on their minds, their guilty feelings, their perceived failures and inadequacies. It is important to realize that these issues are sometimes a by-product of the depression rather than the cause of it. Psychotherapy with depressed persons who have major depression consists of encouragement, support, education—not trying to get them to understand themselves better. When the sufferer is in the midst of a depression, psychotherapy, broadly defined, is definitely part of the treatment, but intensive psychotherapy with a goal of helping a person understand herself better and change her approach to life will not help—in fact, it may make things worse by putting too much responsibility for getting well on the patient. I want to emphasize, however, that support and encouragement are very important parts of treatment.

In "talking therapy," sometimes a lot of talking is necessary to figure out just what kind of therapy should be more important and what the relative importance of medication and psychotherapy should be. If you'll turn back to chapter 2 and review the case of Patty, you'll see what I mean. Patty was the teenager who seemed to have major depression but turned out to be going through some difficult adolescent problems. Her depression was actually a reaction to external events, not a biologically caused problem. Had I simply given Patty a prescription for antidepressants and sent her on her way, she might have been unhappy much longer. The opposite case, a major depression that seemed to be reactive, was illustrated in chapter 3 with the case of Alice.

In both these cases, several sessions—several hours of talking—were required to reach the deeper level of understanding necessary to make the proper diagnosis. As treatment continues, the role of psychotherapy in the treatment can change. In some cases, as the person's mood gets better, the "therapy" issues seem to evaporate and psychotherapy is no longer necessary. Often, however, even as a person's mood improves, it becomes clear that psychotherapy *will* be useful. Exploring one's life history and reflecting on inadequate approaches to life problems are inevitable when one talks about one's feelings for a few hours and has time between sessions to think about them. This often leads people to want to learn more about themselves and use this knowledge to adopt new coping strategies. These are the kinds of processes and goals accomplished in psychotherapy.

In the section on relapse, I mentioned the importance of regularizing life and cutting down on stress as a way to lessen the chances of episodes of mood disorders; psychotherapy can be a very important aspect of this. As we saw in the chapter on the heredity of mood disorders, these illnesses run in families, and a person who grew up in a family disrupted by the illness of a parent or another family member can carry many emotional scars into adulthood. As we have also seen, alcoholism can be associated with these illnesses, and those from homes where there was an alcohol problem are now known to frequently require psychotherapy to deal with their difficult childhoods and disrupted emotional maturation.

Don't forget that living from day to day with a mood disorder can often be, to say the least, a difficult task. If the illness is not diagnosed until several episodes have occurred, the consequences of manic behavior or prolonged depression can cause problems in one's career, one's relationships, and many other important areas of life. In people who are suffering with a mood disorder, past and present can seem to conspire to cause tribulation and distress even when the disorder itself is in remission. When this distress builds up, it may make an episode of illness more likely. The treatment for these sorts of problems is psychotherapy, and in many instances it needs to be part and parcel of the treatment of mood disorders.

Several forms of psychotherapy seem to be especially helpful in the treatment of depression, the most important being *cognitive therapy*. The person most closely associated with this form of psychotherapy is Dr. Aaron Beck who, along with several collaborators, has written many books and articles on depression and its treatment by cognitive therapy. In contrast to the more traditional passive role of the psychotherapist, the practitioner of cognitive therapy is quite active, asking questions, interrupting the patient, giving directions, and even assigning homework. Treatment focuses on current problems—here and now—and does not analyze the past in much detail. The basic premise of cognitive therapy (sometimes called *cognitive-behavioral therapy* because of the emphasis on changing behavior) is that persons with depression usually have attitudes or assumptions about the world and themselves (each assumption is called a *schema*) that can lead to negative thoughts, which in turn lead to or sustain depressed feelings and behaviors.

This theory of depression proposes that depressed persons come to view themselves as inadequate or defective and that they tend to attribute any disappointment or unpleasant experience to this supposed defect in themselves. This view leads to automatic thoughts like "I can't do anything right" whenever a problem comes up. A young woman burns dinner and the thought "I can't do anything right" pops into her head (despite the fact that she has cooked perfect dinners every night for weeks and weeks). The patient berates herself for every failure and never takes credit for (or even takes notice of) her successes. A vicious cycle of negative thoughts and depressed feelings begins.

The cognitive therapist works to get the patient to recognize his negative automatic thoughts (negative cognitions) and see the distortions caused by erroneous schemas. The connections between these thoughts and depressed feelings are identified and the patient is helped to replace negative thoughts with positive, reality-based thoughts and eventually to change their distorted view of themselves. (The young woman would replace "I can't do anything right" with something like "I make mistakes occasionally, but I'm basically a pretty competent person.")

Although some studies indicate that cognitive therapy can be as effective as medication in some patients, whether or not it can substitute for medical treatments is a subject of much disagreement. Nevertheless, this technique appears to offer benefit above and beyond traditional psychotherapy in the treatment of depression and is a welcome addition to the armamentarium of available treatment options for depression. Cognitive therapy for the treatment of bipolar disorder has also been developed.

Neither psychiatrists nor patients should close their minds to either the biological approach to helping mood disorders or the psychological. A combination of both is almost always the quickest way to recovery.

## TREATMENT OVER THE LONG TERM

Like other common illnesses such as high blood pressure and adult-onset diabetes, we now know that mood disorders are caused by a complex interaction of genetic risks and environmental factors. This has important implications for treatment over the long term.

A person's genetic makeup doesn't change over time; your genes, which can be thought of as a set of instructions for building and operating the body, were determined at the moment of conception, when one of your father's sperm, containing his genes, combined with your mother's egg, containing her genes.* The genes that we start out with operate our bodies throughout our lives. The implication this simple fact has for long-term treatment of mood disorders is that whatever genetic risks a person may have for a mood disorders will continue throughout their lifetime. Thus, long-term treatment for mood disorders will be the rule, not the exception.

However, the other important causal factor in mood disorders, our environment, is constantly changing—usually in quite unpredictable ways. We get a new job (or retire), get married (or divorced), have a baby, lose a parent. This list is nearly infinite. Some factors we can control (taking a new job), some we can't. Some changes we can see coming and prepare for (getting married, having a baby), some we may not see coming (the loss of a parent, getting laid off from a job and having financial problems). The implication this has for the long term is that a person who has had a serious depression or manic episode can never know when an event might occur that will cause the mood control system to break down again. He needs as much protection against this possibility as he can manage.

* To be accurate, only one-half of each parents' genes are in sperm and egg. Remember that organisms have a double set of chromosomes, with two of each gene. During the formation of the sex cells (sperm and egg), only one set is "packaged" and passed on to the offspring. Another way to think of this is that we inherit half of our genes from each parent.

These two implications both argue for the same conclusion: mood disorders need to be managed over the lifetime. Thinking about a major depressive episode or an episode of mania as a one-time illness—like pneumonia or a broken arm—doesn't make sense given what we know about the causes of these problems.

Imagine a man who is found to have consistently high blood pressure readings at his doctor's office. The doctor prescribes blood pressure medication. The patient goes in to see his doctor after being on his medication for a while and gets some good news: his blood pressure is now in the normal range. Would he say, "That's great, doc! I can stop taking this medication now, right?" Well, this doesn't really make sense, does it? We know that one normal blood pressure reading doesn't indicate that the condition has been cured. But we also know that if this man loses weight, watches his salt intake, and begins a regular exercise program, he may eventually be able to take a lower dose of medication and perhaps stop taking it completely.

Imagine a woman with diabetes who has been able to control her blood sugar by carefully watching her diet and exercising regularly. She develops a severe kidney infection: she is in severe pain, runs a high fever, can't eat or drink properly, and needs to be hospitalized. In the hospital, it is noted that her formerly well-controlled blood sugar levels are fluctuating wildly. The doctor decides to put her on insulin until the infection is gone and her blood sugars normalize. She asks the doctor, "Does this mean my diabetes is much worse? Will I have to have insulin injections for the rest of my life?" Not at all. We know that when the body of a person with diabetes is under extreme stress from a severe infection, their already impaired ability to regulate blood sugar breaks down still further, and they need more intensive treatment, in the form of insulin treatment, to get their blood sugar under control. The chances are that when the patient is over her infection, what worked before (diet and exercise) will once more be sufficient to keep her symptoms under control.

Like high blood pressure and diabetes, mood disorders must be managed over time with the goal of keeping symptoms under good control. Mood disorders must continually be treated because they cannot be cured. This means that symptoms must be watched and monitored regularly and that treatments will probably change over time as difficulties and stressful events arise and resolve and as the illness goes through its own fluctuations. For reasons we don't understand, medications that once worked well for a patient can sometimes begin to work less well, and the patient will have breakthrough symptoms. Raising the dose can sometimes take care of this problem. Sometimes a switch to a different medication or combination of medications is needed. After a period of stability, doses of medication can sometimes be lowered and a medication discontinued. These facts argue for continuing in treatment with a physician—a psychiatrist if possible—over the long term.

Some people are fortunate to have a very treatment-responsive illness. Perhaps the first antidepressant they are prescribed works well for them (unfortunately, this happens only about 50 percent of the time). Many others must try several medications before one works; perhaps they need to take a combination of medications (now the rule rather than the exception in bipolar disorder) with changes in dosing over time. A person may take one medication for long periods of time but need to be on two during times of stress and difficulties.

My point here is that many persons with mood disorders will see their treatments change over time as their symptoms change. Perhaps the one predictable quality of mood disorders is that they are often very unpredictable. This means that the treatment plan needs to be constantly reassessed for effectiveness and changes in treatment crafted to address problems as they arise.

## THE DEPRESSIVE LIFESTYLE

If a person has struggled with depression over a long period of time, it is possible, especially if the depression has been serious and not aggressively treated, for him to get trapped in what I call the "depressive lifestyle." A person with longer-term depression has often lost interest in many of his usual activities. He may have stopped pursuing avocations such as sports or hobbies and has perhaps even stopped working. He may go out less often with friends, who eventually stop extending invitations.

Shopping can be chore, so, especially if the individual lives alone, the refrigerator is empty and diet becomes unhealthy. This, together with lack of exercise, results in lower energy level and less restful sleep. Perhaps he's stopped attending church or synagogue, dropped out of clubs, stopped gardening or volunteering, or going to sports or cultural events. He gradually loses touch with the people, places, and things that had been sources of pleasure and satisfaction and kept him involved in the world. Eventually, the structure of his life becomes dilapidated, even bleak.

A vicious cycle has been set up: the symptoms of depression have resulted in an environment that makes the depression worse. One day is just like the next; with nothing much to look forward to, day blends into night into the next day.

It's important to talk about this issue because this lifestyle trap makes getting better from depression more difficult. Patients who get into treatment after the depressive lifestyle has become established and experience improvement in their mood will still be hampered by this environment from making progress as quickly as they would otherwise.

I once had a patient who had taken early retirement in the midst of a severe depression. After he stopped working, he'd basically retreated to the home because he was so crippled by anxiety and depression. His depression was very resistant to treatment, and it was over a year before he got the definitive treatment that improved his condition significantly. When his mood finally started to get better, he was suddenly faced with all the complicated issues that retiring persons face: the change in self-concept that comes with the end of working life, for example. It was as if after breaking through one brick wall—severe depression—he had run into another. Because his social life had largely revolved around work friends, friends he now had much less in common with, he felt isolated. He didn't know what to do with all the time he now had on his hands because he'd never had many interests outside of work and family. At one point when he was nearly better, he told me he felt a little like Rip Van Winkle: "It's as if I went into a long, dark tunnel and now that I've come out the other end, I don't know where I am!" Because of the depressive lifestyle he'd been living for a year (not willingly, of course), the work of getting better was much harder—there was simply a lot more to do than if he'd just been out of work for a week or two. He no longer had the support system he'd once had—the structure of the regular work schedule, the support system of coworkers and friends—not to mention that he hadn't been able to prepare for retirement the way he otherwise would have.

There are two main points to note here. One is that it is very important not to let the depressive lifestyle take over. This means aggressive treatment and not giving up—neither the patient nor the doctor—as long as the patient is still impaired from usual activities. If the depression threatens to make a major impact, if going on long-term disability is being considered, for example, it's time to visit a major medical center for a consultation and consider hospitalization or ECT.

The other point is that the person who has been depressed for a long period of time will need more than medication to get back to their usual level of functioning. Psychotherapy is especially important for these patients to help them deal with all the complicated issues that emerging from the depressive lifestyle brings them face to face with and to give them the support and encouragement that their depleted environment no longer gives them. The term *rehabilitation* can be applied to this aspect of treatment. Just as a person needs help readjusting to the environment after a lengthy illness such as surgery and chemotherapy for cancer, the person who's recovering from a long and severe bout of depression (or mania for that matter) needs extra psychological support. I'll be discussing occupational therapy and support groups later in this chapter, interventions that can be extremely valuable for these patients and can significantly expedite their recovery in a way that medication alone cannot.

Mood disorders are potentially fatal illnesses. Self-destructive thoughts and impulses and even suicide attempts are not uncommon in persons suffering from these illnesses. The intensely sad and oppressive feelings mood disorders cause can make life itself seem a difficult, even overwhelming, burden. Minimizing the risk of self-destructive behavior is a necessary part of living with a mood disorder and needs to be discussed in detail.

Perhaps the most effective means of minimizing the risk for suicide is the prevention of episodes of illness. This may seem so obvious as to not bear discussion, yet, as with many ideas that may seem obvious, it is a rather profound truth. Relapse prevention is really suicide prevention, and I invite you to reread the preceding sections dealing with relapse with this idea in mind. Persons with mood disorders should know well all the signs and symptoms of relapse and not hesitate to get in touch with their doctor should they notice these changes. The best preventative action of all in dealing with suicide is to prevent relapse.

Nevertheless, despite the best efforts of all involved, relapses do occur, and the symptoms of a recurrent depression may include suicidal thoughts. The appearance of self-destructive thoughts and impulses is in itself very frightening, both to the patient and to those around him. For many centuries, tremendous stigma and disgrace has been associated with suicide, and this sense of shamefulness still makes some people reluctant to discuss these thoughts when they occur. These ideas, similar to the common misconception that "only crazy people kill themselves," only complicate what is really a simple clinical issue: suicidal thoughts and behavior are a complication of a medical illness, a serious complication that warrants immediate medical attention. For this reason, involvement of a mental health professional to assess the situation and make recommendations is a necessary and very appropriate first step.

Another common misconception about suicide is that asking a person if they are thinking of harming themselves will "plant the idea" and may thus increase the chances of suicide. There is no scientific evidence to support this idea; indeed, many persons who are having suicidal feelings are relieved to be able to talk about them.

Prediction of suicide is very difficult, but one feeling that seems to be associated with suicide attempts is hopelessness. Depressed people who express hopelessness, believe there is "no way out," or feel trapped may be at high risk of self-injurious behavior. Those close to the patient with depression need to become familiar and comfortable with words they can use to ask about suicide: "Are you bothered by feelings that life isn't worth living?" "Are you having thoughts about hurting yourself?" If there is even a hint that the answer may be yes, professional assessment of the situation is necessary. Avoiding the subject may cause the afflicted person to conceal self-destructive thoughts and feelings until they feel overwhelmed and then act on them suddenly.

To reiterate, mental health professionals know how to assess the risk and what steps to take. Change of medication, dosage increase, more frequent therapy visits, hospitalization—there are many options. As I said earlier, discussing these thoughts with a professional trained in the assessment of the potentially self-destructive person can be very encouraging and reassuring for everyone involved and may in itself resolve the situation.

I want to emphasize that professionals can help best in making treatment decisions. If a member of the family with a history of heart problems suddenly developed chest pain, the family wouldn't try to decide whether or not to change medication or hospitalize—the doctor would be called immediately! The appearance of suicidal thoughts should be treated in the same way. It is a serious symptom; its appearance calls for cool heads and a contingency plan. Everyone should know who to call and not hesitate to do so.

Every year or so I will see a patient in my office who is depressed and, after reassuring myself during the interview that the risk of suicide is low, will send them home only to get a panicked phone call from a spouse or parent, "Why didn't you put her in the hospital? Didn't she tell you she had asked me where she could buy a gun?" Contrary to popular belief, psychiatrists cannot read minds! Suicidal thoughts may be accompanied by feelings of shame, or felt by the patient to indicate weakness or being "really far gone," and so might be concealed. It's important to remember that just as there are things a person will tell their therapist and not their family, the converse is true as well. Also, suicidal thoughts, like the mood itself in depression, can change throughout the day or be present on some days and not on others, or at some times of day and not others. All these factors may contribute to the patient not revealing these thoughts to the doctor. The family should not assume that the doctor will figure out in a brief interview everything that they have been observing for weeks or even months. Another key in suicide prevention is free communication—patient, family, and psychiatrist all need to be talking to each other.

Ironically, when people are getting better from their depression they are often more vulnerable to suicide. Sometimes severely depressed persons are so lethargic that *any* action is too much of an effort. When they are getting a bit better and begin to have more energy, it can be a dangerous time. In the next section I will discuss involuntary treatment. When someone is suicidal or even possibly suicidal, one should not hesitate to invoke the legal procedures available to get them the help they need.

Here are a few very simple and practical recommendations that will reduce the risk of suicide and that need to be in place not just during a crisis, but every day in a household in which a person with a mood disorder resides.

I have already mentioned that it is important for people with mood disorders to avoid alcohol. Abstinence becomes even more critical if depression has set in, and it is essential if suicidal feelings develop. Alcohol is disinhibiting—that is, it causes people to lose their inhibitions and become more impulsive. It's not difficult to see how dangerous this is in the depressed person. A significant percentage of persons who commit suicide are intoxicated when they do so; alcohol should be scrupulously avoided by depressed persons.

Suicide prevention measures also include throwing out old and leftover medications and asking family members to take possession of the pill bottles of current medications.

Persons with mood disorders who have access to firearms must seriously examine their need for such. Some studies indicate that in places with more strict gun control laws, there are lower suicide rates. What is true in a population as a whole probably has application in the case of the individual. Is the risk of access to a highly lethal means of self-destruction justifiable for a person at greater risk of suicide than the average person? The answer seems obvious to me: persons with mood disorders should not have guns in the house—ever.

Suicidal persons are almost always ambivalent; they do not want to die but feel they have little choice or option. Patients with mood disorders need to recognize that when the light at the end of the tunnel seems to fade out, this itself is a symptom of their disease, not something to be acted on. Even though mood disorders do not often cause the affected person to lose touch with reality, their perception of reality is colored by the mood state.

When I was in the third grade, I flunked an eye exam at school and was taken off to the optometrist to get glasses. I'll never forget the first time I wore them. I was astonished at the clarity and brilliance of objects as ordinary as street signs and fire hydrants and was jolted to realize that my view of the world had been so dim and foggy without my even knowing it. Perception is reality. The depressed individual must not make judgments about the heaviness of his burden in life. His perception, his reality, is distorted, fuzzy, and inaccurate. The pessimism and hopelessness he feels are the hallmarks of illness; they are symptoms to be treated, not true feelings to be acted upon. At the risk of sounding flippant, I want to quote something a colleague once said to me: "Suicide is a permanent solution to a *temporary* problem." Perhaps this should be the guiding principle and motto in suicide prevention.

"Ruth certainly needs some help, but she doesn't need to be *here*," Ruth's friend told me.

"Here" was the psychiatric unit of the finest general hospital in town. It was only two years old, staffed by expert psychiatric nurses, social workers with mental health backgrounds, occupational therapists, and other professionals. There was no lock on the door; the cafeteria and dining room for patients in an adjacent wing were also used by the hospital to provide dinner when the board of trustees met. The decor was beautiful and pleasant, like the dormitory of an expensive school or perhaps the executive conference and retreat center of a big corporation.

Ruth's family doctor had been almost frantic on the phone that morning. "You must see this patient *today*. I've been trying to get her to see you for weeks because I haven't been able to get her depressive symptoms under control, but she's kept putting it off. Two of her friends brought her in today because she isn't sleeping, hasn't eaten in two days, and can't stop crying. Also, she told me she was beginning to have suicidal thoughts."

When I saw Ruth, she had been distraught and could hardly speak without bursting into tears. She had small children at home, felt overwhelmed by the demands of their care, and was beginning to think that she was a bad mother to them. Her husband was out of town at a business meeting, and she was terrified of being alone. Her friends had been up all night trying to soothe and calm her. I agreed with her family doctor that she was having a major depressive episode.

"I want to admit you to Memorial Hospital; I think it would be best for you to be someplace where someone can take care of you, where you won't have to worry about your home responsibilities. I want to be a bit more aggressive with medications for depression, and this means you might be a bit sedated at first. In the hospital there'll be nurses to check your blood pressure and so forth; they know these medications and can be on the lookout for any side effects or other problems. We can change the treatment plan daily or even hourly if need be."

"Whatever you think is best," was her feeble reply. She was exhausted.

I called the hospital, and there was an empty bed. I sent Ruth home with her friends to get some clothes and toiletries and told them I would meet them at the hospital that afternoon.

When I got to the hospital to write admission orders and get Ruth's treatment started, I was surprised to find her and her friends in the visitors' waiting room. Her bags at her side, she looked as if she was ready to leave rather than to be admitted.

"Doctor, I'm frightened. I don't know if this is the right thing to do. I don't know if this is the right place for me."

"Of course you feel frightened," I said. "No one likes to be in the hospital, and besides, depression makes people feel frightened and uneasy about everything. You'll be in good hands here." I looked to her friends to support me.

I was flabbergasted at one friend's reply: "Couldn't you just give her some sleeping pills and see her as an outpatient?"

I thought to myself, "With friends like you, who needs enemies?" (Psychiatrists probably do more tongue biting than any other medical specialists.)

"Wouldn't it be better for me to be home with my family, in my own house? I don't feel very relaxed in the hospital. I'm not sure I could sleep."

"You told me you were up all last night. I don't think tonight would be much better even with sleeping pills. If being at home with your family was what you needed, you'd be feeling better by now. This is the best psychiatric unit in the city, and we were lucky to get you a bed today. Usually there's a waiting list of several days."

"I don't know what to do."

"Of course you don't. Depression makes people indecisive and unsure of themselves. That's why you came to see me—right? Because you don't know how to help yourself, and you need expert advice. I think you will get better much more quickly in the hospital. I'll be able to be more aggressive with medication doses here." I found I was repeating myself.

"Couldn't I be on a regular medical floor? You could see me every day there."

"Medical floors are noisy and upsetting even for someone who is not depressed. The staff here is experienced in helping with depression. They know how to care for people with symptoms like being frightened and anxious. On a medical floor the staff will give you your medication, but they won't be available to talk or be very reassuring. They're too busy. Also, you need to learn about depression and medication for depression, and your family will want to be involved in your recovery. We have special meetings for family members here to help everyone learn about depression and its treatment."

"Won't it be depressing for me to be around other depressed people or people with worse problems?" Ruth asked.

"Most people find it's comforting to know that others have the same kind of problems, and seeing that you're not the sickest person in the hospital can be a comfort too."

Ruth finally listened to the person she was paying for expert advice—me—and admitted herself to the hospital. As I expected, she was soon home again and feeling much better.

---

Just as some people still have misconceptions about psychiatrists, they also have misconceptions about psychiatric hospitalization. Many of these misconceptions are based on some unfortunate facts about psychiatric treatment in the distant past. You've heard the horror stories and seen the old movies, so I won't repeat those facts except to say that in the days when there was essentially no effective medical treatment for any psychiatric problem, many people with psychiatric illnesses received inadequate care, under poor conditions, in understaffed, poorly funded state hospitals. Fortunately, those days are over.

What are modern psychiatric hospitals and psychiatric units in general hospitals like? Since people with psychiatric illnesses are not usually physically incapacitated or "sick" in a physical sense, psychiatric hospitals, or psychiatric units of general hospitals, are a bit different from medical or surgical units. Patients wear regular clothes, not pajamas or nightgowns, and do not spend much time in their rooms. Psychiatric units are often laid out much like a school dormitory, with bedrooms, a large sitting area or common area, and perhaps some lounges in addition to the usual nursing station and other staff areas. Patients usually eat together in a dining area. They are often responsible for getting their own medication from the nursing station rather than lying in bed and having it brought to them.

There are almost always several group meetings each week, where patients are encouraged to discuss the symptoms that brought them into the hospital. Staff members lead these groups and help people share and learn from one another. Because chemical dependence complicates so many psychiatric problems, AA meetings or other meetings on this subject are sometimes held on the unit.

Besides the doctor, who leads the treatment team and is ultimately responsible for treatment, there are many other staff members who help in the recovery process. Social workers, who usually have special training in working with families, often meet with family members to gather information that will help the doctor educate both patient and family about the treatment. They also can help patients make practical arrangements during and after the hospitalization, such as planning treatment after discharge, finding child care, coordinating transportation home, and coping with insurance and Social Security issues. They often do family therapy or marriage counseling as well, if the psychiatrist requests it.

Almost all units provide some diversions, too. Patients who are depressed often feel like just lying around or restlessly pacing the floor. A physical therapist is often on the hospital staff, and exercise is encouraged—perhaps stretching exercises and calisthenics once a day—to stimulate appetite and promote sleep. Many hospitals have exercise rooms, even gymnasiums and pools. Occupational therapists provide opportunity for more focused activities, such as craft projects. Especially in depression, people tend to be inwardly focused and preoccupied, and a simple project like potting some seedlings or painting a figurine can help them think about something besides their bad feelings for a time, letting them experience the little victory of accomplishing something and seeing the results. Also, occupational therapy provides the doctor with a valuable tool for assessing progress. It gives trained staff an opportunity to observe and measure improvement (or lack thereof) of problems such as impaired concentration, restlessness in depression or motor agitation in mania, impaired self-confidence, or irritability. Occupational therapy is much more than "arts and crafts," however; the name of this specialty comes from its focus on how persons with illness *occupy* their time. Psychiatric occupational therapists are very helpful for people who have drifted into what can be called a "depressive lifestyle."

Psychiatric nurses are the glue that holds a good program together. Nurses encourage, nurture, support, and comfort their patients and answer their questions, and they record all kinds of information for the psychiatrist, from blood pressure and weight to how many hours of sleep a patient had. Good nurses don't just carry out the doctor's orders; they ask the doctor questions and make suggestions. Many hospitals have a "primary nurse" system, in which one nurse is assigned to coordinate care throughout the patient's stay and be a consistent contact between the patient and the rest of the staff.

What kinds of psychiatric problems call for hospitalization? Just as with any other medical problem, the hospital is necessary when symptoms are so severe that people's ability to care for themselves and their families is disrupted, when they need speedy assessment and diagnosis because of rapid appearance of or change in their symptoms, or when an intensity of treatment is warranted that is not possible in an outpatient setting. In earlier chapters I described some of the more serious symptoms of mood disorders—delusions and severe agitation. These symptoms require hospitalization. Sometimes hospitalization is a good idea to *prevent* these symptoms. ECT almost always requires hospitalization (though some hospitals will allow outpatient ECT if the patient will have plenty of care and supervision at home). I also mentioned how hospitalization might be indicated to intensify treatment when disability threatens employment.

Hospitalization speeds up the process of recovery. Instead of taking several weeks to get to know a patient, with the help of a good staff I can make a much better assessment in a day or two. In the hospital, staff members can objectively measure how much the patient is sleeping or eating, and progress is assessed daily by professionals. Treatments, especially medications that are not working, can be changed immediately. Problems can be more easily treated before they become too severe. When a person starts on lithium or antidepressants, blood tests can be done daily if necessary, so the therapeutic dose can be reached quickly. Side effects can be monitored and treated at once.

If the patient is having suicidal thoughts, hospitalization is necessary. Also, patients who are having aggressive feelings, as sometimes happens in the manic state, can be helped to control their impulses much better in the hospital. Hospitalization is a good idea if symptoms are severe or if the patient is in danger of deteriorating—in any situation where time is of the essence.

Do freestanding psychiatric hospitals have advantages over psychiatric units in general hospitals? I think there are advantages and disadvantages to each. The general hospital with a good psychiatric program may be the first choice for those whose health is frail, perhaps because they have been depressed for a long time and are malnourished or dehydrated, because they are elderly, or because they have another illness. The general hospital has more medical support—laboratories, an x-ray department, a large medical staff with many specialties, and other resources.

The advantage of freestanding psychiatric hospitals perhaps is their less "medical" quality. They tend to be smaller and may have more amenities such as a large cafeteria, exercise rooms, meeting rooms, and occupational therapy rooms.

Perhaps the best of both worlds can be found in the university medical center. Because these hospitals are large, they also have large units devoted to psychiatry, and so may have the amenities and physical facilities of the freestanding hospitals and also the range of medical support of the general hospital. That they are part of a medical school means the latest in treatment is often accessible, perhaps including new medications not available to other hospitals. In difficult cases of mood disorders, a trip to a different part of the state or even out of state to go to a university medical center may be well worth the effort.

Sometimes my patients come to the hospital thinking they will be put to bed and left alone to "rest." One patient asked me, "Isn't there a hospital where I don't have to participate in all these activities?" "There is," I replied, "but I don't admit my patients there unless there are no other beds available in town." Good psychiatric programs encourage, even insist upon, activity rather than passivity, socialization rather than withdrawal, and active sharing, learning, and helping each other rather than isolation. They promote wellness and recovery by pushing patients to be as independent and as responsible for their recovery as possible.

## STIGMA

Unfortunately, there is still stigma attached to any type of psychiatric disorder, and mood disorders are no exception. One patient of mine was doing extremely well on lithium for some months after having been ill for nearly a year because she had been incorrectly diagnosed. She told me she was becoming serious about a young man. "When and how do I tell him I take medication to keep my mood stable?" I had no easy answer for her. "What do I tell people when they ask me why I was in the hospital?" patients often ask.

I suppose a good basic fact to remember is that one's medical history is very properly considered a private matter. Those who feel compelled to share every detail of their gallbladder operations with anyone who will listen probably don't realize just how boring these details really are. On the other hand, people who probe even brief acquaintances for information about what a biopsy showed, what medication they are taking, and so forth are going far beyond the boundaries of politeness and good taste and should simply be told that those are personal matters that bear no discussion. Medical records are strictly confidential and cannot be released to anyone without the patient's permission. Some states require special kinds of permission for release of psychiatric records.

Close friends and family will understand about a mood disorder, though they may need some educating. A trusted friend or coworker, someone whom you would feel comfortable discussing any other serious medical matter with and who is in a position to help and support, will be able to handle a mood disorder just as well as any other personal matter. My patients are often surprised at how much support they get when they least expect it. I don't know how many times a patient has told me they were worried about telling their boss about their depression only to have the boss say something like, "My wife was in the hospital last year for depression. I understand what you're going though." Remember that serious depression is a *very* common illness. There are few people whose lives have not been touched by it at some time.

Sometimes patients with a mood disorder ask me, "Do I have a mental illness?" I usually tell them that they certainly have an illness, and that since the most prominent symptoms—feelings, thoughts, and behaviors—are in the realm of things considered "mental" rather than "physical" as most laymen understand those terms, "Well yes, I suppose you do." Unfortunately, the term *mental illness* has come to have all kinds of negative connotations beyond this clumsy definition. Some of the myths are that people with mental illness are dangerous; that mental illness is untreatable; that the symptoms of mental illness are bizarre and shocking; and that victims of mental illness, indeed their whole families, are somehow cursed or tainted.

I won't go through these myths and refute them one by one, for if you have read the other chapters you know such horrors certainly do not apply to mood disorders. Not so long ago these very same myths were held to be true of two other forms of "mental illness"—that is, illnesses with behavioral symptoms—epilepsy and mental retardation. At one time those with epilepsy were confined in state mental hospitals. People with mental retardation were once considered physically dangerous as well as sexually aggressive, and therefore were seen as needing lifelong institutional confinement to protect the community. Education has largely removed the stigma associated with epilepsy and mental retardation, but the connotations of shame, dangerousness, and unpredictability remain with the term *mental illness*. It may be a term to be tossed out of our vocabulary—put into the trash bin with *madness* and *insanity*.

## Community Support and National Organizations

There are more and more organizations in this country dedicated to helping persons with mood disorders and their families understand these illnesses, improving access to good treatment, and most importantly, providing support when times get tough. The Mental Health Association, the oldest of these organizations, was founded at the turn of the century by Clifford Beers, a man who had bipolar disorder and who had been mistreated in asylums. His autobiography, *A Mind That Found Itself*, was influential in American mental health treatment reform. The Mental Health Association, with chapters all over the country, carries on Beers' work in its efforts to provide advocacy for those with psychiatric problems, educate the public about mental health issues, and reduce the stigma of psychiatric illnesses and their treatment. (See "Support and Advocacy Organizations" at the back of this book for a listing of national organizations, with their addresses and phone numbers.)

Scan your newspaper to learn about workshops and lectures on mood disorders and their treatment, sponsored by hospitals, medical schools, and community mental health centers in your area. Your local community mental health center will have a board of directors or community advisory board that would probably welcome your input and feedback. Through membership on such boards, people with mood disorders can have a very direct voice in the development of services and the structure and activities of these agencies.

## The Family

The problems and challenges of recovery and the control of mood disorders affect the entire family. Since the illness can be lifelong, one person's problems can affect several generations. The first task each family member must accomplish is to *understand*. There are so many misconceptions and myths about psychiatric illness, psychiatry, and psychiatric medication that seem ingrained in American thinking that those with mood disorders need all the support and allies they can get. What patients do not need is someone telling them to "shape up" or "snap out of it." The most destructive and cruel thing one can do is to criticize them for being weak or lazy or for having "no willpower."

Perhaps the most important role for family members is to guide the patient into proper treatment and support their staying in treatment. In mood disorders, the affected person often resists treatment; in fact, resistance can be part of the illness.

## How to Help with Depression

Depressed people can be unmotivated, lethargic, and perhaps irritable and complaining. They are pessimistic and self-blaming, and thus tend to reject the idea that any treatment will help. Depression makes people avoid social contact, and this too may make getting them to accept treatment difficult. "What can a doctor do?" is a common question. Those unfamiliar with the medical basis of depression can often see little point in seeing a doctor for a problem with their feelings.

Sometimes this resistance is so frustrating that family members are tempted to give in to the patient's lack of interest in treatment. "You can't help someone who doesn't want help, can you?" Well, sometimes you can. The very important point here is that mood disorders can cripple a vital aspect of the healing process: *the anticipation of getting well.* With this temporary disability, the depressed person is severely handicapped in the ability to seek and continue in treatment. Since some degree of hopelessness is almost always a symptom of the illness, expending energy in the pursuit of getting well seems a waste of time, even a cruel joke.

This is where family and friends come in. *They* must be the source of support and optimism in treatment. When a patient says that medication is not helping and that there's no use in taking it, their spouse, parent, child—whoever—needs to insist that they keep on and that they must not get caught up in the tendency to avoid treatment. Depressed persons sometimes seem to be trying to make others as pessimistic as they are. I sometimes tell family members who wonder why their relative is so complaining and rejecting, "It's the illness talking." It's important not to listen too closely to such talk and to remember that this attitude will disappear when the illness is successfully treated.

Most of all, one must not blame the patient for symptoms or be critical of uncooperativeness. It is crucial to remember that this pessimism and resistance are symptomatic of the illness. To criticize the depressed person for resisting treatment is like blaming someone with a broken leg for not being able to walk. I hope that by now I need not even mention that the symptoms of major depression (and the other mood disorders, for that matter) are beyond the patient's ability to control and that blaming the victim of the disease is very wrong.

On the other hand, one must not let the depressed person remain too passive, and sometimes firmness is necessary. It may seem cruel to make depressed people get out of bed and go to a doctor's appointment when they complain of feeling so bad, but it's the only way for them to get better.

A phrase I've come to use a lot to counter pessimism and resistance is "I'm confident." Friends and family members of people with mood disorders may find it helpful to say things like:

— "I know you don't feel a lot better yet, but I've noticed some improvement, and I'm confident you'll feel better soon."
— "The doctor has started this medication, and I'm confident of his ability to help, so I'm going to remind you to take it every day."
— "I know you don't feel like going shopping, but the doctor said you should be doing as many normal things as possible. I'm confident you'll feel better once we get there."

To feel confident themselves, family members must be armed with knowledge about the illness and work in conjunction with the treating physician to bring about recovery. The spouse or another family member (one person should be appointed in larger families) should accompany the patient to appointments and should be in the office during at least part of the visit; the doctor will appreciate having an objective observer reporting. Remember, the patient's reports will always be colored by the symptoms of the illness, and objective information about improvement or lack of improvement is vital in making treatment decisions. There is little guidance available from the clinical laboratory or radiology department in making these decisions; only observations will help. The family can be the doctor's eyes and ears in the home and provide valuable information.

Many family members ask how much to expect from people recovering from depression. Should they go to work, to school? Basically, I encourage depressed patients to do as many normal things as they possibly can, even if they must force themselves. Though they may lack the motivation to attend to regular duties, when they do complete them they often feel a bit better for having done so. This is a good rule of thumb: *Try to do as much of what you normally do as you possibly can.* Family members should encourage this.

On the other hand, it does no good to force too much, and relatives shouldn't nag or badger the patient. Remember that depressed people are feeling guilty enough from their illness; feeling that they are failing their families too will only add to their distress. They should be encouraged to do those things they can do successfully, especially diverting and physically stimulating activities like exercise, shopping, or gardening. On the other hand, they should be encouraged to stop trying to attend to tasks they aren't doing well; failing to succeed at school or work will only add to feelings of guilt and worthlessness.

## WHEN THE PATIENT DOESN'T *WANT* HELP

The family's role in helping a person who is becoming manic can be trying, even painful, but it is extremely vital. The terrible dilemma with this mental state is that patients can feel very *good.* More often they feel irritable and angry. In either case, sometimes they absolutely refuse any kind of help. Just as depression colors one's vision of the world so that help seems useless, mania can make help seem unnecessary or even threatening. As I hope I made clear earlier, mania can be a dangerous condition (see chapter 4), and early intervention is important.

Our legal system recognizes this problem and provides legal mechanisms to get impaired people the treatment they require even when their symptoms blind them to their need for it. Every state has laws allowing those who are suffering from a psychiatric condition and showing severe symptoms to be evaluated for treatment, against their will if necessary. Sometimes invoking these laws is the only way to get a manic person into treatment. Several sources of information are available about these laws and the procedure for getting someone into treatment. Probably the best source is the local community mental health center, because the staff frequently performs such evaluations. General hospital emergency room staff members also will be familiar with the procedure.

Often a family member must visit the local city hall, courthouse, or police station and give information directly to a magistrate or judge. If on hearing the information the official agrees that a psychiatric evaluation is warranted, an order of some kind will be executed allowing the police or sheriff to transport the patient to the community mental health center, an emergency room, or a psychiatric unit, depending on local procedures. Often police or deputies have special training in dealing with psychiatric patients, and occasionally they will be accompanied by mental health workers to pick up an ill person. The appearance of these authority figures frequently has a calming effect on even the most agitated patients, and people often become much more accepting of the need to get help.

This initial procedure, which allows the authorities to act on the word of family or friends and bring people for evaluation, usually allows only that—an evaluation—and has a short time limit, usually less than forty-eight hours. During this time patients must be examined by a physician, sometimes two physicians, and must be found to meet certain criteria for continued treatment against their will. The criteria vary from state to state but usually include finding that a patient suffers from a psychiatric condition requiring treatment, and that without treatment, he may deteriorate, be violent or suicidal, or otherwise show impaired judgment. A doctor or several doctors can determine that these criteria are met and admit the patient to a hospital. It is essential that a family member talk to the doctor making the evaluation, because direct and objective information must be recorded about the patient's behavior that indicates the need for treatment. Patients who want to avoid treatment can sometimes "pull themselves together" for the doctor, and family members who think the symptoms and need for treatment are so obvious that they need not accompany their relative to the evaluation may find the patient back home in a few hours.

After the physician admits the patient to the hospital, there is always a hearing by a magistrate, judge, or hearing officer, usually a few days after the admission. This hearing determines that the involuntary admission was proper and legal and that the patient does indeed meet criteria for involuntary hospitalization. This is usually done in the hospital, often in a conference room with only a few people present. Although it is a legal proceeding, it is not a big courtroom scene; it is private and there is an effort not to intimidate anyone.

It is important to remember that involuntary treatment involves curtailing a person's freedom and that the law takes it very seriously. There are safeguards to prevent the abuse of these laws, which in some countries makes a mockery of psychiatry and medicine when innocent people with "sick" political views are imprisoned in so-called hospitals. Patients either are assigned an attorney or are allowed to bring their own advocate. Again, it is important that the family be present so that the facts about the person's illness and symptoms can be presented directly by objective observers. If it is clear that treatment is needed to avoid a dangerous situation, the person will be committed to the hospital for a limited period. The doctor can always discharge the patient sooner, but if hospitalization is still necessary at the expiration of the time limit, another hearing must be held.

In some states involuntary treatment of outpatients is possible. The procedures for this type of commitment are usually similar to those for hospitalization. Again, the local community mental health center is the best source of information about these options.

Legal procedures to get a person into a hospital and into treatment do only that. The patient does not lose any other rights, and property or testamentary rights and privileges are not in any way affected.

## OTHER FAMILY ISSUES

Mood disorders take a toll on the family of the affected person as well as on the patient. Living with a depressed person can be demoralizing even for those who do not suffer from the illness, and the manic state can cause great upheaval in the family. As with any other illness that can have a long course, everyone can simply get very tired of dealing with it. Family members need to take care of their own needs for support and encouragement to prevent getting "burned out."

We clinicians can derive support from our colleagues. We go to conventions and meetings to keep up on the latest developments and see the improvements in treatment and the new discoveries that will make our work more effective. Most of all, these activities allow us to reaffirm to ourselves that we are doing good work, and practicing with high standards, and that everyone has challenging patients and feels discouraged at times—that this is not a sign of lack of dedication or commitment. Family members need the same kind of support, and they can get it by participating in the treatment of their relative and by getting involved in organizations that have the same goals—improving the care of those with psychiatric disorders (see "Community Support and National Organizations" in this chapter).

Family members of a person with a mood disorder may at some time find that they need mental health treatment. Sometimes the frustrations and challenges of caring for a person with a severe mood disorder trigger feelings of demoralization and discouragement or anger and resentment. In helping someone else deal with emotional problems, caretakers should be aware of their own emotional needs and get support and treatment when their inner resources are strained. Remember that mental health professionals can help with all kinds of unhappiness, and the unhappiness that can arise from a family member's illness is no exception.

# CHAPTER 8

# Summing Up and Looking Ahead

FIFTEEN YEARS AGO, I WROTE THE FIRST EDITION OF THIS BOOK TO HELP fill a void that became apparent to me when I first started seeing patients in a general psychiatric practice. I saw that many people who came to me for treatment, including highly educated and well-informed people—even people who ran multimillion dollar businesses or were highly trained professionals—hadn't a clue as to the medical basis of the depression, mood swings, and other symptoms of mood disorders that they had come to me for help with. Some may had heard vaguely about "chemical imbalances," but they were very uninformed about an illness they may have had for many years. This has changed only a little over the last fifteen years. More recently, patients may mention seeing a television commercial for an antidepressant or reading a magazine story about a movie star who was treated for postpartum depression, but there are still many misconceptions and a lot of ignorance about the causes and treatment of these illnesses. Compounding this is the stigma that, though much less than previously, is still associated with psychiatric illness and treatment. Add to this inaccurate and frightening media representations of ECT and psychiatric hospitalization, and it becomes clear why, although mood disorders are very common, many sufferers receive inadequate treatment or no treatment at all. I hope that I've helped break down these barriers for some and aided those already in treatment to better understand their illness.

These "illnesses of the mind" are really of the body, but cannot be understood using familiar illness concepts. In many illnesses of the body, abnormal functioning is clearly linked to tissue destruction of one type or another. A tumor grows and presses on a nerve and paralysis or pain results. Remove the tumor and the symptoms may be relieved. The pneumococcus bacterium invades the lungs, cells die, and the lung fills with pus and blood; kill the invader with the proper antibiotic and the lung cells regenerate.

Mood disorders result from a different kind of illness; there are no tumors, bacterial invaders, or tissue or cell death, but rather an inborn defect in a control system in the brain that leads to symptoms when environmental stresses cause the system to break down. I've compared mood disorders to illnesses like high blood pressure and diabetes, in which a control system—for blood pressure and blood sugar regulation, respectively, in those illnesses—breaks down and symptoms result.

Neuroscientists now think that there is a mood regulation system in the brain that, by a complex set of processes, allows mood to change in response to certain events and stimuli and then returns the mood to neutral—to a normal "set point." Just as a temperature center in the brain returns the body temperature to 98.6° Fahrenheit by making us sweat or shiver in response to temperature changes in the environment, a mood center in the brain returns the mood to neutral from low after a disappointment, and from euphoria after some happy event. Mood disorders seem to result from a malfunction in this center. If the set point changes, pervasive, unrelenting depression may result. The system may stop working as efficiently as it should, causing the mood to overshoot in both directions in erratic patterns, resulting in bipolar disorder.

We are making enormous progress in the field of psychiatry. The diagnosis of psychiatric illnesses, including mood disorders, is becoming more accurate all the time. The available treatments for these illnesses have become much more effective, and there are many more of them. But these advances have come about through trial and error, not because of a better scientific understanding of their causes. In the not too distant future, however, this is likely to change. Thousands of scientists work in two related fields that will eventually lead to a fuller understanding of these illnesses and to new and more effective treatment approaches.

The first of these fields is neuroscience: the study of the biology and chemistry of the brain and nervous system. The understanding of the fine details of how neurons develop, link to, and communicate with each other through complex networks, and how brain cells and their networks adapt and change in the living organism in response to experience, continues to grow. Now, new technologies for brain imaging such as *PET (positron emission tomography)* scans and *SPECT (single photon emission computed tomography)* are allowing scientists to see the brain at work in living persons for the first time. These imaging techniques can show changes in blood flow within the brain, locate areas that are hyperactive or abnormally low in activity, or detect abnormally high or low levels of brain chemicals like serotonin and dopamine. This information is revealing how the interplay of activity between different brain areas functions in the regulation of mood, and it is making it possible to identify the responsible circuitry. These techniques are allowing us to see how the brain of a person with a mood disorder functions differently from that of a person who does not have a mood disorder and, perhaps even more important, what changes occur when a person receives treatment and begins to feel well again.

The second of these fields is genetics. The development of advanced biochemical methods and molecular probes has made this exciting new research possible. With the announcement that the Human Genome Project had mapped almost all of the genetic material in the human chromosomes, a new era in the understanding of genetics began. The discovery of more genes is announced every day, and it is only a matter of time before the genetic mechanisms of mood disorders are unraveled. The identification of the genes linked with mood disorders is only one of the goals of work in this field. Just as important will be understanding the mechanisms by which genes turn on and off and other mechanisms that regulate the expression and work of the instructions encoded in the DNA molecule. A subfield within the field of genetics is that of *pharmacogenetics,* which concerns itself with genes associated with therapeutic response to particular medications. The promise of pharmacogenetics is a simple blood test that will indicate which medication will work best for a particular patient, ending the lengthy and frustrating trial-and-error approach we now use to find the right medication.

The two fields of neuroscience and psychiatric genetics are closing in on the causes and mechanisms of mood disorders from different directions. As these two enterprises advance, they will begin to inform each other—that is, advances in one field will lead to advances in the other. Discovering that a gene for a particular protein is linked to a mood disorder will tell neuroscientists that the protein is active in the regulation of mood. The discovery of some new enzyme in neurons that is a factor in neural plasticity will tell the geneticists to focus on the gene for that enzyme in their studies. Little by little the whole picture will become clearer.

As our understanding of the biology of mood disorders improves, we get closer to better diagnostic methods and safer and more effective treatments. The number of new medications continues to grow, and many more new pharmaceuticals are "in the pipeline," some of them based on new understanding of the biological causes of these illnesses. Soon, we will be able to design treatments more effectively and more rationally. More sophisticated use of nonpharmaceutical treatments like transcranial magnetic stimulation may make it possible to use lower doses of medications or may help medications to work more quickly.

As scientists take the step from isolating genes to determining the function of those genes, the possibility of gene therapy arises—repairing the code in the DNA that causes mood disorders. The obstacles to be overcome before we can look for this type of cure can only be called daunting, even monumental. But scientists are closing in on these illnesses little by little, and with enough time and enough hard work, a cure might be possible.

In the meantime, those with symptoms of mood disorders must take advantage of the very safe and effective treatments that are available. The consequences of ignoring these illnesses can be fatal.

Many paths are being taken in the search for better diagnosis and treatment of mood disorders, and most stretch far beyond the horizon There are no dead ends in sight. People who suffer from depression and other mood disorders can be more than just hopeful that the future will be brighter for them; they can be *confident* that it will.

# Further Reading

Samuel H. Barondes, *Better Than Prozac: Creating the Next Generation of Psychiatric Drugs* (New York: Oxford University Press, 2005). For those who are interested in an in-depth history of the development of psychiatric medications and detailed descriptions of how they are thought to work in treating mood disorders.

Max Fink, *Electroshock: Healing Mental Illness* (New York: Oxford University Press, 2002). A detailed, reassuring discussion of the uses, advantages, risks, and technical features of electroconvulsive therapy, including the patient's experience, by an international expert on the treatment.

Robert J. Hedaya, *The Antidepressant Survival Guide: The Clinically Proven Program to Enhance the Benefits and Beat the Side Effects of Your Medication* (New York: Three Rivers Press, 2001). This book sets out an ambitious plan for minimizing the side effects of psychiatric medications through diet, exercise, and other lifestyle changes.

Kay Redfield Jamison, *An Unquiet Mind: A Memoir of Moods and Madness* (New York: Vintage Books, 1996). A powerful and moving narrative written with grace and wit by an international expert on bipolar disorder who suffers from it herself. This treasure of a book contains some of the most engrossing and vivid descriptions of the experience of bipolar disorder ever written. A "must read" for anyone touched by bipolar disorder.

Martha Manning, *Undercurrents: A Life beneath the Surface* (New York: HarperCollins, 1994). A description of descent into and recovery from a life-threatening major depression told by the clinical psychologist who experienced it.

Anne Sheffield, *How You Can Survive When They're Depressed: Living and Coping with Depression Fallout* (New York: HarperCollins, 1999). Practical and sensible advice on self-help for those living with a person who has depressive illness. Includes chapters written especially for partners, parents, and children of people with mood disorders.

William Styron, *Darkness Visible: A Memoir of Madness* (New York: Random House, 1990). I recommend this book as one of the best accounts of the symptoms of depression available. A good book for family members to read to better understand the experience of serious depression.

# Support and Advocacy Organizations

All of the following organizations provide information, resources, and often referrals to support groups as well as to clinicians in your community who are skilled in treating mood disorders. Some provide direct services to consumers; others focus on education, combating the stigmatization of psychiatric illnesses, advocating for better medical insurance coverage of psychiatric disorders, and supporting research.

The Depressive and Related Affective Disorders Association (DRADA)
8201 Greeneboro Drive, Suite 300
McLean, VA 22102
703-610-9026
888-288-1104
www.drada.org

Depression and Bipolar Support Alliance (DBSA)
730 N. Franklin Street, Suite 501
Chicago, IL 60610-7224
800-826-3632
www.dbsalliance.org

National Alliance for the Mentally Ill (NAMI)
200 N. Glebe Road, Suite 1015
Arlington, VA 22203-3754
800-950-6264
www.nami.org

National Mental Health Association
1021 Prince Street
Alexandria, VA 22314
800-969-NMHA
www.nmha.org

American Foundation for Suicide Prevention
120 Wall Street, 22nd Floor
New York, NY 10005
888-333-AFSP
www.afsa.org

National Alliance for Research on Depression and Schizophrenia (NARSAD)
60 Cutter Mill Road
Great Neck, NY 11021
800-829-8289
www.narsad.org

INTERNET RESOURCES

In addition to the Web sites of the organizations listed above, there is an astonishing range of resources on the Internet. But remember that there is also inaccurate information, bias, and just plain nonsense as well. It's important to consider information sources very carefully. Here are several excellent resources:

WebMD
www.webmd.com
   A great source of information on every imaginable medical issue. Many useful articles and links to other resources.

United States National Library of Medicine
www.nlm.nih.gov
   In addition to news and articles on numerous mental health issues written for general readers, this site provides free access to Medline, the most comprehensive medical database in the world. Over 14 million articles published in 4,800 biomedical journals can be accessed. An incredibly valuable resource!

ClinicalTrials.gov
www.clinicaltrials.gov

This site of the National Institutes of Health allows users to search for federally and privately supported clinical research (i.e., studies of new treatments for diseases, including mood disorders). It is possible to get information about a study's purpose, who may participate, locations, and phone numbers to obtain further details.

# Index

Bipolar disorder, 75–102; chemistry of, 85–86; in children and adolescents, 111–12; classification of, 85; depression of, 81–82; length of treatment for, 99–101; mania of, 76–79; relapses of, 99–100, 165; vs. schizoaffective disorder, 131–32; "soft," 101–2; treatment of, 86–102; triphasic, 80

Brain imaging, 9, 192–93

Brain mapping, 121–22

Brain tumor, 150

Bright light therapy, 129–31

Bupropion, 43, 46

Cade, John, 87–88

Carbamazepine, 92, 94–95

Celexa. See Citalopram

Chemical dependency, 141–46

"Chemical imbalance," 12, 191

Children and adolescents, 26–29; bipolar disorder in, 111–12; depression in, 110–11; suicidal behavior in, 112–14

Chlorpromazine, 38–39, 54, 55

Chronobiology, 128, 155

Citalopram, 43

Clergy, 162

Clomipramine, 43

Clonazepam, 137, 148

Clozapine (Clozaril), 56–57, 58

"Club drugs," 145

Cocaine abuse, 145

Cognitive-behavioral therapy, 171

Cognitive therapy, 171–72

Community mental health centers, 165, 185–86, 188

Confidentiality, 184

Constipation, 24

Counseling, 168–69; pastoral, 162

Cyclothymia, 84

Cymbalta. See Duloxetine

Delusions, 54, 69, 72, 131, 132

Dementia syndrome of depression, 108–9

Depakene; Depakote. See Valproate

Depersonalization, 133

Depression, 16–74; biology of, 9–15; of bipolar disorder, 81–82; child/adolescent, 110–11; classification/diagnosis of, 29–37; complicated, 64–72; course of, 25, 41; double, 37; endogenous, 30, 37; family and, 186–88; geriatric, 105–10; major, 26, 33; at menopause, 21; mood in, 4, 22, 23; "normal," 26–29; pain

and, 123–27; panic disorder and, 132–38; postpartum, 20, 115–16, 151; pseudo-dementia of, 108; psychotic, 69–71; reactive, 29, 30, 34, 36, 37; recurrence of, 20; seasonal, 127–31; sleep and, 152–55; stroke and, 119–22; substance abuse and, 141–46; symptoms of, 23–25; treatment of, 38–72; unipolar, 81; in women, 114–19

Depression and Bipolar Support Alliance, 197

Depressive and Related Affective Disorders Association, 197

Depressive lifestyle, 174–75

Depressive syndrome, 30

Desipramine, 39, 43

Desyrel. See Trazodone

Dextroamphetamine, 53

Diagnosis, 30–37

Diazepam, 148

Diet and MAOIs, 47–48

Diuretics, 90

Diurnal variation in mood, 20, 128

Divalproex sodium. See Valproate

Dopamine, in Parkinson's disease, 7–8

Doxepin, 43

Drug hepatitis, 49

Duloxetine, 43, 46

Dysthymic disorder, 37

Early morning awakening, 17, 19, 24, 40, 128

Ecstasy abuse, 145

Effexor. See Venlafaxine

Elavil. See Amitriptyline

Eldepryl. See Selegiline

Elderly persons, depression in, 105–10

Electroconvulsive therapy (ECT), 22, 25; in bipolar disorder, 99; course of, 61; in depression, 58–62, 66, 70, 175; for elderly persons, 108, 109; history of, 58–59; maintenance, 61; mechanism of action of, 15, 60–61; vs. medications, 71–72; procedure for, 59–60, 183; side effects of, 61–62

Electroencephalogram: during ECT, 60; sleep, 152–53

Emsam transdermal system. See Selegiline

Endorphins, 127

Environmental factors, 172

Epitol. See Carbamazepine

Equanil. See Meprobamate

Equitro. See Carbamazepine

Escitalopram, 43

Ethchlorvynol, 148

165; early signs of, 165–66; prevention of, 166–67, 176

Remeron. *See* Mirtazapine

Reserpine, 7, 147

Risperidone (Risperdal), 57, 58

Sarafem. *See* Fluoxetine

Schizoaffective disorder, 131–32

Schizophrenia, 38–39, 54, 131

Schou, Morgans, 88–89

Seasonal affective disorder, 127–31, 149, 152, 155

Seconal, 148

Second messengers, 13–15

Sedative/hypnotics, 53; abuse of, 145; depression induced by, 147–48

Selective serotonin reuptake inhibitors (SSRIs), 43; child/adolescent suicide and, 113–14; mechanism of action of, 12, 44–45; side effects of, 44–46

Selegiline, 43, 48

Self-medication, 144

Seroquel. *See* Quetiapine

Serotonin, 12, 39–40, 54

Sertraline, 43

Serzone. *See* Nefazodone

Sexual behavior: in depression, 19, 25; in manic state, 78

Sexual dysfunction, SSRI-induced, 46, 53

Sinequan. *See* Doxepin

Single photon emission computed tomography, 192

Sleep architecture, 153–54

Sleep deprivation, 154–55

Sleep disturbances, 17, 19, 24, 33, 153–55; 165; sedative/hypnotics for, 53

Social workers, 162

Stelazine. *See* Trifluoperazine

Steroids: adrenal, 148; depression induced by, 70, 147, 151

Stevens-Johnson syndrome, 95, 96

Stigma, 124, 159, 184–85

Stimulant medications, 52–53

Stroke, 105, 119–22

Substance abuse, 141–46

Substance P, 125

Suicidal thoughts/behavior, 33, 35, 66, 176–78; asking about, 176; assessing risk for, 176–77; in children/adolescents, 112–14; prevention of, 177–78

Support and advocacy groups, 185, 197–99

Synapses, 10–12

"Talking therapy." *See* Psychotherapy

Tardive dyskinesia, 56

Tegretol. *See* Carbamazepine

Thioridazine, 55

Thiothixene, 55

Thorazine. *See* Chlorpromazine

Thyroid hormones, 148–49; for depression, 51–52

Tiagabine, 97

Tofranil. *See* Imipramine

Topiramate (Topamax), 97

Toxic epidermal necrolysis, 96

Transcranial magnetic stimulation, 62–63, 194

Tranylcypromine, 43

Trazodone, 43, 47

Tricyclic antidepressants, 42–44; side effects of, 42–44; structures of, 42, 45; therapeutic range for, 51

Trifluoperazine, 55

Trilafon. *See* Perphenazine

Trileptal. *See* Oxcarbazepine

Tuberculosis, 150

Twin studies, 141

Tyramine, dietary, and MAOIs, 47–48

Vagal nerve stimulation, 63–64

Valium. *See* Diazepam

Valproate, 92–94

Vegetative symptoms, 19, 24, 78, 110

Venlafaxine, 40, 43, 46

Viral infections, 150

Vitamin deficiencies, 150

Vivactil. *See* Protriptyline

Weight gain, drug-induced, 48, 57–58

Weight loss: in depression, 19, 40; SSRI-induced, 45–46

Wellbutrin. *See* Bupropion

"Winter blues." *See* Seasonal affective disorder

Women, mood disorders in, 114–19

Xanax. *See* Alprazolam

Ziprasidone, 57, 58

Zoloft. *See* Sertraline

Zonisamide, 97

Zyprexa; Zydis. *See* Olanzapine